I0820357

THE ARCHITECT'S EDGE

INNOVATION
LEADERSHIP
& PRACTICE

Published in 2025 by U
an imprint of Unicorn Publishing
Charleston
Meadow Business C
Lewes BN8
www.unicornpublishir

ISBN 978-1-91745
10 9 8 7 6 5 4

Designed by Stewart
Printed by Fine To

THE ARCHITECT'S EDGE

GARETH STAPLETON

INNOVATION
LEADERSHIP
& PRACTICE

RECOMMENDATIONS

'The Architect's Edge' is a refreshing approach to learning and practicing architecture by integrating the creative, entrepreneurial, and business side of this profession. Having lived through this journey helps Gareth Stapleton bring these various aspects to life. Being involved in leadership and its development myself, I truly appreciate how Gareth does not shy away from bringing together academic thinking and practical doing to assist and nudge architects in their journey toward becoming successful professionals.
Prof Bernd Vogel – *Centre for Leadership, Henley Business School*

'The Architect's Edge' should become a core teaching narrative in architectural education. Its insights provide invaluable guidance and inspiration, ensuring that the next generation of architects is well-prepared to meet the demands of the profession, have agency, and make a significant impact on the world. I highly recommend that all students of architecture and creatives further afield take note!
Maria Kramer - *Senior Lecturer, School of Architecture + Cities, University of Westminster*

As a psychologist who has worked extensively with professionals facing burnout, I can attest to the need to prioritise emotional and mental well-being in a fast-paced industry that demands perfection. Gareth's professional excellence shines through in this book and anyone who has worked alongside him will attest to his passion and commitment to his career. I am proud to endorse his drive to help others and his insights into managing stress, maintaining balance, and preventing burnout whilst being mindful of the limitations of being human. This holistic approach is vital if the profession is to thrive and make a lasting impact on the world.
Dr Christina Johnson – *Counselling Psychologist*

Gareth is a uniquely talented individual, a polymath, who has built an outstanding, award-winning career in the UK and abroad. This book exemplifies why Gareth's work is so remarkable. His unique blend of skills and experiences has allowed him to achieve resounding success in the interrelated fields of architecture, planning, and construction.
What sets this book apart is Gareth's ability to integrate his vast knowledge and practical insights into a cohesive guide for aspiring architects and seasoned professionals. He goes beyond conventional practices, exploring innovative and unconventional methods that address a wide array of societal challenges, both locally and globally. This approach not only enhances the effectiveness of architects but also equips them to contribute meaningfully to resolving some of the most pressing global issues.
Russell Brown, RIBA

"This book expands our understanding of both architecture and entrepreneurship, making architects more effective not only within traditional modes of practice but also by exploring opportunities for unconventional methods to address a broad spectrum of societal challenges, both locally and globally. Gareth Stapleton is leading the way with his innovative thinking, offering invaluable insights that will inspire and guide architects towards a more impactful and adaptive future."
Jack Pringle PPRIBA

Finding an architect who not only comprehends the intricacies of construction management but also has a proven track record of delivering for high-profile clients is rare. Gareth Stapleton exemplifies this unique blend of skills and perspectives. His transition from design practitioner to project leader showcases his exceptional ability to navigate and excel in the complex world of architecture and construction. This book is a testament to his innovative approach, providing invaluable insights that will inspire and guide both aspiring and seasoned professionals towards greater success.
Patrick Walsh – *Founder, Ayton Project Management*

ABOUT THE AUTHOR

Gareth Stapleton OBE is a Partner at Host and is recognised as an award-winning, integrity-driven, and adaptable business leader. His educational background spans Business, Management Consulting, and Architecture, forming the foundation of a global reputation for excellence in delivering high-quality standards. Gareth's leadership has secured multiple commissions from clients, including Oxford University and Apple, where he introduced governance procedures that aligned and advanced real estate portfolios with both legislative requirements and industry best practices.

He has served as project and construction manager on a range of award-winning projects including: the Open Up cultural transformation of the Royal Opera House with Stanton Williams; the Royal Academy of Music with ritchie*studio; the UK Pavilion at Milan EXPO 2015 with Wolfgang Buttress and BDP; Amazon UK HQ; the Serpentine Gallery with Zaha Hadid; the Serpentine Pavilion with both Ai Weiwei and Sou Fujimoto; the Blavatnik School of Government, University of Oxford with Herzog & de Meuron; and the Tree of Trees sculpture by Thomas Heatherwick for the Queen's Platinum Jubilee.

He began his career in architecture at the Stirling Prize-winning practices WilkinsonEyre and Hawkins\Brown, before completing an MBA at Henley Business School and transitioning into project and management consulting. Over the past two decades, he has made a significant impact, co-founding the award-winning consultancy Host (formerly Rise International) and establishing the design practice Assemble Creative alongside Stew Smith.

In 2023, Gareth was named one of the UK's Top 100 Influential People. He has contributed pro bono expertise to initiatives including The Queen's Green Canopy, the Duke of Gloucester Awards Scheme, and the Serpentine Gallery Summer Pavilions. He serves on the Estates & Sustainability Committee at Regent's Park College, University of Oxford; is an advisor to the Branch Trust; and holds a Non-Executive Director role with MOBO Award-winning artist Guvna B.

Gareth is currently pursuing doctoral research at Henley Business School as part of the Management Leadership and Behaviour Research Group. He is a contributor to the *Elgar Encyclopaedia of Leadership* (2024) and the author of *The Architect's Edge: Innovation, Leadership, and Practice* (2025). In recognition of his services to architecture, project and construction management, Gareth was awarded the honour of Officer of the Order of the British Empire (OBE) in the 2025 King's Birthday Honours.

He lives in the Cotswolds with his wife and four children.

CONTENTS

INTRODUCTIONS - BY MICHAEL FREEMAN & IAN RITCHIE

Michael Freeman

To be an architect, one must possess many skills, some acquired through lengthy academic training and others acquired in the workplace.

Architects might mention creativity and craftsmanship, and a passion for designing—and completing—attractive buildings.

An interest in, and decent grasp of, the relevant planning and environmental considerations for any given project are also necessary. This includes assessing the desirability and viability of possible structural, infrastructural and M&E solutions, and evaluating potential building materials and technologies. Architects should also be able to work successfully within, and potentially lead, productive, motivated project teams of specialist consultants.

Equally important, I think, are the following skill sets if you aspire to be a good architect, especially if you hope to rise in the profession or to found your own practice:

- An architect must be able to accept that their own vision is not, and cannot be, the be-all and the end-all of any project. In the real world, that vision will lead to sub-optimum outcomes if it does not align with the client's requirements, those of the client's financiers, or of the intended occupiers of the project.
- In the real world, a good architect needs the skills to win new clients and retain existing ones, and the ability to consistently achieve internal business targets in terms of: costs, profitability, meeting deadlines, and in recruiting, training and motivating staff, and building and sustaining an effective, happy workplace.

I am not an architect, but as co-founder of Argent in 1981 with my brother, Peter (current chair of Homes England), I have for over forty years been involved as a developer on many projects with many architectural firms on schemes ranging from a few thousand square feet to our 70 acre, several billion pound regeneration of the area around King's Cross. I have experienced how very good it can be to work with an architect who possesses the demanding mix of skills outlined above, and how unsatisfactory to downright dreadful it can be working with one who does not.

My friend Gareth Stapleton has seen, learned, and considered much about the relationships between architecture, planning, construction, and real-world considerations in both the private and public sectors. In this book, he offers his own clear, highly readable thoughts, based on his own very considerable experience, about what an architect needs to do to be a good architect and, with luck and persistence, a successful one.

About Michael Freeman

Michael Freeman and his brother Peter founded Argent in 1981. Under their leadership, Argent has grown to become one of the UK's leading developers, renowned for its ability to deliver complex, innovative and high-quality large-scale urban regeneration projects that significantly enhance their environments.

Ian Ritchie

This book is important to our profession.

I can vouch for Gareth Stapleton's passion for performance, having worked with him over many years as he led projects on behalf of clients as project manager or construction director. After learning much in architectural practice he rose high in construction management during his time at PDCM and RISE International, where he formed a powerful tandem with Bob White, establishing their reputation as problem solvers. This role gave Gareth wide international experience and a board-level perspective in business management, enabling him to bridge the gap between client and architect by providing a well-informed and balanced viewpoint.

I am an architect, sometimes an engineer, industrial designer, writer, poet and artist, and have led an architectural practice in London for over four decades—serving as both architect and construction manager for projects in the UK and France. In parallel, I founded and co-led the engineering design firm Rice Francis Ritchie in Paris, which developed a reputation for rescuing challenging projects. During that time, we were frequently consulted by the French government and other architects across Europe due to our uniquely pan-disciplinary expertise.

From this heterogenous perspective, I can fully appreciate Gareth's contributions to the profession, which is why I am pleased to help introduce his book. It addresses both the practicalities and the art of business—for business is indeed an art to be mastered if one is to meet the challenge of delivering high-quality, innovative architecture, particularly on large-scale urban and commercial projects. Gareth also emphasises the need to master the art of interdisciplinary collaboration, which is vital for both intelligent reflection and for delivering coherent, holistic solutions to the challenges any project presents.

Architects 'sell' their creative brain power to clients. This involves the art of engaging with clients and expressing a desire to understand their demands. As Michael Freeman notes in his introduction, clients value professional business acumen as much as your creativity. They are, rightly, as concerned with economy, efficiency and value for money as they are with aesthetics. Resolving this tension between design and execution is key to successfully delivering a project, and it often explains the alignment of specific clients with particular architects.

Gareth's career has spanned a range of professional roles, equipping him with a mastery of the vital aspects of driving and managing the administrative and commercial aspects of both architectural practice and construction delivery. He understands the inherent responsibilities and liabilities of the 'real' world of architecture and building, and how important it is to continue learning, to stay alert to new ways of operating, and equally, how vital it is to share and exchange knowledge. In the chapters that follow, he shares valuable insights from which we can all benefit.

Professor Ian Ritchie CBE RA

Dip Arch (Dist) PCL ARB RIBA MCSA MIABSE FSFE FRSA FSHARE FSIAD // Hon: FRIAS FAIA FRAM MScPdiM DLitt Dhc Royal Academician // Member Akademie der Künste // Honorary Visiting Professor of Architecture Liverpool University Member Politecnico di Milano Academic Board // CABE Commissioner Emeritus

INTRODUCTION

Entrepreneur Me? Yes You!

As an architecture graduate or newly qualified professional, you possess unique creative problem-solving skills and technical expertise. You have the ability to envision beautiful, functional spaces and places that create a sense of community. Your skills extend beyond the field of architecture into a wide range of fields and industries. You can create something new, solve problems no one else has tackled, and make a difference in the world. You have the drive and determination to take risks, push boundaries, and see opportunities where others see challenges. You are dissatisfied with the status quo; you want to innovate, disrupt, and positively impact the world—that is why you have pursued this career.

Entrepreneurship is integral to the architectural profession; once understood and leveraged, it can provide a solid framework for diverse practice models. With an entrepreneurial mindset, you can make use of your strengths, applying your skills and knowledge to identify problems and opportunities others might miss, take calculated risks, and create something new and meaningful.

Section One Equips you with an outline of the knowledge and strategies to leverage your unique skills to become an effective entrepreneur.

Section Two will build on these foundations, focusing on the changing landscape of architectural practice. It will explore real-world examples of innovative practices already reshaping the profession, illustrating how these new forms of engagement can address some of today's most urgent global challenges. Among other topics, it will offer a practical guide to leadership, public relations and human resources, personal health and welfare, and the power of saying 'No'.

In Section Three, you'll learn the essential strategies for building and maintaining strong client relationships, managing your business effectively, and using modern technology to enhance client satisfaction and project success. This volume offers advanced strategies for client engagement, emphasising the importance of personal connections and sustained communication. It also explores critical business management practices like financial stability, resource allocation, and risk management.

Section Three also addresses the ethical dimensions of architectural practice, focusing on integrity, professionalism and social responsibility. You'll learn how to navigate ethical dilemmas, foster a culture of integrity within your firm, and promote sustainability in your projects. By integrating these business strategies and ethical considerations, you'll be equipped to lead your practice with confidence, innovate effectively, and make a positive impact on the built environment and society.

SECTION ONE

01

CHAPTER ONE

Jumping Out of An Aeroplane Without a Parachute and Landing Safely!

Chapter One introduces the attitudes and principles needed to transition from architectural education to entrepreneurship, emphasising the philosophical grounding and skills this requires. It reveals gaps in traditional architectural education, especially the need for business acumen to complement creative talent, and urges architects to critically examine their practices, reflecting on the purpose behind their work.

1.1 // Things They Didn't Teach You at University!

(Like How to Run a Business and Make a Living from Your Talents)

Architectural education usually overlooks the business skills needed to monetise talent and ensure long-term success. This is not to suggest every architect needs an MBA, but that business acumen and creativity are equally important for a successful business career.

Understanding the Concept of Entrepreneurship in Architecture:

Entrepreneurship involves creating value by combining unique resources to exploit opportunities—something architects inherently do when creating impactful designs. Nevertheless, many architects see themselves more as designers or project managers than entrepreneurs. But adopting an entrepreneurial mindset is essential for navigating the business of architecture, and understanding key entrepreneurial principles can help architects seize opportunities that might seem out of reach.

1.2 // Embracing an Entrepreneurial Attitude

(The Core Principles Every Architect Needs to Succeed)

Principle 1 - Starting with Why

Entrepreneurship's first principle is understanding your purpose, a concept popularised by Simon Sinek in *Start with Why*[1]. This ancient concept goes back to Aristotle and modern thinkers

[1] Sinek, S., 2011. *Start with why: How great leaders inspire everyone to take action.* Penguin Books Ltd. London

like Viktor Frankl, both of whom emphasised the importance of purpose and meaning in life and work.

In *Nicomachean Ethics*, Aristotle introduced the idea of 'telos', or purpose, as the ultimate goal of human activities. He argues that every action aims at some good, described as the 'final cause'. Understanding our telos, Aristotle believed, helps us align our actions with our values and is central to achieving 'eudaimonia'—'flourishing' or 'the good life', wherein the individual experiences fulfilment and excellence in personal and professional life.

David Ponders the Meaning of his existence while waiting for the beat to drop

In Man's Search for Meaning, Viktor Frankl, a Holocaust survivor, emphasised the importance of finding meaning and purpose, especially in adversity. He proposed that meaning can be discovered through work (doing something significant), love (caring for another person), and courage during difficult times.

Aristotle would suggest that architects should identify their core values and let these guide their design philosophy and professional endeavours. For instance, an architect who values sustainability might prioritise eco-friendly materials and energy-efficient designs. Such alignment of professional practice with personal values ensures their work is technically proficient, and ethically and morally satisfying.[2]

[2] Aristotle, Nicomachean Ethics, trans. W. D. Ross. (Oxford University Press. 1925.) Book I, Chapter 7.

Another architect might find meaning in designing affordable housing for underserved communities, thus combining professional skills with a humanitarian mission. This would accord with the broader vision of architecture as a discipline that can improve lives and contribute to societal well-being, aligning with Frankl's insights, which suggest architects can find purpose in creating functional spaces that also foster community and address social and environmental challenges.[3]

Applying These Philosophies in Architecture

Before starting your architectural practice, you must clearly understand what you are doing and why. Having a clear purpose is not just about personal fulfillment; it's about positioning your practice to resonate with clients and stakeholders.

Equally, being an entrepreneur is about more than just a good idea or a great product; it's about having a vision, mission, and purpose that go beyond making money. Your 'why' is the foundation of your business, the driving force that guides your decisions, strategies, and actions. Whatever your reasons for becoming an architect, they should be something you deeply care about, giving you meaning and purpose.

Principle 2 - Creating Value

The father of modern management, Peter Drucker, famously said, 'The purpose of a business is to create a customer'.[4] For architects, this means providing solutions that meet the needs and expectations of your clients, whether these be individuals, organisations, or communities.

Creating value does not end with delivering a service; it's about understanding your client's needs and exceeding their expectations, and tailoring your services accordingly. To build a reputation that consistently delivers value and attracts more clients and opportunities, differentiate yourself from competitors by offering something unique and relevant.

Principle 3 - Building Relationships

Your network is your net worth.

Relationships are the backbone of any successful business. In architecture, this means establishing and maintaining relationships with clients, contractors, suppliers, and other stakeholders who can support and promote your practice. Building strong relationships requires trust, transparency, and mutual respect, meeting commitments, and being responsive to the needs of others—so be approachable, communicative, and reliable.

Principle 4 - Managing Resources

Time, money, and energy are your most valuable and limited resources. Effective resource management is critical to the success of any business. In architecture, this means managing your projects, team, finances, and time effectively and efficiently to ensure that projects are

[3] Viktor E. Frankl, 2006. Man's Search for Meaning, Beacon Press. pp. 98-105.
[4] Drucker, P., 2012. The practice of management. Routledge.

completed on time and within budget without compromising quality.

Principle 5 - Learning and Innovating

Architectural innovation is about finding better ways to solve problems and deliver value. Staying at the forefront of the field requires continuous learning, experimentation, and adaptation. It means keeping up with the latest trends, technologies, and regulations while exploring new ideas and approaches to design and construction.

Be curious, open-minded, and proactive in seeking knowledge and feedback. Be creative and daring in experimenting with new materials, techniques, and concepts, pushing the boundaries of your comfort zone.

Entrepreneurship is a mindset, a way of thinking, and a way of being.

It is a journey, not a destination. Success is defined by your impact on the world and the legacy you leave behind, not purely by money or fame. Embrace the spirit of entrepreneurship, and be bold, resilient, and true to yourself.

02

CHAPTER TWO

CHAPTER TWO

Landing on Your Feet: You've Made It to the Start Line!

This chapter highlights how embracing both the successes and challenges of architectural training shapes an architect's professional identity and prepares them for the dynamic nature of the profession. Architects are then encouraged to reflect on their journey through RIBA Parts 1, 2, and 3. By introducing v and reflective practices necessary to build sustainable practices and achieve long-term career success, Chapter Two sets the stage for navigating the complexities of the profession which are examined in greater detail in Sections Two and Three of this book.

2.1 // How Did I Get Here?

(Reflecting on the Journey through RIBA Parts 1, 2, and 3)

As an architect, you may find yourself asking, 'How did I get here?'

Completing RIBA Parts 1, 2, and 3 can evoke emotions ranging from exhilaration and pride to uncertainty and anxiety. It's important to reflect on the highs and lows of your architectural training, understanding how these experiences have shaped your journey and will continue to influence your future.

The end of the beginning

2.2 // Reflecting on the Highs

(Late Nights, Tight Deadlines, and Triumphs)

Although architectural training is rigorous and demanding, it also reveals your passion, creativity, and purpose. Recognising the tangible and intangible, personal and professional milestones and accomplishments that mark your progress is vital.

Some typical highs that bond all architects through shared experience include:

- **Creating impactful design projects** that meet and exceed your tutors' and peers' expectations. The satisfaction of seeing a project come to life from a mere concept to a detailed design that impresses and meets academic standards is incomparable.
- **Passing exams or assessments** that showcase your extensive knowledge and understanding of architecture and its integration with other disciplines.
- **Presenting your work and ideas** to an audience, and receiving recognition and praise that reinforce your confidence and validate your approach. These presentations hone your communication skills, essential for articulating complex ideas and concepts to diverse audiences.
- **Collaborating with colleagues, mentors, and clients,** gaining new insights and perspectives that enrich your work and preparing you for the collaborative nature of architectural practice.
- **Developing your design style, vision, and values** and using them to guide your decisions. This helps you establish a unique identity and approach to architecture, setting the stage for a distinctive career path.
- **Building your portfolio and CV**, showcasing your skills, achievements, and personality to potential employers or clients. A strong portfolio and CV open doors to career opportunities,highlighting your competencies and experiences.
- **Obtaining your RIBA Part 1, 2, or 3 certifications** and becoming a qualified architect ready for new challenges.

These highs provide a sense of fulfilment, validation, and motivation. Whenever you feel overwhelmed or uncertain, recall these achievements and let them guide you towards a brighter future as an architect.

2.3 // Facing the Lows

(Stress, Criticism, and the Occasional Meltdown)

Challenges, setbacks, and failures are inevitable in architecture as in life. These experiences can test your resilience, confidence, and motivation. Common struggles during architectural training include:

- **Facing criticism, rejection, or indifference;** Criticism can be constructive, but also disheartening. Learning to separate constructive feedback from negativity and using it to improve your work is a crucial skill.
- **Dealing with tight deadlines, conflicting requirements, and limited resources;** Managing multiple projects with varying demands teaches you prioritisation, time management, and how to work under pressure—essential skills for professional practice.
- **Struggling with technical or conceptual issues;** These struggles highlight areas for growth and learning, pushing you to seek solutions and expand your expertise.
- **Balancing the demands of studies, work, and personal life;** The intense demands of architectural training require effective time management and self-care strategies to maintain well-being and productivity.
- **Coping with stress, anxiety, or burnout;** Recognising the signs of burnout and developing coping mechanisms is vital for long-term success in the profession.
- **Managing uncertainty, change, or disruption;** The architectural profession is dynamic, requiring adaptability and resilience to navigate changes and uncertainties.

While painful, these lows can also be transformative and empowering. They teach resilience, adaptability, and empathy, helping you better understand yourself and your work. Embracing highs and lows with a growth mindset allows you to leverage these experiences to your advantage.

2.4 // The Reflective Practitioner

(Schön and Kolb Make a Cameo)

Some academic perspectives on the challenges and rewards of architectural training might be useful. For instance, Schön's concept of the 'reflective practitioner' emphasises the importance of reflection in professional practice. This is particularly relevant in architecture, where learning from past projects can significantly enhance future designs and practices. Similarly, Kolb's experiential learning theory posits that learning is a cyclical process involving concrete experiences, reflective observation, abstract conceptualisation, and active experimentation. For architects, each project and interaction provides an opportunity for learning and growth.

Practical Tips for Each Stage of Your Journey:

Here we provide some practical advice tailored to the different stages of your academic architectural journey to help you align your career with your long-term aspirations and ensure sustained success and personal fulfilment.

End of Part One:

- **Embrace the journey, not just the destination**. Architectural training is a lifelong process of learning, exploring, and creating. Appreciate each step of your journey, fostering a positive and resilient mindset.
- **Explore various opportunities** during your placement year. Think about the type of practice you want to work for, the sectors that interest you, and what will benefit you long-term as you prepare for Part 2.
- **Practice empathy.** Architecture is about people, not just buildings. Empathy enhances your design process, ensuring that your projects meet the real needs of those who will use them.
- **Seek advice from those ahead of you.** Glean valuable insights from peers who have completed their placement years. Their experiences can provide guidance and help you navigate common challenges.

During this phase, it's crucial to focus on practical skills and understanding the dynamics of architectural practice. Engaging with mentors and experienced professionals can provide invaluable insights and guidance. This period also allows you to test and refine your design philosophies and methodologies in real-world scenarios, laying a solid foundation for your future career.

End of Part Two:

- **Find your 'why'.** Discover what drives you as an architect and use it to guide your work and decisions. Reflect on your motivations and how they align with your career aspirations.
- **Plan your placement or job.** Consider where you need more experience. Planning ensures that your experiences are comprehensive and aligned with your career goals.

This stage is about deepening your understanding and honing your skills. Engage in diverse projects to build a robust portfolio and expand your expertise. It's also a time to start thinking about the kind of architect you want to become. Reflect on your experiences and use them to shape your professional identity and career path.

[1] Schön, D.A., 2017. The reflective practitioner: How professionals think in action. Routledge..
[2] Kolb, D.A., 2014. Experiential learning: Experience as the source of learning and development. FT press.

End of Part Three:

- **Build your network**. Architecture is collaborative and interdisciplinary. Connect with other professionals to learn from their expertise and experience. Networking opens doors to opportunities and collaborations that can significantly impact your career.
- **Invest in your skills and knowledge**. Stay current with CPD, latest technologies, trends, and best practices. Invest in your professional development. Continuous learning ensures that you remain competitive and proficient in your field.

And so it begins ......

- **Take care of your well-being**. Architecture can be demanding. Prioritise your mental and physical health. A healthy work-life balance is essential for sustained success and personal fulfilment.
- **Never hesitate to ask questions**. There are no stupid questions, even when you are qualified. Seek guidance whenever needed. Curiosity and a willingness to learn from others are essential traits for ongoing professional growth.

As you navigate these stages, keep in mind that technical skills alone are insufficient. Emotional intelligence (EQ) is also critical to your development as an architect.

2.5 // The Role of Emotional Intelligence (EQ)

(Why EQ is Your Secret Weapon)

EQ involves understanding and managing your emotions while effectively navigating interpersonal dynamics. Popularised by Daniel Goleman's 1995 work,[3] the concept highlights the synergy between EQ and technical skills (IQ) in architecture. EQ equips architects to manage client interactions, team collaborations, and design challenges with sensitivity, fostering an environment conducive to innovation and responsive design.

Research underscores EQ's role in leadership, decision-making, and creativity—key components of architecture. Architects can elevate their practice by understanding and integrating EQ, ensuring projects are both technically sound and emotionally resonant with clients and stakeholders.[4]

The Importance of EQ at Different Career Stages

University

Studies show that students with higher EQ perform better academically and handle stress more effectively.[5][6] Emotional self-awareness, self-regulation, and empathy help students manage the pressures of academia, and collaborative projects benefit significantly from students who communicate and work well within diverse teams.

Early Career

High EQ helps early-career architects face challenges like adapting to workplace culture, managing client expectations, and working within interdisciplinary teams. Resilience and adaptability, key components of EQ, help them cope with inevitable temporary setbacks and rejections. Early-career architects with high EQ can position themselves as valuable team members and proactive problem-solvers.[7][8]

Practicing Architect

For practicing architects, high EQ helps architects manage complex projects and lead teams effectively by mediating conflicts, maintaining strong client relationships, and navigating diverse cultural dynamics. The last is vital as the architectural profession becomes increasingly global and diverse. Architects with high EQ can better understand client visions, anticipate their needs, and deliver exceptional projects, quickly building a reputation for excellence and reliability.[9][10]

[3] Goleman, D., 2020. *Emotional intelligence: Why it can matter more than IQ.* Bloomsbury Publishing.
[4] Salovey, P. and Mayer, J.D., 1990. Emotional intelligence. *Imagination, cognition and personality,* 9(3).
[5] Schutte, N.S., Malouff, J.M., Hall, L.E., Haggerty, D.J., Cooper, J.T., Golden, C.J. and Dornheim, L., 1998. Development and validation of a measure of emotional intelligence. *Personality and individual differences,* 25(2) pp.167-177.
[6] Parker, J.D., Summerfeldt, L.J., Hogan, M.J. and Majeski, S.A., 2004. Emotional intelligence and academic success: Examining the transition from high school to university. *Personality and individual differences,* 36(1), pp.163-172.
[7] Gardner, L. and Stough, C., 2002. Examining the relationship between leadership and emotional intelligence in senior level managers. *Leadership & organization development journal,* 23(2), pp.68-78.
[8] Boyatzis, R.E., 2006. An overview of intentional change from a complexity perspective. *Journal of management development,* 25(7), pp.607-623.
[9] Bar-On, R., 2006. The Bar-On model of emotional-social intelligence (ESI) 1. *Psicothema,* pp.13-25.
[10] Cherniss, C. and Goleman, D., 2001. The emotionally intelligent workplace: *How to select for, measure and improve emotional intelligence in individuals, groups and organizations.* Jossey-Bass.

As you navigate these stages, keep in mind that technical skills alone are insufficient. Emotional intelligence (EQ) is also critical to your development as an architect.

2.6 // Strategies for Developing EQ in Architecture

(How to Be Less of a Robot and More of a Human)

- **Self-Awareness and Reflection:** Regularly reflect on your emotions and reactions to different situations. Understanding your emotional triggers can help you manage them more effectively.
- **Empathy Training:** Engage in activities that enhance your ability to understand and share the feelings of others.
- **Stress Management Techniques:** Learn and practice stress management techniques to help you remain calm and focused under pressure.

- **Seeking Feedback and Learning:** To improve your EQ skills, actively seek feedback from peers, mentors, and clients to gain insights into how your emotional responses impact your professional interactions.
- **Conflict Resolution Skills:** Develop your conflict resolution skills by learning how to approach disagreements constructively. This involves active listening, empathy, and finding mutually beneficial solutions.

2.7 // Developing Leadership Skills

(From Architect to Jedi Master)

While good business leadership is vital to a successful architectural practice and is thoroughly covered in Book Two, it also warrants mentioning here. Leadership in architecture is closely linked to having a clear and compelling vision that serves as a compass to navigate the profession's complexities and challenges while also keeping architects aligned with their core values.

The Importance of Vision

A well-defined vision helps maintain a forward-thinking perspective that integrates design with social, environmental, and ethical considerations. By articulating and adhering to a clear vision, architects can inspire and motivate teams and stakeholders to pursue shared goals, fostering a collective sense of purpose and direction.[11]

Developing Leadership Skills

Leadership in architecture goes beyond managing projects and teams; it involves inspiring others, fostering innovation, and driving positive change. Architects with strong leadership skills can guide their teams through challenges, encouraging collaboration, are adept at conflict resolution. By integrating EQ into their leadership style, architects can create a supportive work environment that cultivates talent and promotes continuous learning.[12]

Visionary Projects

Case studies of work by visionary architects such as Norman Foster, whose sustainable and innovative designs include the Gherkin in London, or Shigeru Ban, whose humanitarian architecture has provided relief and dignity to disaster-stricken communities, illustrate how a strong vision, emotional intelligence, and leadership skills can lead to meaningful contributions to the field and society.

It's important to recognise that purpose-driven leadership is rooted in a deep understanding of one's core values and vision. By defining and living their purpose, architects can create work that is not only innovative and functional but also meaningful and impactful. Chapter Three will explore how to articulate your purpose and align it with your professional practice.

[11]Senge, P.M., 2006. The fifth discipline: The art and practice of the learning organization. Broadway Business.
[12]Northouse, P.G., 2021. Leadership: Theory and practice. Sage publications.

LANDING ON YOUR FEET

10 Key Learning Points //

1. **Reflect on Your Architectural Journey** Regularly reflect on your experiences during your architectural training. Use these reflections to inform your future actions and continuously improve your practice.
2. **Recognize and Celebrate Milestones** Identify and celebrate key milestones in your education and career. Celebrating these moments can boost your motivation and confidence.
3. **Manage Criticism and Setbacks** Develop a resilient mindset to handle criticism and setbacks. Use constructive criticism to enhance your work and grow professionally.
4. **Develop Emotional Intelligence (EQ)** Improve your EQ by practising self-awareness, empathy, stress management, and effective communication.
5. **Balance Work and Personal Life** Maintain a healthy work-life balance and prioritise your mental and physical health.
6. **Build and Leverage Your Network** Actively engage in networking opportunities; building a strong network can open doors to new opportunities, collaborations, and career advancements.
7. **Continuously Learn and Innovate** Stay updated with the latest trends, technologies, and best practices in architecture. Invest in continuous learning through courses, workshops, and reading. Experiment with new ideas and approaches to design and construction.
8. **Develop Leadership Skills** Cultivate leadership skills by taking on roles that require managing projects, teams, or initiatives. Focus on inspiring and motivating others, resolving conflicts, and fostering a collaborative work environment.
9. **Define and Communicate Your Vision** Articulate a clear and compelling vision for your architectural practice. Ensure your vision aligns with your core values and resonates with clients and team members. Use your vision to guide decision-making and project direction.
10. **Embrace Purpose-Driven Practice** Identify your purpose as an architect and let your purpose drive your professional practice and decision-making.

CHAPTER THREE

Finding Your True North:
Because Wandering Aimlessly Isn't a Career Plan

As already indicated in Chapter Two, leadership requires a well-defined sense of purpose. This chapter provides a guide to defining and articulating your core values and integrating leadership theories and principles of purpose-driven organisations into your practice to foster a culture of innovation, collaboration, and ethical decision-making. Case studies provide real-life examples of architects who have successfully founded their own innovative, purpose-driven practices.

3.1 // Applying Leadership Theories to Purpose-Driven Architecture

(Incorporating Leadership Principles to Drive Impact)

Purpose-driven leadership involves having a clear sense of personal values and using them to guide ethical decision-making.[1] By understanding our talents, passions, and values, we can align them with our leadership purpose. Key principles include:

- **Reflect on Your Personal Values and Leadership Purpose:** Take time to understand your talents, passions, and values and align them with your leadership purpose. Use this to guide ethical decision-making and inspire and motivate others.
- **Craft a Compelling Vision and Communicate It Effectively:** Develop a clear and convincing vision for yourself and your firm. Use effective communication skills to engage and inspire team members, clients, and stakeholders. A compelling vision aligns everyone involved and fosters a sense of shared purpose.
- **Foster a Culture of Innovation and Collaboration:** Create a culture that values learning, experimentation, and innovation. Foster collaboration and teamwork, encouraging everyone to contribute ideas and perspectives. This culture drives continuous improvement and creativity.
- **Measure and Communicate Your Impact:** Regularly evaluate your practice's social, environmental, and economic impact. Use data and storytelling to communicate this impact to stakeholders. Transparent communication builds trust and demonstrates your commitment to your purpose.

Integrating Purpose-Driven Leadership into Architectural Practice:

The concepts of purpose and values have taken on new significance in the context of purpose-driven organisations and sustainability challenges. Companies like Patagonia, Unilever, and Tesla exemplify this trend by making their mission and values central to their strategy and operations, aiming to positively impact society and the environment while building trust, loyalty, and reputation.

From an architectural perspective, by integrating sustainability, social equity, and beauty into their design philosophy and practice, architects can contribute to a purpose-driven organisation's mission and value proposition.

To become purpose-driven leaders, architects can benefit by:

- **Studying and Applying the Principles of Purpose-Driven Organizations:** Learn about mission alignment, stakeholder engagement, and social impact. Apply these principles to your practice to ensure that your work is aligned with your purpose and adds value to society.

- **Developing Leadership Skills:** Strong leadership skills are essential for inspiring and guiding your team towards achieving your vision. Enhance your emotional intelligence, communication, and ethical decision-making through training, coaching, and mentorship.
- **Collaborating with Other Professionals and Stakeholders:** Collaboration enhances the impact of your work and broadens your perspective. Work with community leaders, policymakers, and NGOs to create interdisciplinary solutions to complex problems.
- **Measuring and Communicating Your Impact:** Effective communication demonstrates your commitment to your purpose and engages stakeholders. Use tools such as life-cycle assessment, social return on investment, and storytelling to measure and communicate your work's social, environmental, and economic impact

3.2 // Pulling the Ripcord: No Time Like the Present

(Taking Bold Steps to Align with Your Authentic Self)

In life, there are times when we feel trapped in a situation that is no longer fulfilling or meaningful.

So, why is it so hard to take action? Why do we often settle for the status quo, even when it's not serving us well? 'Pulling the ripcord' is a metaphor for taking bold and decisive action to break free and pursue a path that aligns with our authentic selves and aspirations. While it requires courage, clarity, and commitment, this leap opens the possibility for growth, learning, and fulfilment.

Understanding the Challenge:

Change is inherently stressful because it confronts us with uncertainty. Fear of leaving our comfort zone can be paralysing, causing us to cling to familiar but unfulfilling situations. In the context of architectural practice, this can manifest as feeling trapped in a firm misaligned with your values, stuck in uninspiring projects, or overwhelmed by the bureaucratic aspects of the profession.

// Strategies for Pulling the Ripcord:

1. Focus on the Long Game:

Maintaining a long-term perspective and focusing on the bigger picture rather than immediate gratification helps you assess whether staying in your current situation or pursuing a new path aligns better with your purpose and values in the long run.

2. Embrace the Discomfort:

Discomfort challenges us to develop new skills and perspectives; embrace discomfort as part of the journey. Seek opportunities to take on challenging projects, step into leadership roles, and learn new technologies. Each experience, though initially uncomfortable, will lead to greater confidence and fulfilment and can significantly enhance your skills and career prospects

3. Surround Yourself with Support:

Connect with people who share your values, vision, and goals who can offer encouragement, or individuals who have had similar experiences and can share their insights.

4. Take Action:

Waiting for the perfect circumstances may prolong our discomfort and delay our progress. Every journey begins with a single step, and each step leads us closer to our goals. Don't let fear or doubt hold you back; pull the ripcord today and see where it takes you.

3.3 // Inspiration from Architectural Leaders

(Learning from Visionaries in the Field)

Many architects face significant challenges when starting their businesses, including discrimination, scepticism, and difficulty finding work. However, through perseverance, many achieve great success and recognition for their innovative designs.

Kazuyo Sejima

Kazuyo Sejima co-founded the architectural firm SANAA (Sejima and Nishizawa and Associates) with Ryue Nishizawa. Early in her career, Sejima faced significant difficulties as a woman in a male-dominated field but remained committed to architecture, demonstrating resilience and determination. Her persistence led to the establishment of SANAA, which gained international acclaim for its minimalist and innovative design characterised by simplicity, clean lines, and transparency. Notable projects include the 21st Century Museum of Contemporary Art in Kanazawa, Japan, completed in 2004, and the Rolex Learning Center at the École Polytechnique Fédérale de Lausanne (EPFL) in Switzerland, completed in 2010.

In 2009, SANAA designed the Serpentine Summer Pavilion in London, a project that further enhanced its international reputation. It featured a delicate, floating aluminium canopy, creating an ethereal, light-filled space. Like many of SANAA's works, this design blurs the boundaries between interior and exterior, emphasising harmony with the surrounding environment.

Kazuyo Sejima's visionary approach and her work with SANAA has earned her numerous accolades, including the prestigious Pritzker Architecture Prize in 2010, and inspired a new generation of architects. Her ability to transcend traditional architectural norms while creating innovative, human-centred designs underscores her significant impact on the field.[2]

[2] Martínez, P.G. and Ramos, F.J.M., 2022. Emerging patterns in the construction of Sejima's, Sanaa's and Nishizawa's domestic spaces, from 1987 to 2010. Frontiers of Architectural Research, 11(3), pp.375-401.

Dior Omotesando, Tokyo by SANAA

Bjarke Ingels

Bjarke Ingels founded BIG (Bjarke Ingels Group), in 2005 at age 30, determined to make a significant impact in the world of architecture despite scepticism from established architects who doubted his ability to succeed at such a young age. Ingels remained undeterred, and his unique approach to design and architecture has solidified his reputation as one of the leading architects of his generation.

Ingels' innovative designs blend functionality with sustainability and aesthetic appeal. One of his notable early projects is the '8 House' in Copenhagen, completed in 2010. It features a distinctive figure-eight layout, integrating apartments, townhouses, and commercial spaces while promoting community interaction with green roofs and bike paths. Another remarkable project is the Kistefos Museum, known as 'The Twist', in Jevnaker, Norway, which opened in 2019. Twisting its way across the Randselva River, the museum is both a functional bridge and an art gallery, showcasing Ingels' ability to merge art with utility.

Ingels designed 'VIA 57 West' in New York City, completed in 2016. Its distinctive tetrahedral shape offers residents stunning views of the Hudson River while maximising natural light and ventilation. Ingels' 2016 Serpentine Summer Pavilion in London was an 'unzipped wall' that was transformed from straight line to undulating structure that played with light and shadow.

Bjarke Ingels apartments in Copenhagen, Hovedstaden, Denmark

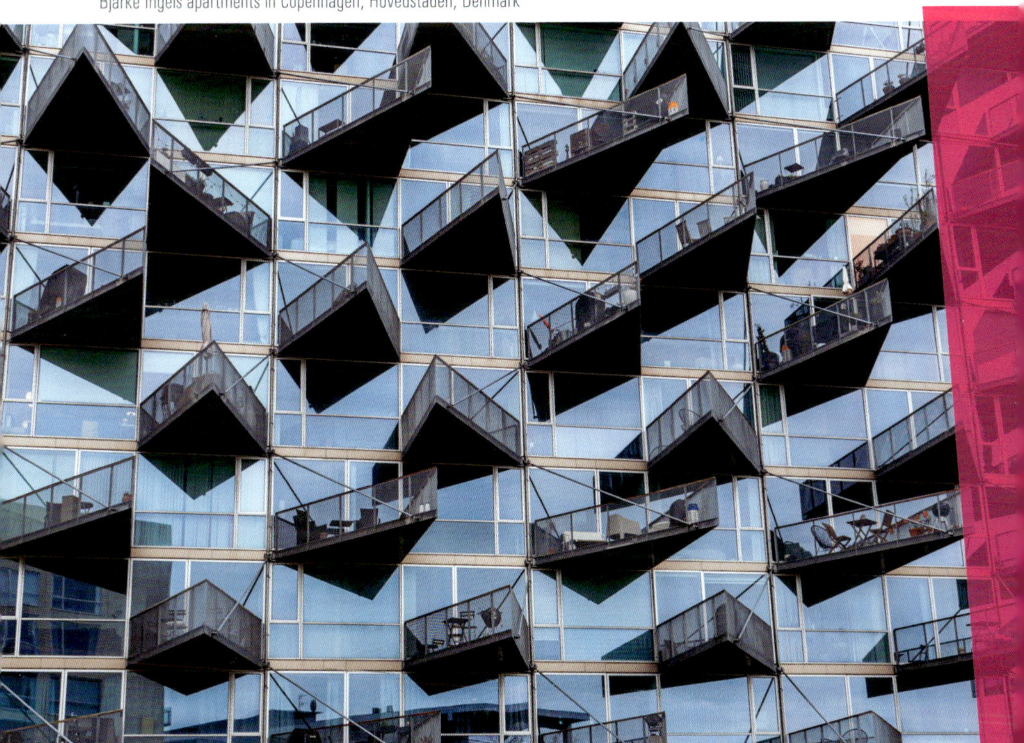

Worcester Cathedral Visitor Centre and Crypt refurbishment by Clews Architect

Case Study Clews Architects by David Finlay

The story of Clews Architects, founded by Michael Clews in 1972 in his rented cottage in Kings Sutton, Oxfordshire, illustrates the benefits of pulling the ripcord in architectural practice. After Heather Clews joined in 1980, the small team of five aimed to establish its identity. They nearly won a prestigious Oxford College Competition, which would have established the practice for years. However, the competition process brought them exposure that led to a key commission: a government-funded project to re-survey and then assign new or amended listing descriptions to all historic buildings in England. Clews Architects was awarded the counties of Oxfordshire, Northamptonshire, and Warwickshire to re-survey, providing a significant workload and source of revenue during a recession, and allowing the practice to develop their qualifications working in and around historic buildings.

Working in the heritage sector alongside surveyors, archaeologists and researchers provided a strong grounding in conservation and, ultimately, set the firm on its path to working with historic structures by enabling them to design new contemporary buildings in sensitive heritage locations. The

[3] Ingels, B., 2015. BIG. Hot to cold. An odyssey of architectural adaptation. Taschen.

experience defined the practice's ethos. Their early design rigor, a product of working in sensitive locations, has remained a constant, becoming the practice's core identity. The defining characteristic of all their work is a sensitivity to context and the creation of bespoke quality solutions.

Once the practice had gained a foothold in conservation and it was clear they could win work within this field, there was a deliberate decision to diversify and apply this experience to educational, residential, and community buildings to stabilise workflow and reduce commercial risk during economic downturns. Clew Architects, like most architectural practices, faces the ongoing challenge of conveying their diverse experience to prospective clients. In their case, they need to overcome misconceptions that being an expert in conservation limits their architectural capabilities.

Learning from Clews Architects

Clews Architects' success underscores the importance of embracing early career challenges as opportunities for growth and learning, and the necessity of clear purpose, willingness to embrace discomfort, and the importance of building a supportive network. It demonstrates how early experiences shape a practice's identity and ethos, enabling architects to create impactful, innovative work aligned with their values. By pulling the ripcord and embracing new paths, architects can achieve fulfilling and successful careers, contributing meaningfully to society and the built environment.

Worcester Cathedral Visitor Centre

LANDING ON YOUR FEET
10 Key Learning Points //

1. **Reflect on Personal Identity** Continuously reflect on your unique talents, passions, and values to align your professional work with your deeper purpose. This ongoing reflection is crucial for personal and professional growth.
2. **Define Your Purpose Statement** Create a clear and compelling purpose statement that encapsulates your values, contributions, and impact. This statement serves as a guiding star, inspiring both you and your team.
3. **Align Work with Core Values** Ensure your projects and professional decisions are aligned with your core values and aspirations. This alignment enhances fulfilment and impact in your architectural career.
4. **Communicate Your Purpose** Effectively communicate your purpose to your team, clients, and stakeholders using storytelling and visuals to ensure everyone is aligned with your vision.
5. **Evaluate Impact Regularly** Continuously assess your work's social, environmental, and economic impact. Use data, feedback, and metrics to measure and refine your approach, ensuring ongoing alignment with your purpose.
6. **Embrace Leadership Principles** Integrate leadership principles into your practice by developing a compelling vision, fostering a culture of innovation and practicing ethical decision-making.
7. **Study Purpose-Driven Organizations** Learn from successful purpose-driven organisations like Patagonia, Unilever, and Tesla. Apply their principles of mission alignment, stakeholder engagement, and social impact to your architectural practice.
8. **Embrace Discomfort for Growth** Accept that discomfort is a natural part of growth and learning. Step out of your comfort zone to embrace new challenges, learn new skills, and enhance your professional capabilities.
9. **Build a Support Network** Surround yourself with supportive peers, mentors, and communities that share your values and vision. A strong support network provides encouragement, feedback, and accountability.
10. **Take Bold Action** Take bold and decisive actions to pursue paths that align with your authentic self and professional aspirations. Each step, no matter how small, moves you closer to your goals.

[1] Wright, F.L., 1939. An organic architecture; the architecture of democracy. Mit Press.

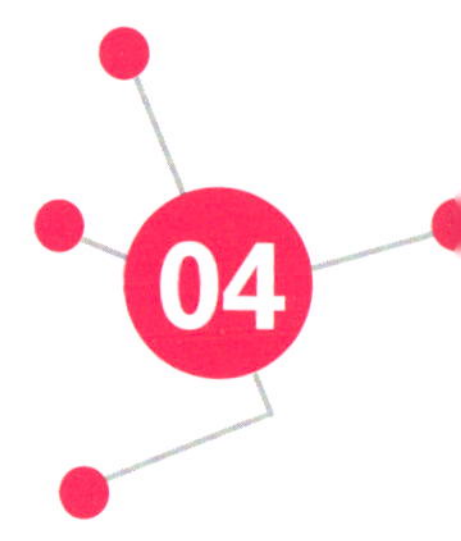

CHAPTER FOUR

Who Are You Really?
Finding Your Architectural Identity Without a Crisis

As discussed in the previous chapter, architectural identity transcends mere design aesthetics; it embodies the core beliefs, motivations, and ethical standards that navigate architects through their careers.

Developing a distinct architectural identity is essential for success, setting you apart in a competitive market. In this chapter we examine the elements contributing to this vital attribute. By reflecting on these, you can develop a Unique Selling Point (USP) that resonates with your target market and clearly communicates why clients should choose you over competitors. Through practical examples, case studies, and actionable insights, we provide the tools needed to build a distinctive architectural identity.

4.1 // Architectural Identity - Who Exactly Are You?

(Defining Your Unique Architectural Persona)

During university, architecture students are exposed to many design theories and styles and start developing their creative vision. However, relying solely on what one learns in university is insufficient to develop a strong architectural identity. The distinct identities adopted by architectural practices that guide their design philosophy, project approach, and overall practice development are influenced by factors that include the architects' vision, values, influences, and prevailing industry trends. These can significantly shape a practice's early development, influencing adoption of technology, collaboration strategies, material choices, and innovation decisions.

Frank Lloyd Wright and Zaha Hadid are, respectively, the most iconic and the most influential architects of the 20th and 21st centuries. Their distinct and unique design styles significantly impacted the field of architecture. Frank Lloyd Wright's architectural principles were influenced by his upbringing in rural Wisconsin, where he developed a deep appreciation for the natural world. His organic architecture, which uses natural materials, integrates with the surrounding environment, and

focuses on functionality[1]. In 1911 he built the first iteration of his Wisconsin home/studio Taliesin on those principles. By 1950 his fame was such, that when three young Irish architecture students were awarded Fellowships to study with him there yet lacked the funds for steamship tickets, they risked a transatlantic crossing from Ireland to New York in an 11-meter wooden sailboat called the 'Ituna' they had renovated themselves. The adventure gained Tony Jacob, Sean Kenny, Des Dalton and their friend, Kevin O'Farrell, who had 'come along for the ride', considerable publicity and fame.

On the other hand, Zaha Hadid was known for her avant-garde and futuristic designs, pushing the boundaries of what was architecturally possible. Her designs were characterised by their fluid forms, sharp angles, and use of cutting-edge materials and technology. Hadid's design principles were influenced by her upbringing in Baghdad and early experiences as an architect in London.

4.2 // Developing a Unique Selling Point (USP)

(Standing Out in a Sea of Blueprints)

Identifying and cultivating a USP is crucial for architects seeking to differentiate themselves in a crowded market. It involves identifying and communicating what makes your architectural practice or approach unique, valuable, and appealing to your target clients. As you curate your unique positioning, your brand emerges as a channel to express this essence. It's a dynamic encapsulation of your principles, aspirations, and creative inclinations.

Action Points

1. **Understand Your Target Market**
   - **Research:** Understand your target clients' needs, preferences, and pain points. Are they commercial developers, residential homeowners, or perhaps institutions like schools or hospitals?
   - **Segmentation:** Narrow your target market to those that would most benefit from your unique services.
2. **Analyse Your Competition**
   - **Identify Key Players:** Look at other architects operating in your target market. What services do they offer? What are their strengths and weaknesses?
   - **Differentiation:** Find gaps in the market or areas where you can excel beyond what is already offered.

[1] Wright, F.L., 1939. An organic architecture; the architecture of democracy. Mit Press.
[2] Hadid, Z., 2004. Zaha Hadid: complete works. Thames & Hudson

3 **Identify Your Strengths and Specialties**

- **Expertise:** Pinpoint your areas of expertise. Are you specialising in sustainable design, historic restoration, or cutting-edge technology like BIM (Building Information Modelling)?
- **Approach:** Consider what makes your design process or approach unique. Do you have a participatory design process, or do you integrate advanced technologies or materials in a novel way?

4. **Develop Your USP Statement**

- **Concise and Clear:** Your USP should briefly communicate what makes you different and why clients should choose you over competitors. It should address your target market's needs and your competitive advantage.
- **Benefit-focused:** Focus on the benefits your clients will gain from working with you. Will they save money in the long run, enjoy a uniquely personalised design process, or benefit from innovative, sustainable design practices?

5. **Communicate Your USP**

- **Marketing Materials:** Incorporate your USP into all your marketing materials, including your website, portfolio, social media, and pitch presentations.
- **Consistency:** Ensure the message is consistent across all channels to strengthen brand recognition.

6. **Deliver on Your Promises**

- **Quality:** Ensure that your work consistently reflects the quality and uniqueness promised in your USP.
- **Feedback:** Regularly solicit feedback from clients and adjust your practices as necessary to ensure you continue to meet or exceed expectations.

7. **Continuous Improvement**

- **Stay Informed:** Keep abreast of new trends, technologies, and methodologies in architecture to refine and update your USP continually.
- **Evolve:** As your practice grows and the market changes, be prepared to adjust your USP to remain relevant and competitive.

.Developing a strong USP is an ongoing process that involves a deep understanding of your market, continuous improvement, and clear, consistent communication. It's your key to standing out and building a loyal client base.

4.3 // Examples of Architectural Practices with Strong Identities and USP

(Learning from the Greats Without Copying Their Homework)

A well-defined USP communicates a practices' unique attributes clearly and persuasively, enabling potential clients to understand why they should choose your services. Here, we give examples of architectural practices with strong identities and effective USPs to illustrate how aligning your core values and strengths with market needs can create a distinctive brand that resonates with clients and stakeholders.

As you read through these examples, consider how their strategies might inspire and inform your own practice, helping you to carve out a distinctive and successful niche in the industry.

Technological Innovators

Practices that embrace technology as the core of their identity lead in adopting advanced design visualisation and construction tools. They prioritise digital advancements like Building Information Modeling (BIM) and parametric design techniques to create intricate and responsive structures. Snøhetta, a Norwegian design firm known for using advanced software in projects like the Oslo Opera House and the San Francisco Museum of Modern Art expansion, exemplifies this approach.

Collaborative Visionaries

The transformative power of teamwork shapes the architectural philosophy of practices that embrace a collaborative identity. This spirit facilitates the exchange of ideas and fosters innovative

Snohetta, Oslo Opera House

thinking. SHoP Architects, with projects like the Domino Sugar Refinery redevelopment, typify this approach.

Material Explorers

Architectural identities focused on material exploration prioritise using innovative construction materials. Kengo Kuma & Associates blend traditional craftsmanship with contemporary technology, as seen in the V&A Dundee Museum.

Sustainable Pioneers

Sustainable practices prioritise eco-friendly design and construction methods. They integrate green technologies, energy-efficient systems, and resilient design strategies. William McDonough + Partners specialise in cradle-to-cradle design principles, creating buildings and environments that are regenerative and beneficial for all life.

Case Study: Tomas Miller Architect

Some of my earliest memories were of a small, hippy island in Canada where I lived with my parents for 6 months. There, houses emerged from driftwood, shaped by the hands that would call them home. When I returned to that island after my Part 1 studies, I expected my trained eye to find amateurish attempts. Instead, I found genius in their simplicity, the heartfelt artistry of untrained builders.

Back in Gloucestershire, after failing my Part II and moving in with my parents, I was adrift. Then, an old friend from Edinburgh invited me to help build a treehouse. It was like finding that island spirit again. What began as a single project turned into three years of designing and building whimsical, beloved structures. We became architects who built with our own hands, blending traditional craftsmanship with innovative technology, and people were drawn to that dual identity.

As we evolved into a more traditional practice, something was missing. Professional practice felt like pushing uphill. On weekends, I found solace in tech projects—another childhood passion—rigging stepper motors from printers to Raspberry Pi devices, crafting time-lapse camera sliders. A business coach noticed my enthusiasm and suggested integrating tech into our practice. This gave me permission to be at play with work again.

We began capturing sites in 3D with drones, VR headsets, photogrammetry, and game software like Unreal Engine, iterating designs rapidly, and presenting them in virtual reality. Clients were enthralled, and the work was exhilarating. This blend of tech and architecture felt exciting. Delving into project management literature, I discovered 'Creative Inc.' and 'The Lean Startup', which resonated deeply, emphasising quick iterations, learning, and discovery over rigid planning.

Drone Photogrammetry Scan - Tomas Millar, Millar Howard Workshop

However, architecture's business model—hourly rates—felt constraining. Despite our innovations, the gains were marginal. We explored property development but quickly veered away from becoming traditional developers. Inspired by the self-built homes of Hornby Island, we sold serviced plots, letting end-users infuse their creations with love and care. This approach mirrored my roots and brought immense satisfaction.

Collaborating with other architects, we embraced a broader vision. Now inspired by Y Combinator's startup ethos, we aimed to revolutionise homebuilding, making it personal and heartfelt yet

The Dursley Treehouse, Gloucestershire, Millar Howard Workshop.

tech-enabled. Angel funding propelled us forward. The emergence of AI nurtured my coding abilities. Now, merging tech, architecture and traditional craft, we strive to transform how homes are built, focusing on innovation, end-users, and the joy of creation. It feels like a new beginning, yet it's built on the foundation of all that came before.

Reflecting on this journey, I see a tapestry of influences and ideas. The takeaway? Lean into your passions. Venture off the beaten path, and you'll discover uncharted landscapes where you lead the way. Whether finding a niche within your profession or crafting a new business model, pursuing what you love can be personally fulfilling and commercially rewarding.

Millar Howard Workshop Offices, Stroud; Millar Howard Workshop (Isaac Orr)

Livedin Custom Build, Designs by Project Orange, Image Copyright - Livedin Custom Build.

The Yarrows Deck - Early Project Designed and Built by Tomas Miller.

Reflection on Tomas Miller's Journey

Tomas Miller's journey illustrates the transformative power of integrating personal passions with professional practice to find joy and fulfillment in one's work. His practice, which began with hands-on construction of whimsical structures, evolved into a technologically advanced architectural practice that incorporates drones, VR, and photogrammetry. His initial struggles and subsequent success in blending traditional craftsmanship with cutting-edge technology underscore the importance of perseverance and continuous learning.

By integrating his love for technology and innovative building techniques into his practice, Miller not only differentiated his firm but also found renewed passion and creativity, which led to a more satisfying and sustainable career. Miller's journey also underscores the value of adaptability and openness to new ideas, and how embracing new technologies can create unique value.

Finally, this case study emphasises the importance of engaging with mentors, collaborating with diverse stakeholders, and staying open to new ideas and technologies to enhance your professional growth and contribute more effectively to communities and the broader field of architecture.

WHO ARE YOU REALLY?
10 Key Learning Points //

1. **Defining Architectural Identity:** Understand Your Unique Persona: Reflect on your talents, passions, and values to create a distinct architectural identity that guides your professional decisions and actions.
2. **Developing a USP:** Stand Out in a Crowded Market: Learn how to create a Unique Selling Point that highlights your unique strengths and appeals to your target clients, making your practice easily distinguishable.
3. **Continuous Improvement:** Embrace Lifelong Learning: Emphasize the need for ongoing learning, adaptation, and staying abreast of technological advancements to remain relevant and competitive in the field.
4. **Visionary Impact:** Drive Lasting Innovation: Recognize that true success in architecture is defined by the lasting impact and innovative solutions you bring to the field.
5. **Ethical Considerations:** Promote Social and Environmental Responsibility: Prioritise ethical design practices that promote social equity, environmental sustainability, and community well-being in all your projects.
6. **Community Enrichment:** Design for Social Interaction: Create spaces that enhance social interaction, inclusivity, and the overall quality of life for communities, ensuring your work contributes positively to society.
7. **Client Satisfaction:** Meet and Exceed Client Needs: Focus on understanding and fulfilling client needs to build strong, lasting relationships and gain referrals, ensuring your practice thrives on reputation and trust.
8. **Mentorship and Education:** Foster Continuous Learning: Invest in sharing your knowledge and experience with the next generation of architects to foster a culture of continuous learning and professional growth within the industry.
9. **Cultivate Resilience and Adaptability:** Overcome Challenges with Innovation: Leverage your unique strengths and embrace new approaches to overcome challenges, ensuring resilience and adaptability in your professional journey.
10. **Take Bold Action:** Pursue Authentic Paths: Take bold and decisive actions to pursue paths that align with your authentic self and professional aspirations, moving closer to your goals with each step.

CHAPTER FIVE

VALUES OVER VALUABLES

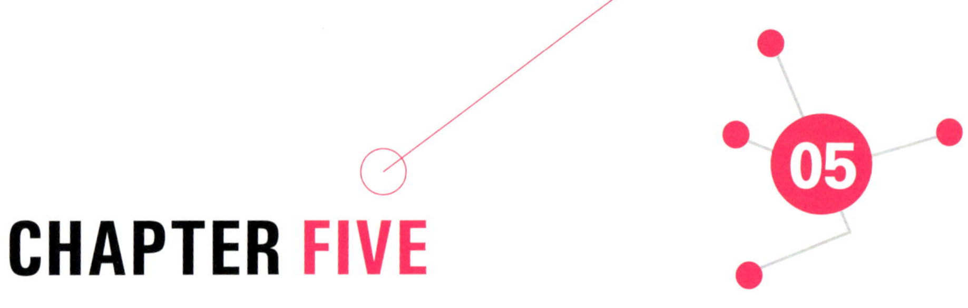

CHAPTER FIVE

Values Over Valuables: Redefining Success Beyond the Bank Account

Often narrowly defined by material achievements, success can also be defined by other criteria. It can encompass visionary impact, design innovation, ethical considerations, community enrichment, awards, client satisfaction, education, mentorship, and broader cultural and social influence.

This chapter provides examples of successful architects whose work embodies these aspects of architectural achievement. QR codes linking to videos and podcasts offer a dynamic way to explore their projects. This chapter also offers tools with which to identify and articulate your unique talents and perspectives and how to make use of them to best advantage. By ensuring your designs embody your architectural vision and core values, and by prioritising these over profit alone, you can achieve a lasting impact on the built environment and society. And remember; an architect's journey is one of continuous learning, adaptation, and reflection.

5.1 // Redefining Success

(More Than Just a Fat Wallet)

Architects who make an enduring imprint on the built environment, introduce groundbreaking design paradigms, and uplift communities embody a deeper, more comprehensive form of success.

Visionary Impact

Architects who embrace this holistic view of achievement recognise that their creations are not solely financial commodities but enduring reflections of their vision and dedication. Consider Zaha Hadid's fluid and dynamic forms: her structures, characterised by their sweeping curves and bold forms, challenged conventional notions of space and structure, redefining architectural aesthetics and inspiring countless other architects. Hadid's work demonstrates how visionary impact can transcend traditional architectural practices and invite us to see the built environment in new ways.

 **Explore the following 360-degree video tours of Zaha Hadid's projects.**

Her iconic project at **520 West 28th Street** in New York is one example that illustrates her innovative designs.

The sustainable design of the **King Abdullah Petroleum Studies and Research Center** in Riyadh can be seen in this virtual tour.

Watch this video to learn about the sinuous forms of the **BEEAH Headquarters** designed by Zaha Hadid Architects.

Design Innovation

Pioneering architectural concepts that push the boundaries of creativity and innovation constitute another facet of success. Architects who challenge conventions and introduce novel design approaches contribute to the field's evolution.

Apple Headquarters Building, Cupertino by Foster & Partners

Foster + Partners' design for the Apple Park campus sets a benchmark for environmentally conscious architecture. The circular design is aesthetically pleasing and symbolises the infinite loop of innovation and sustainability the company strives towards. The building incorporates renewable energy sources, efficient ventilation systems, and lush landscaping, highlighting how innovative design can merge functionality with sustainability, creating beautiful and environmentally responsible spaces.

5.2 // Ethical Considerations and Community Enrichment

(Doing Good While Doing Well)

Diébédo Francis Kéré's approach to architecture is deeply rooted in the principles of social equity and sustainability, and demonstrates how ethical considerations can enhance architectural design. By engaging local communities and using indigenous materials, he creates buildings that are environmentally sustainable and culturally resonant. He exemplifies ethical principles in his design for the Gando Primary School in Burkina Faso, which provides a functional and sustainable educational facility and empowers the local community by involving them in the construction process.

Social Entrepreneurship

Alejandro Aravena, a Chilean architect and a key figure in the firm Elemental, is renowned for his socially driven architectural solutions. Elemental's 'Half a House' project in Chile addresses the critical issue of affordable housing by providing residents with a basic structure they can complete over time according to their needs and financial capacity. This incremental housing approach simultaneously makes homeownership more accessible and empowers residents by involving them in the building process. Aravena's work exemplifies how architecture can directly address social issues, blending innovative design with social entrepreneurship, showcasing architecture's potential to improve lives.

Explore the innovative **Half a House project** by Alejandro Aravena through this TED interview.

Awards and Recognition

Recognition through prestigious awards such as the Pritzker Architecture Prize, often called the 'Nobel Prize of Architecture',[5] and other accolades validates an architect's expertise and vision and brings global recognition. Awards celebrate the recipient's contributions to humanity through the art of architectural excellence in design, innovation, and sustainability.

Client Satisfaction

When clients are content with the final result and feel that their needs and aspirations were genuinely understood and realised, architects achieve a level of success that resonates on a personal and professional level. Satisfied clients become ambassadors of an architect's work, leading to referrals and long-lasting relationships. For example, the collaborative process in designing the Louvre Abu Dhabi involved effective client-architect collaboration to ensure the design met aesthetic and functional requirements.[6] This resulted in a project that fulfils its purpose and stands as a cultural landmark.

Education and Mentorship

Architects who share their knowledge and experience with emerging professionals contribute to the growth and evolution of the profession by ensuring that architectural success also becomes a collective endeavour. Mentorship can take many forms, from formal teaching roles in universities to informal guidance offered to young architects in the workplace.[7] By nurturing the next generation of architects, seasoned professionals ensure their legacy extends beyond their projects and influences the discipline's future.

[3] Kéré, D.F., 2012. School in Gando, Burkina Faso. Architectural design, 82(6), pp.66-71.
[4] Boano, C. and Vergara Perucich, F., 2016. Half-happy architecture. Viceversa, (4), pp.58-81..

Cultural and Social Influence

Architectural success can also be gauged through the influence of an architect's work. Successful projects become a testament to an architect's unique approach. Designs that influence the broader cultural and social context, challenge conventions, and influence the trajectory of architectural discourse contribute to a deeper understanding of architecture's impact on society. Frank Gehry's Guggenheim Museum in Bilbao not only became an iconic piece of contemporary architecture, it also spurred economic rejuvenation in the city, demonstrating how architecture can catalyse urban transformation.

Case Studies

To illustrate the diverse pathways to achieving architectural success and its multifaceted nature, let's explore some additional case studies.

Creative Entrepreneurship in Architecture - Jeanne Gang and Studio Gang:

Jeanne Gang, the founder of Studio Gang, demonstrates the power of creativity in driving sustainable design solutions.[9] Her projects are known for their innovative design and environmental sensitivity. The Aqua Tower in Chicago, with its undulating balconies, creates a striking visual effect and optimises natural light and energy efficiency. Gang's success is measured by the aesthetic appeal of her designs and her commitment to sustainable urbanism and social responsibility.

Aqua Tower Chicago - Studio Gang

In this podcast interview, **Jeanne Gang** discusses her approach to sustainable urbanism and the design of the **Aqua Tower.**

[5] Mahdavinejad, M. and Hosseini, S.A., 2019. Data mining and content analysis of the jury citations of the Pritzker Architecture Prize (1977–2017). Journal of Architecture and Urbanism, 43(1), pp.71-90..

[6] Morgan, C.L. and Nouvel, J., 1998. Jean Nouvel: The elements of architecture. Universe Pub

[7] Senge, P.M., 2006. The fifth discipline: The art and practice of the learning organization. Broadway Business.

[8] Yücesan, D., 2004. The effects of interdisciplinary relations on architecture: A case study Frank Gehry (Master's thesis, Middle East Technical University)..

Take a video tour of the **V&A Dundee Museum** and see how **Kengo Kuma** blends traditional craftsmanship with modern technology.

Victoria & Albert Museum (V&A) designed by Kengo Kuma & Associates

Material Explorers - Kengo Kuma & Associates:

Kengo Kuma is renowned for his masterful and innovative use of natural materials in contemporary architecture. His design for the V&A Dundee Museum demonstrates how a synthesis of traditional craftsmanship and modern technology can create iconic structures. Kuma's work demonstrates how the choice of materials can significantly impact both the aesthetics and sustainability of a building.

Storytellers - Architects who reflect cultural narratives in their work:

Architects who excel as storytellers weave rich cultural narratives into their designs, creating spaces that resonate deeply with users and communities. This approach involves a profound understanding and appreciation of a project's cultural context. Storytelling architects, such as Taller de Arquitectura, engage with local communities, traditions, and histories to create buildings and spaces that reflect the cultural identity of the communities they serve.

The following examples show how thoughtful and sensitive design can demonstrate architecture's power to create lasting connections between people and places.

[10] Dewey, J., 1933. A restatement of the relation of reflective thinking to the educative process. DC Heath.
[11] Humphrey, A., 2005. SWOT Analysis for Management Consulting. SRI Alumni Newsletter, SRI International.

Urban Visionaries - OMA (Office for Metropolitan Architecture)

Led by Rem Koolhaas, OMA is famous for its visionary approach to urban design and architecture. His work often challenges conventional urban planning paradigms, proposing innovative solutions that address the complexities of contemporary cities. Projects like the Taipei Performing Arts Centre and the Park Grove residential towers in Miami illustrate OMA's commitment to revitalising urban spaces and enhancing the quality of urban life.

Watch **Rem Koolhaas** discuss his visionary urban projects in this in-depth interview.

Adaptive Re-Users - Wilkinson Eyre

Wilkinson Eyre's transformation of the Battersea Power Station in London is a prime example of adaptive reuse. This project preserves the historic character of the power station while revitalising it as a mixed-use development that includes residential, commercial, and public spaces. Their approach demonstrates how historical preservation and modern functionality can coexist, creating spaces that honour the past while serving contemporary needs.

Social Responsibility - MASS Design Group

MASS Design Group focuses on socially impactful projects such as schools, hospitals, and community centres, using architecture as a tool for social justice. Their work, such as the Butaro Hospital in Rwanda, prioritises empathy and community engagement and shows how architecture can improve health outcomes and promote social equity.

Detail Victoria & Albert Museum (V&A)

5.3 // Tools for Self-Reflection

(A Mirror for Your Architectural Soul)

Self-reflection is key to uncovering your unique talents and perspectives.[10] Deep self-exploration demands a deliberate and thoughtful examination of your professional and personal ethos. To gain clarity about your professional identity and chart a path for growth aligned with your deepest values and aspirations, tools like a SWOT analysis are useful to evaluate your professional standing and potential growth areas.

The SWOT Analysis

This method involves a detailed examination of your Strengths, Weaknesses, Opportunities, and Threats (SWOT), offering a structured way to identify and leverage individual strengths, address and mitigate weaknesses, capitalise on opportunities within the industry, and navigate potential threats.

Developing your SWOT Analysis

1. **Identify Strengths:** Reflect on the unique skills, experiences, and qualities that distinguish you in the architectural field. Consider technical proficiency, creative thinking, and any specialised knowledge you possess. Document these strengths clearly and concisely.
2. **Acknowledge Weaknesses:** Evaluate areas for improvement, such as gaps in technical knowledge, design skills, or soft skills like communication and teamwork. Recognising these weaknesses is the first step toward addressing them.
3. **Spot Opportunities:** Research the architectural industry's current trends and future directions. Look for niches or emerging areas where your skills and interests could fill a gap.
4. **Assess Threats:** Consider the external factors that could challenge your career progression, such as market competition, technological changes, or economic downturns. Understanding these threats enables you to develop strategies to mitigate their impact.

An Example of a SWOT Analysis for an Architect Moving from Part 2 Study into Early Career

The transition from Part 2 study into an early career phase is characterised by a shift from theoretical learning to practical application, requiring a blend of technical skills, creative vision, and professional acumen. To navigate this transition successfully, conducting a SWOT analysis will help you create a targeted action plan that positions you for success in your early career.

Strengths	Weaknesses
- Technical Proficiency: Strong skills in CAD software, 3D modeling, and BIM (Building Information Modeling).	- Limited Practical Experience: Lack of extensive real-world project management experience.
- Creative Thinking: Proven ability to develop innovative design concepts and solutions.	- Soft Skills: Need to improve communication and teamwork abilities.
- Specialized Knowledge: Experience in sustainable design and green building practices.	- Network: Limited professional network within the industry.
- Educational Background: Comprehensive architectural education with hands-on project experience.	- Portfolio: May need more diversity and completed projects to showcase a full range of abilities.
- Adaptability: Quick to learn and adapt to new tools and methodologies.	- Business Acumen: Limited understanding of business and financial aspects of architectural
Opportunities	**Threats**
- Industry Trends: Growth in sustainable and eco-friendly design offers opportunities to leverage specialized knowledge.	- Market Competition: High competition from other graduates and experienced professionals.
- Technological Advances: Increasing use of digital fabrication and parametric design can be areas to explore.	- Technological Changes: Rapid technological advancements requiring continuous learning and adaptation.
- Market Demand: Rising demand for community-focused projects and affordable housing solutions.	- Economic Downturns: Potential for reduced investment in new projects during economic slowdowns.
- Continued Education: Opportunities for further certifications or specialized training in emerging areas like smart buildings.	- Regulatory Changes: Changes in building codes and regulations that could impact project requirements and timelines.
- Networking: Joining professional organizations and attending industry conferences to expand network.	- Firm Consolidations: Larger firms merging or acquiring smaller firms, reducing job opportunities.

Example of a Swot Analysis

Developing and Maintaining Your Action Plan

After creating an action plan, implement measures to enhance your strengths and improve your weaknesses. Regularly review and update your SWOT analysis to reflect your growing experience, shifting goals, and changes in the architectural field, to ensure your professional identity remains dynamic and responsive to new challenges and opportunities.

Below is an illustration of how to develop and maintain your action plan based on your SWOT analysis.

Enhance Strengths	Improve Weaknesses	Seize Opportunities	Prepare for Threats
- Continue Learning: Stay updated with the latest trends in sustainable design and digital tools.	- Gain Experience: Pursue internships or part-time work to gain real-world project management experience.	- Target Emerging Areas: Focus job search and project proposals on sustainable design and digital fabrication.	- Stay Competitive: Continuously update skills and knowledge to remain competitive in the job market.
- Showcase Skills: Develop a strong portfolio highlighting technical skills and creative projects.	- Develop Soft Skills: Enroll in communication and teamwork workshops or courses.	- Pursue Certifications: Obtain certifications in smart building technology or other emerging fields.	- Adaptability: Be prepared to quickly learn and adapt to new technologies and methodologies.
- Seek Feedback: Regularly seek feedback from mentors and peers to continuously improve design and technical skills.	- Expand Portfolio: Take on diverse projects to showcase a wide range of abilities and completed works.	- Network Actively: Join professional organizations, attend industry events, and participate in online forums to build connections.	- Economic Awareness: Stay informed about economic trends and be flexible with career plans during downturns.
	- Learn Business Basics: Take introductory courses in business and finance related to architectural practice.		- Regulatory Updates: Keep abreast of changes in building codes and regulations to ensure compliance in projects.
			- Explore Various Firms: Consider opportunities in both large and small firms to diversify job prospects.

Action Plan based on Swot Analysis

5.4 // Emerging Trends in Architecture

(Keeping Up with the Joneses (and the Jetsons)

By staying informed about emerging trends and proactively incorporating them into their practice, architects can ensure that they remain relevant and competitive in a rapidly evolving field. Two significant trends currently shaping the field are biophilic design and smart cities.

The Bosco Verticale skyscrapers in Milan

Biophilic Design

Biophilic design integrates natural elements into architectural spaces to promote the health, productivity, and overall well-being of the occupants. Examples of biophilic design include using natural materials, incorporating indoor plants and natural lighting, and creating green spaces within urban environments.

- **Theoretical Foundation:** The concept of biophilic design is grounded in the biophilia hypothesis proposed by E.O. Wilson, which suggests that humans have an innate affinity for nature.[12]
- **Practical Application:** The Amazon Spheres in Seattle exemplify biophilic design. These office spaces feature a lush indoor rainforest, providing employees with a tranquil and inspiring work environment.[13] By prioritising biophilic design, architects can create spaces that are not only beautiful but also support mental and physical health.

Smart Cities

Smart cities harness technology and data to enhance the quality of life for residents. Key features of smart cities include intelligent transportation systems, energy-efficient buildings, and the integration of Internet of Things (IoT) devices to monitor and manage urban resources.

- **Theoretical Foundation:** The concept of smart cities is supported by theories of urban informatics and cyber-physical systems, which explore the integration of digital technology with physical urban infrastructure to enhance efficiency and sustainability.[14]
- **Practical Application:** Songdo International Business District in South Korea is a prime example of a smart city. Integrated, cutting-edge technology is used to manage resources efficiently, reduce energy consumption, and provide residents with a high quality of life.[15]

[14] Townsend, A.M., 2013. Smart cities: Big data, civic hackers, and the quest for a new utopia. WW Norton & Company.

[15] Rugkhapan, N.T. and Murray, M.J., 2019. Songdo IBD (International Business District): Experimental prototype for the city of tomorrow? International Planning Studies, 24(3-4), pp. 272-292.

Strategies to Stay Ahead and Leverage These Trends

- **Collaborative Innovation:** Collaborating with technologists, urban planners, and environmental scientists can help architects integrate cutting-edge solutions into their designs. Interdisciplinary collaboration fosters innovation and ensures that architectural projects meet modern standards of sustainability and efficiency.[16]
- **Client Education:** Educating clients about the benefits of biophilic design and smart city principles can help secure buy-in for projects that incorporate these trends. Clear communication of the long-term advantages, such as improved well-being and cost savings, is essential.[17]
- **Adapting to Change:** Architects must be flexible and willing to adapt their practices to incorporate new trends. This might involve adopting new design software, learning about the latest materials, or exploring innovative construction techniques.[18]

Smart Cities

[12] Krčmářová, J., 2009. EO Wilson's concept of biophilia and the environmental movement in the USA. Klaudyán: Internet J Histor Geogr Environ History, 6(1/2), pp.4-17..
[13] Jamawat, J., 2019. Redesign, redeploy, and re-envision urban corporate headquarters: Amazon's Seattle campus case study (Doctoral dissertation, Massachusetts Institute of Technology).

VALUES OVER VALUABLES

10 Key Learning Points //

1. **Defining Architectural Identity:** Understand the importance of having a distinct architectural identity that reflects your values, principles, and creative vision.
2. **Developing a USP:** Learn how to create a Unique Selling Point that sets you apart in a crowded market and appeals to your target clients.
3. **Continuous Improvement:** Emphasize the need for ongoing learning and adaptation to stay relevant and competitive in the field.
4. **Visionary Impact:** Recognize that true success in architecture is defined by the lasting impact and innovation you bring to the field.
5. **Ethical Considerations:** Prioritize ethical design practices that promote social equity, environmental sustainability, and community well-being.
6. **Community Enrichment:** Design spaces that enhance social interaction, inclusivity, and the overall quality of life for communities.
7. **Client Satisfaction:** Focus on understanding and meeting client needs to build strong, lasting relationships and gain referrals.
8. **Awards and Recognition:** Seek recognition through awards and accolades to validate your expertise and elevate your professional reputation.
9. **Mentorship and Education:** Invest in sharing your knowledge and experience with the next generation of architects to foster a culture of continuous learning.
10. **Cultural and Social Influence:** Aim to create designs that provoke thought, challenge conventions, and contribute positively to the broader cultural and social context.

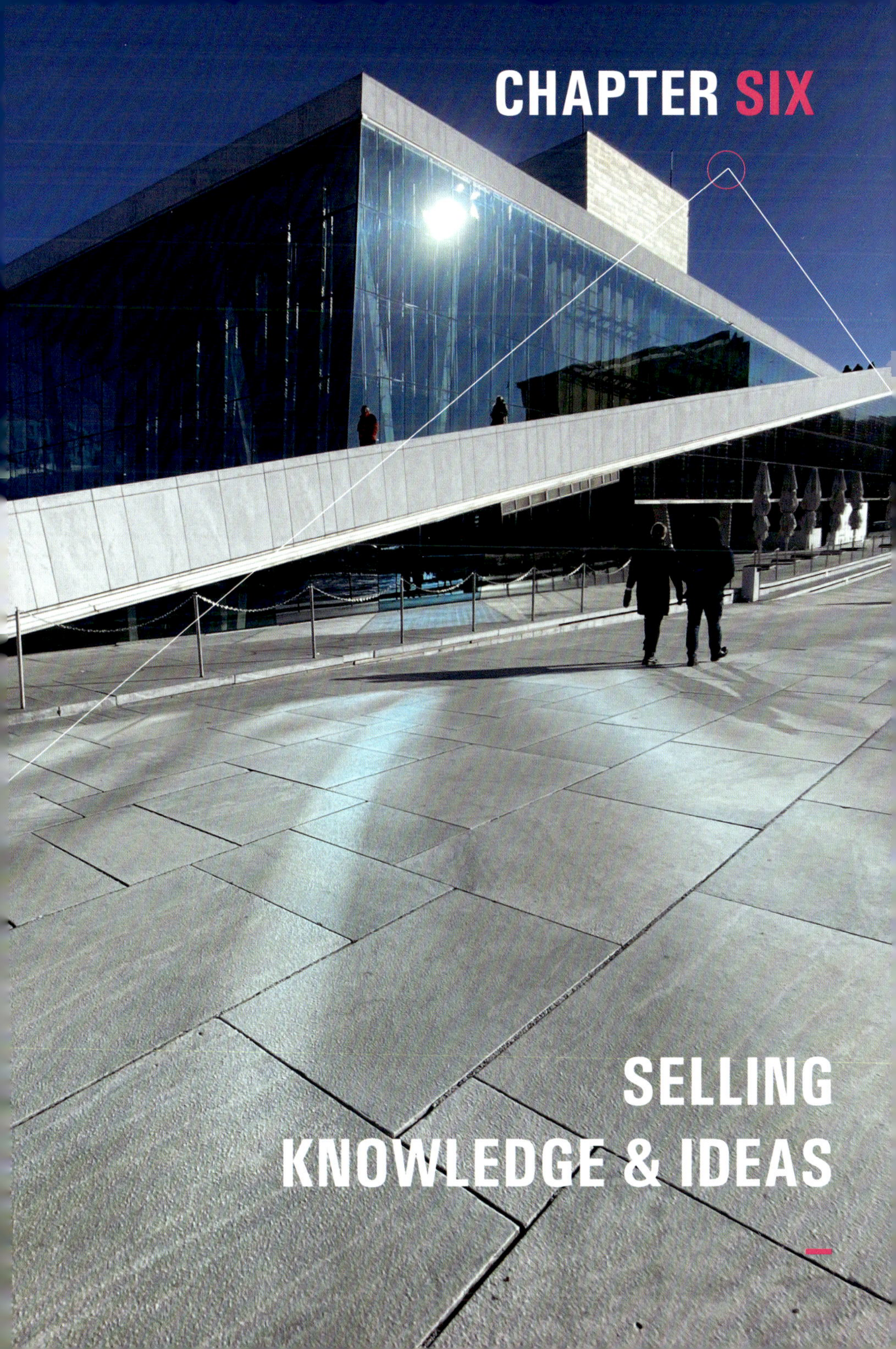

CHAPTER SIX

SELLING KNOWLEDGE & IDEAS

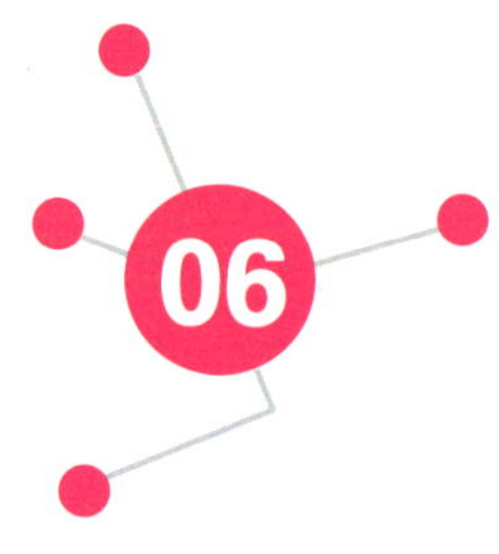

CHAPTER SIX

Selling Knowledge and Ideas: Persuading Clients Without Selling Your Soul

Chapter Six explores the world of professional branding and persuasive communication, guiding architects to present their compellingly and handle client objections effectively. It covers ways to enhance networking and offers insights into developing a compelling portfolio that showcases individual talent, collaborative efforts, and problem-solving skills to build a strong, evolving personal brand. The chapter also emphasises adding value through education and free consultations, positioning architects as trusted advisors rather than mere service providers.

6.1 // Mastering the Art of Communication

(Talking the Talk: Making Sure Your Ideas Don't Get Lost in Translation)

In this section, we propose an 8-principle methodology to help you to share your vision effectively, shaping the discourse of your academic journey and beyond.

Principle One Articulating Architectural Concepts

As an architect, your ideas are valuable, albeit intangible, assets that can generate income.[1] However, selling ideas differs from selling physical products.

For undergraduates, it begins with design critiques, where selling ideas means conveying a concept's essence to peers and mentors. Weekly design reviews provide a platform for presenting creative concepts and architectural visions, and this structured approach teaches students to articulate their design rationale clearly and transform presentations into narratives that integrate concept, function, and context.

Graduates face the challenge of selling their ideas during examinations, judged against real-world parameters. Here, the methodology helps refine presentation skills, showcase design expertise, and

[1] Sinek, S., 2009. Start with why: How great leaders inspire everyone to take action. Penguin.

demonstrate their understanding of the nuances shaping the built environment. Success at this stage is crucial for exams and lays the groundwork for their professional reputations.

Early career professionals must master selling ideas to clients. Here, the architect's profile serves as inspiration. The methodology becomes a toolkit for crafting persuasive narratives that convey both the architectural form and its deeper purpose, helping establish trust and rapport with clients by inviting them into a shared vision that aligns the architect's ideas with the client's goals and expectations.[2]

Action Points for Selling Knowledge and Ideas:

- **Engage in Active Storytelling:** Use storytelling techniques to convey the essence of your ideas. Create a narrative highlighting your designs' concept, function, and context.
- **Utilise Digital Tools:** Leverage software and online platforms to create visually appealing presentations and maintain an updated digital portfolio.
- **Engage with Social Media:** Share insights and project updates on platforms like Instagram and X to build a broader community and reach potential clients.
- **Host Webinars:** Conduct webinars to showcase your expertise and engage with a broader audience.
- **Seek Feedback:** Regularly seek feedback from peers and mentors to refine your presentation skills and methodologies.

6.2 // Creating and Maintaining a Dynamic Portfolio

(Portfolio Magic: Turning Your Work into a Visual Masterpiece)

Principle Two Creating and Maintaining Your Portfolio

A well-crafted portfolio acts as a visual résumé, showcasing your skills, design philosophy, and approach to potential clients, employers, and collaborators. For students and recent graduates, the portfolio is crucial for securing internships and entry-level positions by demonstrating the ability to apply theoretical knowledge to real projects.

As you progress, your portfolio shows your evolving expertise and breadth of work. Detailed case studies of significant work highlight your problem-solving and technical skills, strategic thinking, and your ability to manage complex projects. Illustrating your progress with sketches, diagrams, and progress photos illustrates your methodology and attention to detail.[3] Digital platforms can enhance accessibility and reach, allowing architects to present their work to a global audience.

[2] Goodyear, P. and Carvalho, L., 2014. The architecture of productive learning networks. Routledge.
[3] Samuel, F., 2018. Why architects matter: Evidencing and communicating the value of architects. Routledge.

Action Points for Creating and Maintaining a Portfolio:

- **Regular Updates:** Keep your portfolio current by regularly adding new projects and removing outdated work.
- **Showcase Process and Outcome:** Include a mix of process work (sketches, models) and finished projects to demonstrate your approach and final solutions.
- **Reflect on Collaborations:** Clearly articulate your role in team projects, focusing on how you contributed to and influenced the outcomes.
- **Incorporate Feedback:** Seek feedback on your portfolio from mentors and peers and use this to refine and improve your presentation.
- **Leverage Digital Platforms:** Use online portfolio platforms to reach a wider audience and ensure your work is accessible and engaging.

6.3 // Establishing a Strong Personal Brand

(Brand You: Making Yourself Unforgettable in the Architectural World)

Principle Three Establishing Your Brand Identity

Developing a personal brand as an architectural student lays the foundation for your later professional identity, unique perspectives and values. Your brand should evolve to reflect your ethos and growing expertise, becoming a vital tool to attract clients and collaborators.[4]

A solid personal brand differentiates you in the architectural profession. By clearly communicating your value and what you have to offer, it helps potential clients and employers understand why they should choose to work with you. For students and young professionals, establishing a personal brand helps build a supportive network of mentors, peers, and industry connections for career growth.

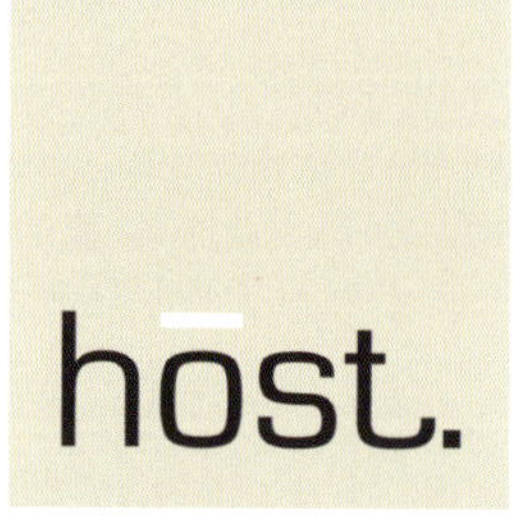

Develop Your Brand

[4] Neumeier, M., 2005. The brand gap. Peachpit Press.

Personal branding includes your visual identity, communication style, and online presence. Consistent use of your logo, colour scheme, and design style across all platforms creates a cohesive and recognisable brand. Your communication style, whether formal or conversational, should consistently reflect your personality and values to build credibility.[5]

Engaging on platforms like LinkedIn, Instagram, and X allows you to share your work, thoughts, and insights. Regularly updating your website with content keeps your audience interested. Networking, both online and offline, further enhances brand visibility and opens doors to new opportunities.

Action Points for Developing a Brand:

- **Identify Your Unique Selling Points:** Reflect on what makes your architectural vision unique.
- **Consistent Brand Presentation:** Ensure your brand is consistently presented across all platforms.
- **Engage with Your Audience:** Use social media and other platforms to share your work, thoughts on architecture, and insights into your creative process.
- **Iterate and Evolve:** As your career progresses, revisit and refine your brand to reflect your current position and aspirations.
- **Leverage Networking Opportunities:** Attend industry events, participate in online forums, and connect with peers and professionals.

Principle Four Building a Professional Reputation

As a student, your reputation is based on your academic performance. It develops as you showcase work through online platforms, industry events and conferences.[6] In the professional world, your reputation is shaped by your work on real-world projects and interactions with clients and colleagues. Keeping your knowledge and skills current enhances your expertise and shows commitment to excellence.[7]

Action Points for Establishing Your Reputation:

- **Curate a Targeted Digital Portfolio:** Focus on showcasing projects that align with your niche or expertise. Highlight your design process, challenges you've overcome, and the impact of your work.
- **Speak at Industry Forums:** Seek opportunities to speak or present at industry events. Sharing your unique insights or case studies can significantly boost your professional standing.

[5] Wheeler, A., 2014. Designing brand identity: An essential guide for the whole branding team. John Wiley & Sons.

- **Publish Thought Leadership Pieces:** Write articles or blog posts on architectural topics you're passionate about.
- **Create Engaging Visual Content:** Utilise platforms like Instagram or Pinterest to share high-quality images or videos of your work, design inspirations, and behind-the-scenes looks at your projects.
- **Mentorship and Collaboration:** Offer to mentor students or younger professionals. Collaborate with peers on projects or research. This also enriches your professional experience.

Principle Five Persuasive Communication in Architecture

Sales skills, while not typically associated with architecture, are essential to success. They involve learning how to communicate the values of your designs and persuading clients to invest in your ideas. A consultative approach focuses on understanding the client's needs and tailoring recommendations to show how your design solutions address them.[8] Highlighting the benefits your designs bring to the project rather than just their features, creates a compelling narrative that resonates with the client.[9]

Learning to handle objections is crucial, as clients may question cost, feasibility, or other elements. Addressing these concerns with evidence and examples can help alleviate them and build trust. Using case studies and testimonials can further strengthen your position and increase the likelihood of client buy-in.

Action Points for Developing Sales Skills:

- **Practice the Consultative Approach:** Engage in active listening during client meetings. Ask open-ended questions to uncover their vision and challenges.
- **Learn to Handle Criticism:** Respond to common criticisms by researching potential client concerns about your projects. Practice addressing these criticisms constructively and confidently.
- **Showcase Your Expertise:** Use your portfolio and past successes to demonstrate your capability and build credibility with potential clients.
- **Continuous Learning:** Attend sales training workshops and read up on sales strategies to refine your approach. Gain insights by networking with sales professionals in the architecture field.
- **Feedback and Adaptation:** After client meetings, identify areas for improvement. Seek feedback from mentors or peers to enhance your sales approach.

[6] Cialdini, R.B. and Cialdini, R.B., 2007. Influence: The psychology of persuasion (Vol. 55, p. 339). Collins.
[7] Kegan, R. and Lahey, L.L., 2002. How the way we talk can change the way we work: Seven languages for transformation. John Wiley & Sons.
[8] Carnegie, D., 2024. How to win friends and influence people. ببلوماني اي للنشر والتوزيع.
[9] Miller, D., 2017. Building a story brand: clarify your message so customers will listen. HarperCollins Leadership.

6.4 // Providing Added Value

(Going the Extra Mile: Making Clients Love You for More Than Just Your Designs)

Principle Six Delivering Added Value

Providing value beyond basic architectural services is crucial for selling your knowledge and ideas. It sets you apart from competitors, builds trust with potential clients, and establishes you as a reliable source of knowledge.[10] Offering additional insights and resources shows your commitment to client success and positions you as a trusted advisor.[11]

Added value can encompass educational content like blog posts, articles, and webinars that showcase your expertise and provide valuable information. Sharing knowledge on relevant topics positions you as a thought leader in your field. Free consultations or design reviews demonstrate your capabilities.

Action Points for Providing Value:

- **Offer Free Consultations or Design Reviews:** Provide potential clients with a no-cost evaluation of their existing spaces or future projects to demonstrate your expertise and the benefits of your services.
- **Create Insightful Content:** Write blog posts or articles highlighting your architectural solutions, innovative approaches, and case studies to establish thought leadership.
- **Host Educational Events:** To engage and educate your audience, organise webinars or workshops on trending topics in architecture, such as sustainable design or smart homes.
- **Highlight Your Unique Value Proposition:** Clearly articulate how your specific skills provide clients tangible benefits.
- **Demonstrate Expertise and Trustworthiness:** During all interactions, emphasise your comprehensive knowledge and reliability, positioning yourself as not just a service provider but a valuable partner in achieving transformative outcomes.

Principle Seven Highlighting the Impact of Design

In architectural design, distinguishing between features and benefits is important. Features are tangible design elements, while benefits connect these features to the client's needs and aspirations.[12] To convey the benefits of your designs, understand the client's needs and demonstrate how your solutions address them. A proposal for an office design with open floor plans and natural lighting becomes more persuasive when you explain how these features foster collaboration and boost employee well-being, leading to increased productivity. This shifts the focus from the design's

[10] Kumar, V., 2012. 101 design methods: A structured approach for driving innovation in your organization. John Wiley & Sons.
[11] Lencioni, P.M., 2010. The five dysfunctions of a team: A leadership fable. John Wiley & Sons.

physical attributes to its positive impact on the client's daily operations and overall objectives, creating a more compelling narrative

Life cycle cost analysis helps illustrate long-term benefits of your designs by comparing the costs and advantages of different design options over time. It can highlight the financial and environmental benefits of using sustainable, high-quality materials and technologies, for example, aligning with the values and objectives of clients who seek to reduce their carbon footprint and contribute to a sustainable future.[13]

Action Points for Emphasising Benefits:

- **Identify Client Goals:** Begin by understanding the client's broader objectives and tailor your proposal to align with them.
- **Translate Features into Benefits:** For each design feature, explicitly state the benefit it provides to the client.
- **Use Relatable Scenarios:** Illustrate benefits through scenarios or stories that resonate with the client, showing the real-world impact of your design.
- **Highlight Emotional and Financial Benefits:** Don't just focus on the design's practical advantages; also consider its financial implications for the client and its effect on users' emotional well-being.
- **Gather Testimonials and Case Studies:** Support your claims with examples from past projects where similar features provided substantial benefits, demonstrating your track record of delivering value.
- **Incorporate Life Cycle Cost Analysis:** Demonstrate how your design minimises costs over its entire lifespan, including maintenance, energy, and operational expenses.
- **Highlight Carbon Footprint Reduction:** Provide data or estimates on how your design features contribute to lower carbon emissions, aligning with sustainability goals.
- **Use Sustainable Materials and Technologies:** Specify using materials and technologies that have less environmental impact and promote energy efficiency.
- **Educate Clients on Sustainability Benefits:** Explain the long-term value and impact of sustainable design choices on the environment and the client's financial bottom line.
- **Provide Comparative Analyses:** Compare traditional designs to underscore your proposals' cost savings and environmental benefits.

[12] Anderson, C., 2016. TED Talks: The official TED guide to public speaking: Tips and tricks for giving unforgettable speeches and presentations. Hachette UK.
[13] Heschong, L., 1979. Thermal delight in architecture. MIT press.

6.5 // Networking and Building Professional Relationships

(Schmoozing with Purpose: Networking Without the Nonsense)

Principle Eight Building Networks and Partnerships

Successful architectural practice thrives on robust collaborative relationships with clients, contractors, and stakeholders,[14] while selling knowledge and ideas hinges on forging meaningful connections. Networking is crucial for building these relationships.[15] Cultivating a network of peers and potential clients keeps you fresh in their minds and also creates new business opportunities.

Action Points for Fostering Collaborative Relationships:

- **Initiating Relationships:** Begin with targeted networking. Identify potential clients or collaborators through industry events, online forums, or professional associations. Initiate contact with a personalised approach, focusing on their work and expressing genuine interest.
- **Resources for Relationship Building:** Equip yourself with business cards, a professional website, and a portfolio of your work. These tools are essential for making a solid first impression and provide easy ways for new contacts to remember you and your work.
- **Conducting Research:** Before meetings, research the client or collaborator's recent projects, their company culture, and any standard connections. This preparation shows your dedication and enables more meaningful conversations.
- **Utilising Social Media:** Leverage social media platforms to showcase your work, share industry insights, and engage with the architectural community.
- **Active Listening and Insightful Queries:** In conversations, practice active listening and ask insightful questions that reveal a deeper understanding and interest in their challenges and goals to establish a foundation of trust and mutual respect.

[14] Gladwell, M., 2006. The tipping point: How little things can make a big difference. Little, Brown.
[15] Cross, N., 2024. Designerly ways of knowing. In Designerly Ways of Knowing and Thinking (pp. 1-14). Springer London.

Case Study Communication at all levels: Ian Ritchie CBE

Delivering a high performance in the art of communication is fundamental to securing new work, and rapidly finding the best language to enable effective communication with each client is key to a successful start.

Arkan Theatre Cairo 0- Ian Ritchie Architects

Completely understanding a new client at the first encounter is rare, so it is professionally sound to take care in the marketing language you use, being particularly careful not to exaggerate your track record, resources and skills. That said, many have done so successfully. This tactic requires the architect to maintain illusions in the practice's early performance with the client. Calm frankness is the opposite approach, using the language of marketing to convey an air of confidence without arrogance—perhaps less superficially glamorous, yet also appealing to the right client.

The ethical culture of your practice will soon become apparent, and, as your practice develops, is likely to define the type of client you are best suited to work with.

v

Arkan Theatre Cairo

Deciding in which markets you wish to practice will influence your future and how you approach and manage communications. Seeking independent and regular mention of your practice's work in printed and online news is a tactic often employed by 'driven' firms, while the more subtle approach of publishing books is another method of revealing your practice's values. At a certain point, clients will have formed their picture of who you are and it is often difficult to create another perception without resorting to exaggerated marketing.

Arkan Theatre Main Auditorium

However, for many architects, competitions—open or invited—is where they most often find potential work. Based on my experience, the following are some headline questions to consider when entering competitions, and some strategies to win.

Is the brief crystal clear? Is the jury identified and of high quality? Will there be a live presentation with the client?

Decipher the challenge; look for the 'unspoken' information; combine pragmatism with inspiration. Above all, follow your concept based upon the context, and never design for the jury.

One example from my own practice that illustrates a somewhat unusual approach was for a competition to design a theatre in Cairo, Egypt.

As known architects in the theatre world, we and several other practices were approached by email. The question posed in our studio was how to avoid wasting time and energy, and the key was to understand how this potential client's mind worked.

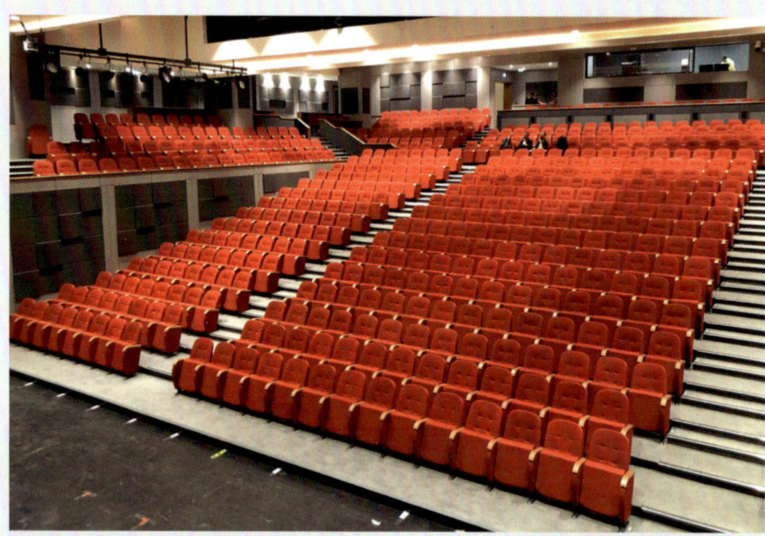

Arkan Theatre Cairo - Main Auditorium

Because we have a Euro-Asian network of offices we were able to contact an Egyptian colleague in Hamburg. Their advice was 'Go to Cairo straightaway!', because Egyptians prefer face-to-face contact. Within days the client's team was grilling us on our knowledge of theatre technicalities: eyelines, seating, acoustics, lighting, ventilation, fire stage equipment—not a word about design. In the evening, we discussed the project over a family dinner. Within a few hours the conversation became personal, and a stark contrast with the earlier technical audition. The client's wife enjoyed poetry, and we spoke French together, and he was a Liverpool FC supporter (Mo Salah), as am I. Done!

We assembled our team, agreed design scope and RIBA contract conditions, all within a few days.

The Arkan Theatre was designed and delivered with very few visits to Cairo—thanks to the wonder of telecommunications and the trust that was established in one face-to-face meeting.

Reflection

Ian Ritchie's case study illustrates the critical role of effective communication in securing architectural projects. By balancing professional expertise with personal interactions, Ritchie established trust and secured this significant international project. The case underscores the value of ethical communication, leveraging professional networks, and adapting to digital communication challenges. Ritchie's quick recognition of the client's cultural and personal preferences enabled him to tailor his approach, making the client feel understood and valued. His ability to shift from technical discussions to more personal, relatable conversations illustrates the importance of emotional intelligence in client interactions. This dual approach demonstrated his technical competence and genuine interest in the client's broader context, fostering a deeper connection.

Furthermore, Ritchie's use of face-to-face meetings, despite the potential for digital communication, illustrates the enduring value of personal interactions in building trust. This approach is particularly relevant in an era where digital communication sometimes feels impersonal. By engaging directly with the client, Ritchie conveyed sincerity and commitment, which are crucial in establishing long-term professional relationships.

The case study also emphasises the importance of flexibility and responsiveness in communication. Ritchie's willingness to adapt his communication style and approach based on the client's responses shows that successful architects must be agile and perceptive, able to modify their strategies in real-time to align with the client's needs and expectations. During a conversation with me while this book was being written, he expressed the essence of his design process in relation to the client as follows: 'Listen to your client. Listen some more. Think. Write. Write again. Think some more. Write. Think. Now start to draw.'

Ritchie's experience shows the value of being able to combine technical proficiency with strong interpersonal skills. Effective communication is not just about conveying information—it's about creating a narrative that resonates with the client, addressing their concerns and building a relationship based on trust and mutual respect. By adopting these principles, architects can enhance their ability to secure projects, build lasting client relationships, and ultimately achieve greater professional success.

SELLING KNOWLEDGE AND IDEAS

10 Key Learning Points //

1. **Master the Art of Communication:** Use clear, persuasive language tailored to the client's needs to convey your concepts compellingly.
2. **Understand Your Client:** Take the time to deeply understand your client's needs, preferences, and goals. This understanding is key to tailoring your proposals and building trust.
3. **Create and Maintain a Dynamic Portfolio:** Regularly update your portfolio to reflect your latest work and skills. Showcase both process work and final projects to demonstrate your design approach and problem-solving abilities.
4. **Establish a Strong Personal Brand:** Develop a consistent personal brand that reflects your unique perspectives and values. Use various platforms to express this brand and distinguish yourself in the competitive architectural field.
5. **Network Effectively:** Engage in industry events, join professional organisations, and participate in online forums to build a robust professional network. Networking opens doors to new opportunities and collaborations.
6. **Embrace Digital Tools and Platforms:** Use digital tools to create visually appealing presentations and maintain an updated digital portfolio. Active engagement on social media can broaden your reach and establish your expertise.
7. **Provide Added Value:** Where appropriate, offer free consultations, educational content, and insightful articles to establish yourself as a knowledgeable advisor. Providing added value builds trust and attracts potential clients.
8. **Highlight the Benefits of Your Designs:** Focus on the benefits rather than just the features of your designs. Articulate how your design solutions meet clients' needs and contribute to their goals.
9. **Prepare for Competitions Strategically:** When entering competitions, ensure you understand the brief and jury. Craft proposals that align with the context and deliver inspired, pragmatic solutions.
10. **Combine Professional and Personal Interactions:** Blend professional expertise with personal interactions to build stronger client relationships. Personal connections, as shown in Ian Ritchie's case study, can significantly enhance trust and collaboration.

CHAPTER SEVEN

CULTIVATING EXCELLENCE

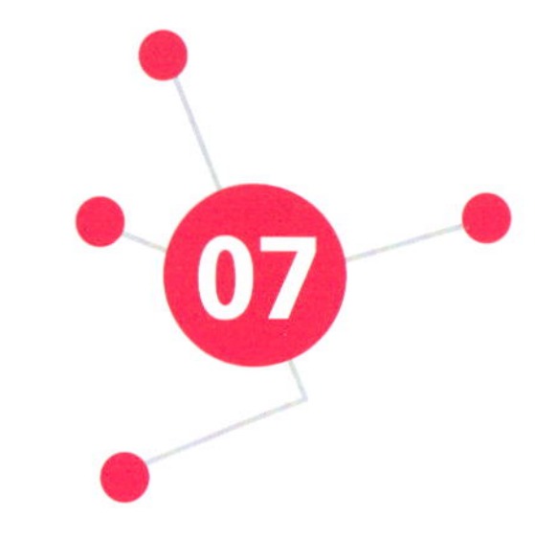

CHAPTER SEVEN

Cultivating Excellence: Strategies for Recognizing and Nurturing Potential

This chapter explores how to build a culture of innovation, collaboration, and continuous learning within architectural firms. It focuses on recognising and nurturing potential, sharing credit, enhancing motivation, and fostering mutual respect and encouragement. It also provides strategies for identifying and developing high-potential employees, ensuring that architectural firms can leverage fresh perspectives and creative solutions.

7.1 // Recognising Potential

(Diamonds in the Rough)

Recognising and nurturing potential is vital for architectural firms aiming to cultivate a growth-centric culture, because such employees can significantly contribute to a firm's success. Yet it requires a keen eye to identify high-potential individuals who may not yet have extensive experience but exhibit intrinsic qualities that suggest future growth. Some characteristics to look out for when evaluating possible high-potential employees are:

Soft Skills

According to Goleman, emotional intelligence, which encompasses self-awareness, self-regulation, motivation, empathy, and social skills, is a significant predictor of professional success. Architects with high emotional intelligence are better equipped to handle the interpersonal and collaborative aspects of their roles, making them valuable assets to any firm.

Innovative Thinking and Creativity

Design creativity and the ability to envision unique, functional solutions to address complex requirements and constraints are critical for success.

Risk-Taking and Resilience

Risk-taking in architecture requires balancing between creativity and pragmatism to ensure innovative designs are also viable. Individuals who embrace calculated risks are more likely to propose bold ideas and solutions that, while unconventional, might lead to breakthroughs that can advance the field and propel their firms toward innovative and successful outcomes.

Architecture projects are typically often long-term and complex, with many potential pitfalls. Resilient individuals stay motivated, adapting and learning from each challenge.

Practical Strategies for Identifying and Encouraging Potential

Structured interviews can assess technical and soft skills, personality assessments can gauge emotional intelligence and resilience, and project-based evaluations allow candidates to demonstrate their problem-solving abilities and creativity in real-world scenarios.

1. Structured Interviews

Structured interviews use predetermined sets of questions to elicit detailed responses that reveal a candidate's abilities, experiences, and potential. By standardising the questions, firms can ensure a fair comparison between candidates.

Example: To assess their problem-solving skills, creativity, and resilience, an architectural firm might ask candidates to describe a challenging project they worked on and how they overcame obstacles.

Practical Application:

- **Technical Skills Assessment:** Ask candidates about specific architectural software they have used, such as AutoCAD or Revit, and request examples of how they have applied these tools in previous projects.
- **Soft Skills Evaluation:** Pose scenarios that require candidates to demonstrate their communication and teamwork skills, such as handling a disagreement within a project team or presenting a design concept to a client.

2. Personality Assessments

Personality assessments are valuable tools for identifying candidates that might excel at managing client relationships and navigating team dynamics.

Example: Tools like the Myers-Briggs Type Indicator (MBTI) or the Emotional Intelligence Appraisal can provide insights into how candidates manage stress, interact with others, and approach problem-solving.

Practical Application:

- **Emotional Intelligence:** Use assessments to evaluate a candidate's ability to understand and manage their emotions and empathise with others.
- **Resilience Measurement:** Implement resilience scales to determine how well candidates cope with stress and recover from setbacks. This can be particularly useful in high-pressure architectural practices.

3. Project-Based Evaluations

Project-based evaluations allow candidates to demonstrate their practical skills and creativity in real-world scenarios.

Example: An architectural firm might provide candidates to develop a design solution for a small project. This allows the firm to assess technical proficiency, creativity, and the ability to communicate design ideas effectively.

Practical Application:

- **Design Challenges**: Provide a hypothetical design brief and ask candidates to develop a solution, complete with sketches, materials selection, and a project timeline.
- **Team Projects**: Ask candidates to collaborate to solve a complex design problem. This can reveal leadership qualities, teamwork skills, and the ability to integrate diverse perspectives.

7.2 // Nurturing Potential

(From seeds to success)

Continuous Learning and Development Opportunities

To help identify and nurture potential in current employees, provide learning opportunities to help them enhance their skills.

Practical Application:

- Establish structured professional development programs that include mentorship, skill-building workshops, and opportunities for further education.
- Workshops, seminars, and access to online courses enable team members to stay current with industry trends.
- Regular feedback and performance reviews that highlight accomplishments and areas for improvement encourage employees to set and achieve professional development goals.

Encouragement and Creating Opportunities for Growth

Architectural firms should help employees develop new skills and gain confidence in their abilities. Assigning them to lead small projects, accompanied by appropriate responsibilities, is a way of nurturing potential. Encouraging participation in design competitions, or involving them in client meetings and presentations are also ways of pushing employees out of their comfort zones.

Encouraging Risk-Taking and Innovation

Architectural firms should encourage a culture that values risk-taking and innovation by creating an environment where employees feel safe to experiment and propose new ideas. This leads to innovative solutions and enhances employee engagement and satisfaction.

Real-Time Feedback and Mentorship

Real-time, constructive feedback enables employees to stay on track with development goals, while mentorship provides guidance and support for their professional growth.

Practical Application:

- **Feedback Mechanisms:** Create a system for regular, structured feedback sessions that focus on continuous improvement and skill development.
- **Mentorship Programs:** Establish formal mentorship relationships where experienced architects can provide junior team members with insights and advice, and guide them through their career progression.

Internship and Apprenticeship Programs

Internship and apprenticeship programs are excellent for identifying and nurturing potential. They offer practical experience that complements academic learning, preparing individuals for the complexities of the profession.

The Apprenticeships in Architecture Trailblazer Group

The Apprenticeships in Architecture Trailblazer Group, established in response to the UK's apprenticeship levy, offers structured architectural professional development through apprenticeships at Levels 6 and 7, equivalent to bachelor's and master's degrees. These programs combine on-the-job training with academic coursework, equipping apprentices with the skills for success in modern architectural practice.

Structure and Benefits of the Level 7 Apprenticeship

By integrating practical assignments, workshops, mentorship and continuous feedback the Level 7 Apprenticeship ensures learning is not confined to the classroom but is continuously reinforced through hands-on experience.

Practical Assignments: Practical assignments bridge the gap between academic learning and professional practice by simulating the challenges and tasks that architects face daily. By working on actual projects, apprentices can better understand design principles, project management, and client interactions.

Workshops and Seminars: These are typically led by experienced professionals and academics who provide valuable insights and foster an interactive learning environment to encourage apprentices to actively engage with the material, ask questions, and participate in discussions that enhance their understanding and skills.

Mentorship: Mentorship is integral to the Level 7 apprenticeship, helping young architects develop their skills and gain confidence in their abilities. Apprentices and junior team members are provided with valuable insights, feedback, guidance and support from seasoned architects, who offer personalised advice and share their experiences to help apprentices navigate the complexities of the profession. Mentorship plays a crucial role in helping apprentices reach their full potential, and also helps them build a professional network, which can be invaluable for their career progression.

Feedback from Employers and Academics: Continuous feedback from both employers and academics ensures that the curriculum remains relevant and aligned with industry standards, ensuring apprentices are well-prepared to meet the challenges of their future careers.

Practical Tips for Recognising and Nurturing Potential

- Identify Key Characteristics of High-Potential Individuals
- Implement Structured Internship and Apprenticeship Programs
- Create Opportunities for Growth
- Provide Regular Feedback and Support
- Foster a Culture of Innovation

7.3 // Giving and Taking Credit

(Altruism and Encouragement)

Architecture is inherently collaborative. This section discusses the importance of attributing credit appropriately to foster mutual respect and encouragement and provides practical examples of recognising and celebrating achievements within a team setting.

The Importance of Sharing Credit

Sharing credit among colleagues builds trust and mutual respect, and reduces workplace conflicts and competition. Teams that share credit are more supportive of each other, more cohesive, and more likely to come up with innovative design solutions. This is essential in a profession where input from multiple specialists is required during a project.

Enhancing Motivation and Performance

According to Ryan and Deci, when employees see their hard work and contributions recognised, their intrinsic needs for competence and relatedness are fulfilled. Recognition also strengthens their sense of belonging within the team. This is especially important when complex projects require sustained effort over long periods; acknowledging individual contributions helps maintain enthusiasm, preventing burnout and disengagement.

Practical Examples

- **Public Acknowledgment:** Recognising employees in front of peers during team meetings or company events boosts their morale and sets a standard for others, especially when highlighting achievements like innovative designs or strong project management.
- **Written Commendations:** Letters or emails of appreciation serve as tangible proof of contributions and achievements, and can enhance an employee's professional portfolio.
- **Informal Expressions of Gratitude:** Simple, informal gestures, like a thank-you note or a verbal acknowledgement in casual conversation, can motivate employees and significantly enhance the overall work atmosphere and individual job satisfaction.

Encouraging Peer Recognition

When team members acknowledge each other's efforts, it fosters a culture of mutual respect and support. Implementing a peer nomination system for awards or recognition can help build a more inclusive and appreciative work environment.

Building a Culture of Mutual Respect

Fostering a culture where sharing credit is the norm builds mutual respect. This enhances communication and collaboration, promoting the free exchange of ideas and leading to more open and constructive engagement. This is important in architecture, where integrating diverse perspectives often leads to innovative solutions and successful project outcomes.

Practical Strategies for Building Mutual Respect

- **Egalitarian Project Management:** Organise regular team meetings where everyone's input is solicited and valued and ensure all team members have a voice in decision-making processes.
- **Transparent Communication:** Encourage honest feedback and constructive criticism to create an environment where team members feel safe to express their ideas. This transparency helps build trust and respect among team members.
- **Recognition of Diverse Contributions:** Acknowledge all contributions, from research and drafting to project management, to reinforce the value of every role within the team.
- **Conflict Resolution Mechanisms:** Provide conflict resolution training and a clear process for addressing grievances to ensure a fair and respectful resolution of issues to maintain a positive team dynamic.

Long-term Benefits

Building a culture of mutual respect and recognition creates a productive environment. This boosts individual and team performance and contributes to the firm's long-term success and reputation. Valued employees are more likely to remain with the organisation, ensuring a stable, experienced workforce, while a culture of mutual respect also attracts top talent, as potential employees seek workplaces where their contributions will be recognised and respected.

7.4 // Creating a Culture of Growth

(Growing Pains: How Challenges Turn Into Opportunities)

The Impact of Encouragement

According to Bandura, self-efficacy is an individual's belief in their ability to succeed in specific situations. Leaders who offer encouragement help team members build confidence in their abilities, leading to increased motivation and performance. This helps create a culture where employees feel empowered to take risks and innovate without fear of failure, knowing their contributions are valued and supported. Encouragement also fosters resilience, helping employees persist in the face of challenges. This is crucial when projects involve navigating unexpected obstacles and adapting to changing circumstances.

Practical Strategies for Encouragement

- **Regular Feedback and Praise:** Constructive feedback helps employees understand what they are doing right and where they can improve. It should be specific, actionable, and highlight how their work contributes to the project's success. By recognising accomplishments and providing guidance, leaders foster a sense of progress and competence among team members.
- **Job Rotation Programs:** Job rotation programs help employees develop their skills by exposing them to different aspects of the business. According to Campion, this approach also enhances job satisfaction and performance by offering a broader perspective and reducing monotony.
- **Professional Development Opportunities:** Encouraging employees to pursue opportunities for continuous learning shows that the firm values its employees' growth and development. Noe et al. emphasise this enhances employees' knowledge, skills, and abilities, leading to improved performance and job satisfaction.
- **Open Communication Channels:** According to Schein36 open communication is fundamental to building a positive organisational culture, by allowing team members to feel comfortable sharing their ideas, concerns, and feedback, which fosters a culture of trust and mutual respect.
- **Work-Life Balance:** Kossek et al. emphasise that work-life balance is critical for employee satisfaction and productivity. A supportive work environment recognizes that employees have lives outside of work and values their overall well-being. Flexible work hours or remote working options can help employees balance personal and professional responsibilities. Encouraging employees to disconnect after work hours and during vacations ensures that they return to work refreshed and motivated.
- **Recognition Programs:** Formal recognition programs, including awards for outstanding performance, innovation, and teamwork, can significantly motivate employees and boost their morale. Employers should ensure employees at all levels are acknowledged for their contributions. According to Cameron and Pierce, both monetary and non-monetary rewards can effectively motivate employees.

7.5 // A+ (Positive) Influence

Being Modest and Influencing People

The importance of modesty and mentorship cannot be overstated in the architectural profession. This chapter explores how these virtues contribute to building successful and sustainable careers. It underscores mentoring's pivotal role in fostering a robust professional community and highlights the significance of practicing modesty to remain grounded and continually open to learning. The chapter delves into the transformative impact of mentoring, drawing on historical examples like Frank Lloyd Wright's mentorship of his apprentices, which has left a lasting legacy in architecture.

Additionally, this chapter examines the art of effective influencing and persuasion, essential skills for architects aiming to articulate their ideas and visions compellingly. By understanding the psychology of persuasion and practicing ethical influence, architects can build strong, trust-based relationships with clients, stakeholders, and colleagues.

Through case studies and practical insights, such as the adventurous journey of the Irish sailing boat "Ituna" and the subsequent professional achievements of its crew, this chapter illustrates the profound impact of mentorship and humility. The chapter also outlines strategies for positively influencing architectural practice, including mastering visual storytelling and cultural sensitivity, fostering user-centered empathy, and advocating for sustainable practices.

By embracing these principles, architects can cultivate a professional environment that supports continuous learning, innovation, and ethical practice, ultimately contributing to a more collaborative and compassionate architectural community.

Mentoring

Mentoring is not merely a professional duty; it serves as a cornerstone for establishing successful and sustainable architectural businesses. Architects who nurture positive relationships with clients, stakeholders, and staff are more likely to see their projects thrive and their reputations expand.

I cannot stress enough the significance of practising modesty and mentoring early in one's career. These virtues are indispensable for building successful and fulfilling careers, allowing individuals to learn from their limitations and help others achieve their potential. Modesty keeps individuals grounded, preventing them from becoming complacent or arrogant. It facilitates learning from one's mistakes and enables individuals to grow and evolve in their careers. Moreover, modesty fosters trust and respect, facilitating solid and healthy relationships with colleagues and clients alike.

Conversely, mentoring empowers individuals to share their knowledge and experience with others and helps them develop and succeed. It provides a platform for individuals to pass on their skills, insights, and wisdom to the next generation of professionals, fostering a diverse and robust workforce. Mentoring also cultivates leadership skills and expands one's networks as mentees seek guidance and wisdom from trusted and respected mentors. Mentees, in turn, benefit greatly from mentoring, gaining valuable insights and experiences that can help them grow and succeed in their careers. Mentoring offers a valuable opportunity to learn from those with more experience and knowledge, allowing them to develop their skills and expertise while building strong professional relationships.

As a trainee or young architect, feeling overwhelmed and unsure of yourself is sometimes normal. You may hesitate to ask questions for fear of looking foolish or incompetent. But the truth is, there's no such thing as a stupid question, and asking for help is a sign of strength, not weakness. Remember, your mentor is there to help you grow and develop as an architect. Don't be afraid to ask for help; don't let the fear of looking foolish hold you back. By seeking guidance and showing a willingness to learn, you'll set yourself up for success.

Above all others, one architect is often cited as a great influencer and mentor: the legendary American architect Frank Lloyd Wright. In addition to being a practising architect, he was also a prolific writer and educator who believed in sharing his knowledge and experience with the next generation of architects.

One notable example of Wright's mentorship is his work with the Taliesin Fellowship, a group of apprentices who lived and worked with him at his Taliesin studio in Wisconsin. Wright saw the Fellowship as a way to pass on his philosophy and techniques to young architects, and many of his apprentices became successful architects. His most famous apprentice was the Japanese architect Arata Endo. Endo came to work at Taliesin in the 1950s and spent several years studying under Wright's guidance. After returning to Japan, Endo incorporated Wright's organic style into his work and became a leading figure in the modernist movement in Japan. Wright's influence as a mentor also extended beyond his apprentices; he taught at several universities throughout his career, including the University of Wisconsin and the Taliesin Associated Architects School of Architecture, where he inspired and influenced countless young architects.

Case Study "Ituna" By Prof Chris Dalton

"When I Nearly lost my life due to being knocked overboard at night 800 miles from Bermuda ......"

The Irish sailing boat "Ituna" set sail on a remarkable voyage from Ireland to New York in the summer of 1950, carrying a crew of four young men. Among them were three aspiring architects, students at Dublin's School of Architecture in the College of Technology, who had been awarded a Fellowship to study under the renowned Frank Lloyd Wright at his iconic Taliesin farm in Wisconsin. With their shared dream and a lack of funds for the usual transatlantic passage, they decided, with youthful bravado and a typical Irish spirit, to sail themselves across.

Their journey began a year earlier, in 1949. With a combination of funds and support from friends and family, they managed to acquire a neglected 11-meter gaff-rigged cutter, originally built in Scotland in 1912. Their goal was to transform this vessel into a seaworthy craft, ready for a daring transatlantic crossing the following summer.

The Ituna story is one of adventure, determination, and transatlantic exploration. Sailing in June 1950, the crew were Tony Jacob, Sean Kenny, Des Dalton (my father), and Kevin O'Farrell, who was the only one with any sailing experience.

Crossings of this kind were extremely rare, and the students' voyage became the stuff of legends. They meticulously documented their experiences in a log, which was later serialised in newspapers on both sides of the Atlantic, captivating readers with tales of their perilous journey. The crew battled unpredictable weather, treacherous waves, and the vast expanse of the ocean. They made an unscheduled stop in northern Spain to sell their malfunctioning engine, narrowly avoided a surfacing submarine in the Bay of Biscay, and almost lost their skipper, Tony, overboard at night mid-way (a dramatic moment immortalised in an Eric Fraser illustration in a Rolex advertisement). They had a radio that could receive but not transmit and just about evaded a hurricane that threatened to blow them onto the Long Island shore.

The boys received a rousing welcome at their triumphant Arrival in New York in late September. Treated like stars in every port along the way, their story captured the imagination of the bustling metropolis, turning the boat into a celebrity on both sides of the Atlantic. All four enjoyed this fame, and Frank Lloyd Wright had to send several telegrams reminding them of their obligation.

Des, Tony, and Sean all eventually made it to Taliesin, though only Sean Kenny stayed the full course of the Fellowship in Wisconsin and Arizona. The Fellowship did not have formal classes or keep many records, so few details are known about their activities. However, several apprentices recall Sean Kenny being around at Taliesin West in oral history interviews. John Geiger stated that his sailing experience proved useful in the construction of the Cabaret Theater at Taliesin West, where his rope-tying skills were put to use. The Cabaret is sunken into the ground but is open to the desert on one side with canvas, later wood, and flaps that could close it off. Kenny evidently came up with the

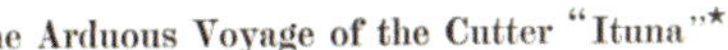

...he Arduous Voyage of the Cutter "Ituna"*

"...when I nearly lost my life, due to being knocked overboard at night, 800 miles from Bermuda..."

EVEN in these prosaic modern days, young men still have a habit of hearing a loud clear call of adventure and launching themselves trustingly into the hands of Providence. Consider, for example, the journey that Tony Jacob made. This Irishman from Co. Wexford, with three companions, sailed 3,000 treacherous miles from Rosslare to Bermuda, fighting the Atlantic in the "Ituna," a cutter only 36 feet from stem to stern.

Stores and equipment were of the sketchiest. Here was no radar, no intricate asdic; their navigational chronometer, for instance, was a wrist-watch. But it was no ordinary wrist-watch; its distinguished service proves that. "Its accuracy was such that after 2800 miles at sea we picked up Bermuda (an island only 15 miles by 3) so exactly that we did not have to alter course one degree."

And this, remember, was after the severest treatment. Temperatures ranged from equatorial to near freezing point. The watch was continually exposed to salt spray; and "on one occasion when I nearly lost my life, due to being knocked overboard at night, 800 miles from Bermuda, it was on my wrist. I was in the water for over twenty minutes, but the watch never lost a second."

The performance that Mr. Jacob's watch put up was a wonderful achievement; but wonder lessens to understanding at the realization that the watch was a Rolex Oyster Perpetual. What magnificent watches they are! Soldiers, airmen, Everest climbers, young men in small boats — we've had letters from them all, praising the infallibility of the Oyster case, the efficiency of the self-winding Perpetual "rotor," the absolute accuracy of Rolex.

But we value just as highly letters from men and women whose lives are directed into quieter channels, whose watches are never subjected to the strains and stresses of high adventure, who write to tell us that their Rolex watches give them perfect service year after year.

And what all these letters help to prove (if, indeed, proof were needed) is that there are many watches, but few as good as Rolex.

* This is a true story, taken from a letter written by Mr. Tony Jacob to The Rolex Watch Company. The original letter can be inspected at the offices of the Rolex Watch Company, 18 rue du Marché, Geneva, Switzerland.

This is a Rolex Oyster Perpetual Datejust — and it is in a class by itself. The accuracy is of the highest standard — *Rolex* standard. The waterproof Oyster case protects that accuracy, and the Perpetual self-winding "rotor" safeguards it by maintaining an even tension on the mainspring. (The Rolex Red Seal is a sign used by Rolex to show that the watch to which it is attached has been successfully submitted to the tests of the official Testing Stations of the Swiss Government, and has been awarded its own Official Timing Certificate together with the proud title of *chronometer*.)

...OLEX

...the history of Time measurement

...PANY LTD. (*H. Wilsdorf, Governing Director*), GENEVA, SWITZERLAND, and THE AMERICAN ROLEX WATCH CORPORATION, 580 FIFTH AVE, NEW YORK

...x Advert – Graphis 43, 1953- "The Arduous Voyage ...e Cutter Ituna"

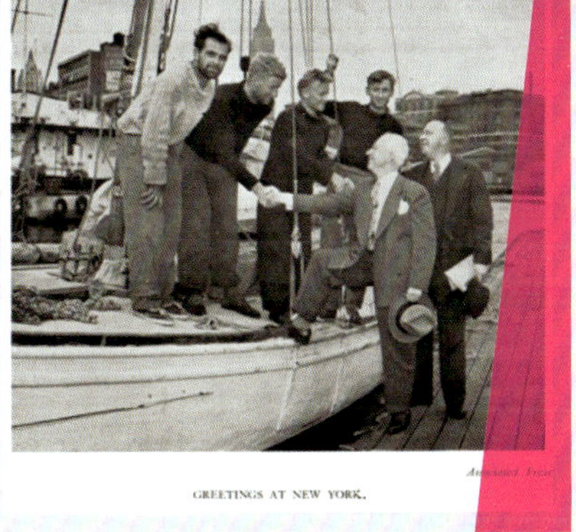

GREETINGS AT NEW YORK.

Itunas arrival in New York

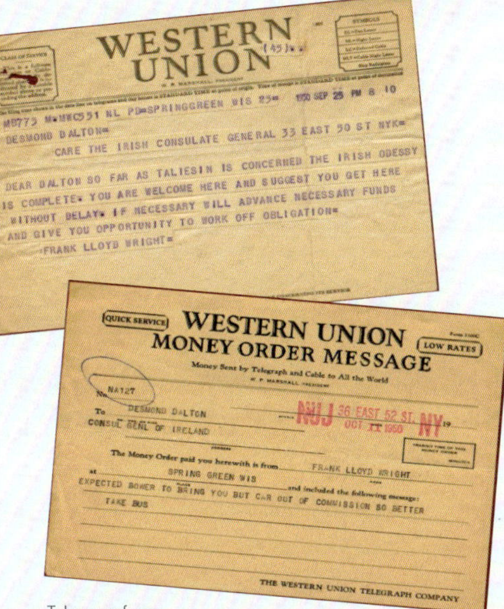

WESTERN UNION

M0773 M•MWC551 NL PD=SPRINGGREEN WIS 25= 1950 SEP 25 PM 8 10

DESMOND DALTON=

CARE THE IRISH CONSULATE GENERAL 33 EAST 50 ST NYK=

DEAR DALTON SO FAR AS TALIESIN IS CONCERNED THE IRISH ODESSY IS COMPLETE• YOU ARE WELCOME HERE AND SUGGEST YOU GET HERE WITHOUT DELAY• IF NECESSARY WILL ADVANCE NECESSARY FUNDS AND GIVE YOU OPPORTUNITY TO WORK OFF OBLIGATION=

FRANK LLOYD WRIGHT=

QUICK SERVICE — WESTERN UNION MONEY ORDER MESSAGE — LOW RATES

Money Sent by Telegraph and Cable to All the World

No. NA127

To DESMOND DALTON

CONSUL GENL OF IRELAND

NUJ 36 EAST 52 ST. NY OCT 11 1950

The Money Order paid you herewith is from FRANK LLOYD WRIGHT

at SPRING GREEN WIS and included the following message:

EXPECTED BOWER TO BRING YOU BUT CAR OUT OF COMMISSION SO BETTER TAKE BUS

THE WESTERN UNION TELEGRAPH COMPANY

Telegrams from
Frank Lloyd Wright to Desmond Dalton

system that allowed them to operate as they opened in an unusual way. He later went on to acclaim as an award-winning theatre and film set designer. Des worked in various Dublin firms dealing with planning and architecture and then in publishing connected with the Building Industry, but – quite the character - was better known in the private gambling clubs of London in the 1960s. Tony operated a successful yacht chartering business in the Caribbean.

Their achievement is a testament to human resilience and the spirit of adventure. Wright later commented on the journey, stating that they had "the kind of courage that is needed in Architecture".[2] The timing of their trip is interesting, as Wright visited the UK in July 1950, accepting an award from the Royal Institute of British Architects. Thus, they would have been travelling on the Atlantic simultaneously.

[1] https://www.rolexforums.com/The Rolex Oyster: 39 Years of Advertising History
[2] Wrighttalisian 'Instagram'- March 17th 2022

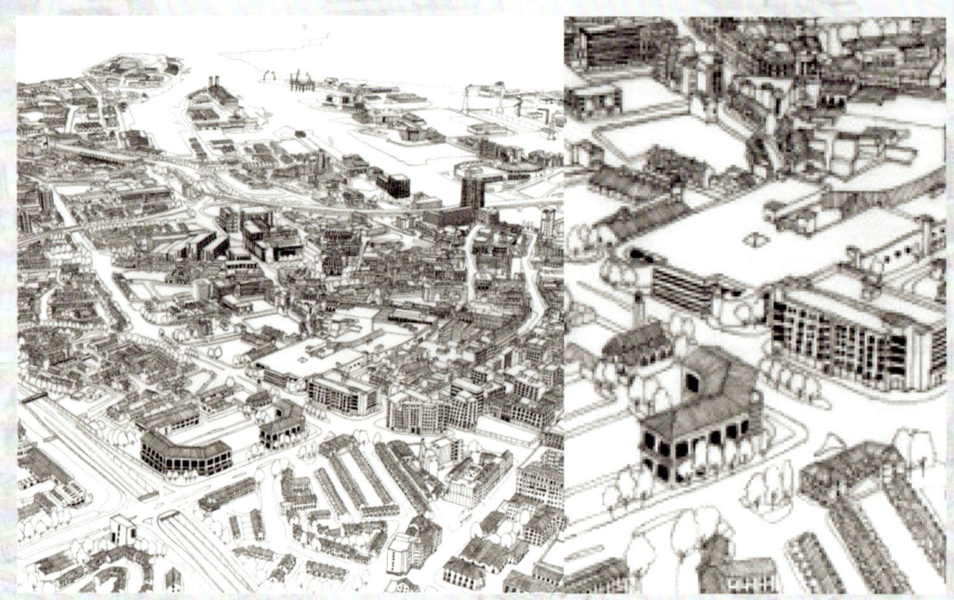

'Belfast Stories'- City scale hand drawing of Belfast

External view of Archive Square

Case Study Laura McClorey FaulknerBrowns Architects

The route to qualification as an architect is usually long and expensive. The Degree Apprenticeship at Northumbria University was established in 2018 to create a more diverse cohort of architecture students, unburdened by the fees of their full-time student counterparts. The Level 7 Apprenticeship affords students the opportunity to 'earn while they learn' by offering four years of part-time RIBA Part II and III study alongside working in a professional practice.

External view of Archive Square

City View Terrace

I completed the Degree Apprenticeship in 2023 whilst working for FaulknerBrowns Architects in Newcastle-Upon-Tyne. During my time as an apprentice, I benefitted greatly from exposure to real-life projects, gaining critical design and construction experience by working on various cultural and leisure schemes. My project highlight was Nottingham Central Library, a job I began working on at Concept Stage (RIBA Stage 2) on the first day of my apprenticeship. I ultimately handed over to the client as Project Architect four years later. Seeing the project come to life and attending the library's launch day in November 2023 was an unforgettable moment for me both personally and professionally.

'Belfast Stories' – Perspective section

My work-based experience fuelled my academic endeavour. My Master's thesis project, 'Belfast Stories', centred on the design of a cultural building in Belfast City Centre. This project went on to win several prestigious student awards, including the RIBA North East Student Award. I strongly equate the success of my academic work with the experience I gained on-the-job as an apprentice. Whilst balancing an extensive workload with a quality output in a finite amount of time could, at times, be challenging, being able to access workplace expertise and resources enabled me to push my capabilities and design. I benefitted greatly from being able to work alongside technical experts in the office when developing the detail of my academic work. This ultimately enabled me to become more competent in my practice-based technical delivery. The apprenticeship benefits both the apprentice and the host practice that can retain architects whose talent they have nurtured if their skills are attuned with the practice's approach.

For me, apprenticeship is a key vehicle for ensuring that architecture is an inclusive profession. Whilst it can be a challenging route to qualification, there are undeniable financial and professional benefits that can help apprentices to flourish as rounded, competent architects.

Reflection on Learning and Application from Laura McClorey's Case Study

Laura McClorey's case study reveals how the 'earn while you learn' model mitigates financial burdens and equips students with real-world skills essential for their professional growth. It also confirms the transformative power of apprenticeships in architecture and the broader benefits of apprenticeship programs for architectural firms in helping them identify and nurture talent.

Her journey through the Degree Apprenticeship at Northumbria University and her tenure at FaulknerBrowns Architects validates the critical role of integrating academic learning with hands-on professional experience. This invaluable blend of theory and practice fosters a holistic educational experience that purely academic routes often lack.

From concept to completion, working on high-profile projects like the Nottingham Central Library provided her with practical insights and a comprehensive understanding of architectural processes. Her real-world experience directly informed her academic projects, leading to innovative and award-winning designs. Laura's success in winning prestigious awards for her Master's thesis highlights how the synergy between academic endeavours and practical application creates excellence.

Technical model

A key takeaway from Laura's journey is the significant impact of mentorship, which was instrumental in her development. It helped her to refine her skills, gain confidence, and understand the nuanced demands of the profession. It also showed that guidance from seasoned architects is crucial in shaping the next generation of industry leaders.

CULTIVATING EXCELLENCE
10 Key Learning Points //

1. **Recognising Potential:** Identify individuals who exhibit emotional intelligence, innovative thinking, a willingness to take risks, and a strong drive to achieve their goals, even without extensive experience.
2. **Leveraging Structured Interviews and Assessments** Use structured interviews, personality assessments, and project-based evaluations to identify and nurture high-potential employees effectively.
3. **Emphasising Soft Skills:** Recognise the importance of soft skills, which are essential for success in collaborative environments.
4. **Fostering Innovative Thinking:** Create an organisational culture that values and rewards creativity, allowing individuals to explore and experiment with new ideas.
5. **Promoting Risk-Taking and Resilience:** Encourage a culture where taking calculated risks and learning from failures are seen as opportunities for growth and innovation.
6. **Supporting Continuous Learning:** Provide opportunities for continuous learning and professional development through workshops, seminars, and access to online courses.
7. **Sharing Credit and Enhancing Motivation:** Recognise and celebrate the contributions of all team members to foster a positive work environment and enhance motivation.
8. **Creating Growth Opportunities:** Assign challenging projects and responsibilities that push employees out of their comfort zones and encourage participation in design competitions and client meetings.
9. **Encouraging Work-Life Balance:** Foster a supportive work environment that values employees' overall well-being by promoting work-life balance, providing regular feedback, and recognising achievements.
10. **Implementing Mentorship Programs:** Establish formal mentorship programs to provide junior team members guidance, support, and real-time feedback.

CHAPTER EIGHT

COLLABORATION

CHAPTER EIGHT

Collaboration - The Ideas Exchange

This chapter outlines the fundamentals of effective interdisciplinary collaboration within architectural projects. It covers how such collaboration enhances innovation during planning and construction, emphasises the importance of engaging clients in the design process to meet their needs, and offers practical strategies like using collaborative technologies, regular meetings, and clear communication channels.

To bring these concepts to life, I will share my personal experience as the Project Director for the 2013 Serpentine Pavilion designed by Sou Fujimoto. This case study exemplifies how proactive client engagement, advanced communication tools, centralised CAD modelling, and off-site manufacturing can lead to successful and innovative project outcomes.

8.1 // The Essence of Collaboration in Architectural Innovation

(United We Create: Harnessing Diverse Expertise for Innovation)

Interdisciplinary collaboration's primary advantage lies in the diversity of expertise it brings to the table: architects that focus on aesthetics and spatial functionality, designers on usability and visual appeal, and engineers on structural integrity and technical feasibility. This creates a highly creative environment where ideas are critiqued and refined from multiple perspectives, leading to more innovative solutions and ensuring early identification and resolution of potential issues. This is particularly valuable when innovative architectural designs challenge conventional building techniques.[1] In such cases, an engineer might foresee structural challenges that a designer might not have considered, permitting early modifications to avoid costly changes later.

1 Allen, E. and Rand, P., 2016. Architectural detailing: function, constructibility, aesthetics. John Wiley & Sons.
2 Kibert, C.J., 2016. Sustainable construction: green building design and delivery. John Wiley & Sons.

Holistic Approach

The holistic approach inherent in interdisciplinary collaboration ensures projects are functional, sustainable, and cost-effective as well as visually appealing. For example, sustainability experts can recommend energy-efficient materials and practices, which architects and engineers can integrate from the start, resulting in significant long-term savings and environmental benefits.[2]

Teamwork Delivers Projects - Serpentine Summer Pavilion

Improved Communication

For a successful project, effective interaction is essential, enabling team members from different disciplines to clarify their requirements, share insights, and resolve misunderstandings promptly. This keeps everyone aligned, helps meet deadlines and maintain project coherence.

Using collaborative tools and technologies like project management software, communication platforms, and collaborative design tools ensures everyone has access to the latest information. For example, Building Information Modeling (BIM) allows architects, engineers, and designers to collaborate on a single digital model, ensuring everyone clearly understands the project and can contribute their expertise effectively.[3]

Efficiency

Collaborative technologies also streamline project workflow, saving time and resources. Weekly interdisciplinary meetings help address potential issues early, and keep the team aligned with project goals and timelines. Early collaboration, such as between architects and engineers, ensures structural requirements are integrated from the start, preventing the need for major modifications later.

[3] Becerik-Gerber, B. and Kensek, K., 2010. Building information modeling in architecture, engineering, and construction: Emerging research directions and trends. Journal of professional issues in engineering education and practice, 136(3), pp.139-147.

8.2 // Client Collaboration

(Clients as Partners: Engaging Clients for Success)

Involving clients early in the design process allows architects and designers to better understand their expectations and deliver a product that aligns with their vision, needs, and budget.

Importance of Engaging Clients

Engaging clients early and consistently ensures that their vision and needs are accurately understood and met. Clients will feel valued and heard, leading to higher satisfaction and more successful project outcomes.

Transparency

Transparency is a fundamental aspect of effective client collaboration. Regular updates and feedback sessions keep clients informed and involved, fostering trust and confidence in the process—essential for navigating complex projects.

Customisation

Understanding the client's vision and requirements allows the design team to customise the project to align with their expectations.

Satisfaction

Meeting and exceeding clients' expectations through thoughtful and responsive design solutions enhances client satisfaction and strengthens the firm's reputation.

Ownership

When they are actively involved in the design process, clients develop a sense of ownership and connection to the project. Engaged clients are more likely to understand the reasoning behind design decisions, leading to a stronger overall relationship.

Communication Tools and Techniques

Digital tools such as project management software, collaborative platforms, and VR can enhance communication and client engagement by allowing clients to visualise the project in real-time and provide more effective feedback.

Case Study My Personal Experience

The Role of Client Collaboration in the Sou Fujimoto Serpentine Pavilion

In December 2012, I was appointed as the Project Director for the 2013 Serpentine Pavilion, designed by the Japanese architect Sou Fujimoto. This project showcases the power of advanced communication technologies, centralised CAD modelling, off-site manufacturing, and proactive client engagement. The project was managed by Rise, with myself overseeing the overall delivery, along with the client representative Julie Burnell. The project adopted a construction management (CM) mindset, emphasising collaboration and efficient workflows, which were essential for meeting the unalterable public launch deadline.

Sou Fujimoto Serpentine Pavilion

Project Overview

Sou Fujimoto, known for his innovative and organic designs, was the thirteenth architect to be invited to design the Serpentine Pavilion. His concept for the 2013 pavilion was a delicate, cloud-like structure made from a lattice of 20mm steel poles. The design aimed to merge natural and man-made elements, creating a semi-transparent space that encouraged visitors to explore and interact with the environment in new ways. The pavilion occupied 357 square meters of lawn in front of the Serpentine Gallery in Kensington Gardens, London.[10]

Interdisciplinary Collaboration

Collaboration involved Fujimoto's architectural team based in Japan, engineering and technical design services provided by AECOM in London, and construction management by Stage One in York. This geographically dispersed team overcame logistical challenges by using advanced communication tools and techniques.

[10] Pop, D., 2015. Theorising Between Space and Place: A Case Study on Perceptive Architecture - Serpentine Gallery Pavilions. Philobiblon, 20(2), p.356.

Sou Fujimoto Serpentine Pavilion

The team also had to navigate strict planning, building control, and licensing deadlines. Achieving these regulatory milestones was essential for the project's success and required meticulous planning and close collaboration with local authorities.

Proactive Client Engagement

From the outset, client engagement was a priority. Julie Burnell, representing the Serpentine Gallery, played a crucial role in maintaining open lines of communication between the client and the project

Sou Fujimoto Serpentine Pavilion

team. Regular feedback sessions ensured the client's vision was fully integrated into the design and execution phases. This proactive approach fostered trust and ensured that the project aligned with the client's expectations and requirements.

Early Adoption of Video Communications

Given the global nature of the team, communication was crucial. The project utilised video conferencing to facilitate seamless communication between Fujimoto's team in Japan and the UK engineering and construction teams. This facilitated real-time discussions, decision-making, and problem-solving, ensuring that everyone was aligned and that the design intent was faithfully executed. Daily meetings were held to keep track of progress and address any issues promptly, which was critical given the immovable programme linked to the public launch.

The communication protocols were informed by lessons learned from the previous year's project with Ai Weiwei. This iterative learning process was vital for the project's success, ensuring that best practices were implemented and potential pitfalls were avoided.

Centralised CAD Modeling

A centralised CAD model played a pivotal role in the project. It allowed all team members to work from a unified digital representation of the Pavilion, which was continuously updated and refined. This model facilitated real-time collaboration and ensured consistency across all design and construction stages. By working from a single source of truth, the team effectively coordinated the complex lattice structure and navigated engineering challenges.[12]

Space frame detail

Off-Site Manufacturing

To minimise on-site construction time and permit higher precision and quality control, the Pavilion's intricate lattice structure was prefabricated off-site by Stage One, a construction company based in York. The components were then transported to London and assembled on-site. This also reduced environmental impact and disruption in Kensington Gardens.

Ted Featonby at Stage One played a crucial role in the process, ensuring the prefabricated components were manufactured to the highest standards and delivered on time.

[12] Pop, D., 2015. Theorising Between Space and Place A Case Study on Perceptive Architecture-Serpentine Gallery Pavilions. Philobiblon, 20(2), p.356.

Project Outcome and Further Collaborations

The 2013 Serpentine Pavilion was completed three days ahead of schedule and within budget, demonstrating the effectiveness of the collaborative approach and the technologies used. The Pavilion received multiple accolades for its architectural significance and innovative use of materials. It served as a flexible, multi-purpose social space that blended seamlessly with its natural surroundings, embodying Fujimoto's vision of merging natural and constructed environments. It was also recognized for its successful execution, highlighting the effectiveness of interdisciplinary collaboration and advanced construction techniques.

This project's success led to further collaborations between the same teams. Notably, we worked together on the 2015 British Pavilion at the Milan World Expo, showcasing our ability to deliver innovative and complex projects on time and within budget.

Reflection on Learning and Application from the Sou Fujimoto Serpentine Pavilion Case Study

The Sou Fujimoto Serpentine Pavilion case study exemplifies how effective interdisciplinary collaboration and cutting-edge technology can streamline complex processes and enhance project efficiency.

Key lessons include the importance of integrating advanced communication tools early in the project. Regular video conferencing and daily meetings ensured seamless communication between geographically dispersed teams, facilitating real-time decision-making and problem-solving. Regular feedback sessions with the client representative ensured that the client's vision was fully integrated throughout.

Centralised CAD modelling maintained consistency and coordination among team members, minimising errors and streamlining the integration of complex design elements. Off-site manufacturing demonstrated the benefits of precision and quality control, and prefabrication reduced on-site construction time and environmental impact, illustrating how innovative construction methods can enhance efficiency and sustainability.

Overall, the Sou Fujimoto Serpentine Pavilion project highlights the importance of leveraging advanced technologies, fostering client collaboration, and employing innovative construction techniques. For young graduates and early career professionals, understanding and applying these principles is crucial for achieving excellence and driving innovation in the architectural field.

8.3 // Stimulating Innovation and Creativity

(Sparking Ideas: Fostering Innovation through Collaboration)

This section explores how interdisciplinary collaboration fosters innovation and creativity, noting the benefits of idea exchange, cross-fertilisation, risk mitigation, and continuous learning.

Idea Exchange

Open, regular communication and brainstorming sessions enable team members to share and develop ideas collaboratively. This can lead to creative breakthroughs that might not occur in a more siloed working environment.

Cross-Fertilisation

Combining insights from different disciplines can result in unique and creative solutions. For example, an engineer's knowledge of sustainable materials might inspire a designer to integrate these materials into their aesthetic vision.

A practical example of this is the use of biomimicry in architecture, where design solutions are inspired by nature. Engineers and biologists collaborate with architects and designers to create buildings that mimic natural processes, leading to innovative and sustainable designs.
The Eden Project in Cornwall, UK, is a prime example of architectural biomimicry, where the structure's design was inspired by natural forms, resulting in a visually stunning and environmentally sustainable project.

Eden Project Cornwall - Grimshaw

Risk Mitigation

By examining a project from varying perspectives, collaborative teams can foresee, identify and mitigate risks early, saving time and resources in the long run. During the London Olympics 2012 project, diverse teams worked together to identify hazards and potential design solutions to ensure the safety and success of the event's infrastructure.

Continuous Learning

Collaboration promotes continuous learning, where exposure to diverse perspectives enhances professional development and keeps the team abreast of the latest trends and innovations in their respective fields.

For young professionals and graduates, working in a collaborative team provides an invaluable opportunity to learn from more experienced colleagues and gain insights from different disciplines. The collaborative design process used in the Argents Kings Cross redevelopment in London shows how continuous learning and interdisciplinary collaboration can transform urban spaces into innovative public amenities.[13]

Action Learning Points:

- Encourage team members to voice their unique perspectives and create an inclusive environment where all ideas are considered.
- Implement regular brainstorming sessions and idea-sharing workshops. Use collaborative tools to facilitate open communication and idea development.
- Promote interdisciplinary collaboration by organizing cross-disciplinary workshops and encouraging team members to explore ideas from other fields.
- Integrate risk assessment into the collaborative process by conducting regular risk analysis sessions with input from all disciplines to ensure potential issues are identified and addressed early.
- Encourage a culture of continuous learning by providing opportunities for professional development and knowledge sharing. This can include workshops, seminars, and access to industry publications and resources.

[13] Dunnett, N. and Kingsbury, N., 2008. Planting green roofs and living walls. Timber Press.

8.4 // Practical Strategies for Effective Collaboration

Tools of the Trade: Practical Strategies for Seamless Collaboration

Effective collaboration during architectural projects requires a structured approach to ensure seamless communication, coordination, and cooperation among team members. This section outlines practical strategies for fostering effective collaboration.

Collaborative Technologies

Collaborative technologies are essential for facilitating communication and coordination, especially in geographically dispersed teams. These tools ensure that all stakeholders are aligned and informed throughout the project lifecycle by enabling real-time collaboration, document sharing, and project management.

- **Project Management Software:** Tools like Asana, Trello, and Microsoft Project allow team members to assign tasks, set priorities, and monitor the status of various project components.
- **Building Information Modeling (BIM):** BIM software like Autodesk Revit and ArchiCAD enables teams to create and manage digital representations of the physical and functional characteristics of places. BIM facilitates collaboration by providing a centralised model that all team members can access and update.
- **Communication Platforms:** Tools like Slack, Microsoft Teams, and Zoom support instant messaging, video conferencing, and file sharing, enabling teams to stay connected in real time and collaborate effectively.
- **Cloud Storage Solutions:** Services like Google Drive, Dropbox, and OneDrive provide secure cloud storage for project documents and files. These platforms ensure that all team members have access to the latest versions of documents, facilitating collaboration and reducing the risk of errors.

Regular Meetings

Regular meetings are crucial for making collaborative decisions by providing a platform for discussing progress, addressing issues, and ensuring that all team members are aligned with project goals.

- **Weekly Progress Meetings:**

  Purpose: To review the progress of the project, discuss any issues, and plan the upcoming tasks

  Format: Typically includes a review of completed tasks, discussion of ongoing work, and planning for the next week

  Benefits: Keeps the project on track, ensures that all team members are aware of their responsibilities, and provides an opportunity to address any challenges promptly

- **Design Charrettes:**

  Purpose: To brainstorm and develop design ideas collaboratively

  Format: Intensive workshops that bring together various stakeholders to develop design solutions

  Benefits: Encourages creativity, integrates diverse perspectives, and fosters a sense of ownership among team members

- **Daily Stand-Up Meetings:**

  Purpose: To provide quick updates on progress and address any immediate issues

  Format: Short meetings where each team member briefly discusses what they accomplished the previous day, what they plan to do today, and any obstacles they are facing

  Benefits: Enhances communication, identifies issues early, and keeps the team focused and aligned

- **Client Meetings:**

  Purpose: To ensure that the client's vision and requirements are understood and integrated into the project

  Format: Regular meetings with the client to review progress, discuss changes, and gather feedback

  Benefits: Builds trust with the client, ensures that the project meets their expectations, and allows for adjustments based on client feedback

Clear Communication Channels

Establishing and maintaining clear communication channels ensures that all team members are informed and engaged throughout the project.

1. **Communication Protocols:**

   Purpose: To establish guidelines for how communication should be conducted within the team

   Components: Includes protocols for meetings, email communication, instant messaging, and document sharing

   Benefits: Reduces misunderstandings, ensures that important information is communicated effectively, and maintains a professional standard of communication

2. **Centralized Information Hub:**

   Purpose: To provide a single source of truth for all project-related information

   Components: Includes a project management platform or intranet where all documents, plans, and updates are stored and accessible to all team members

   Benefits: Ensures that everyone has access to the latest information, reduces duplication of work, and improves coordination

3. **Regular Updates and Reports:**

   Purpose: To keep all stakeholders informed about the project's progress and any changes

   Format: Regular progress reports, status updates, and newsletters

   Benefits: Keeps everyone informed, enhances transparency, and builds trust among team members and stakeholders

Effective, multidisciplinary collaboration in architectural projects requires a combination of collaborative technologies, regular meetings, and clear communication channels. By implementing these strategies, teams can deliver more successful and innovative project outcomes. For young graduates and early career professionals, developing skills in these areas is crucial for achieving professional success and contributing to collaborative and innovative projects.

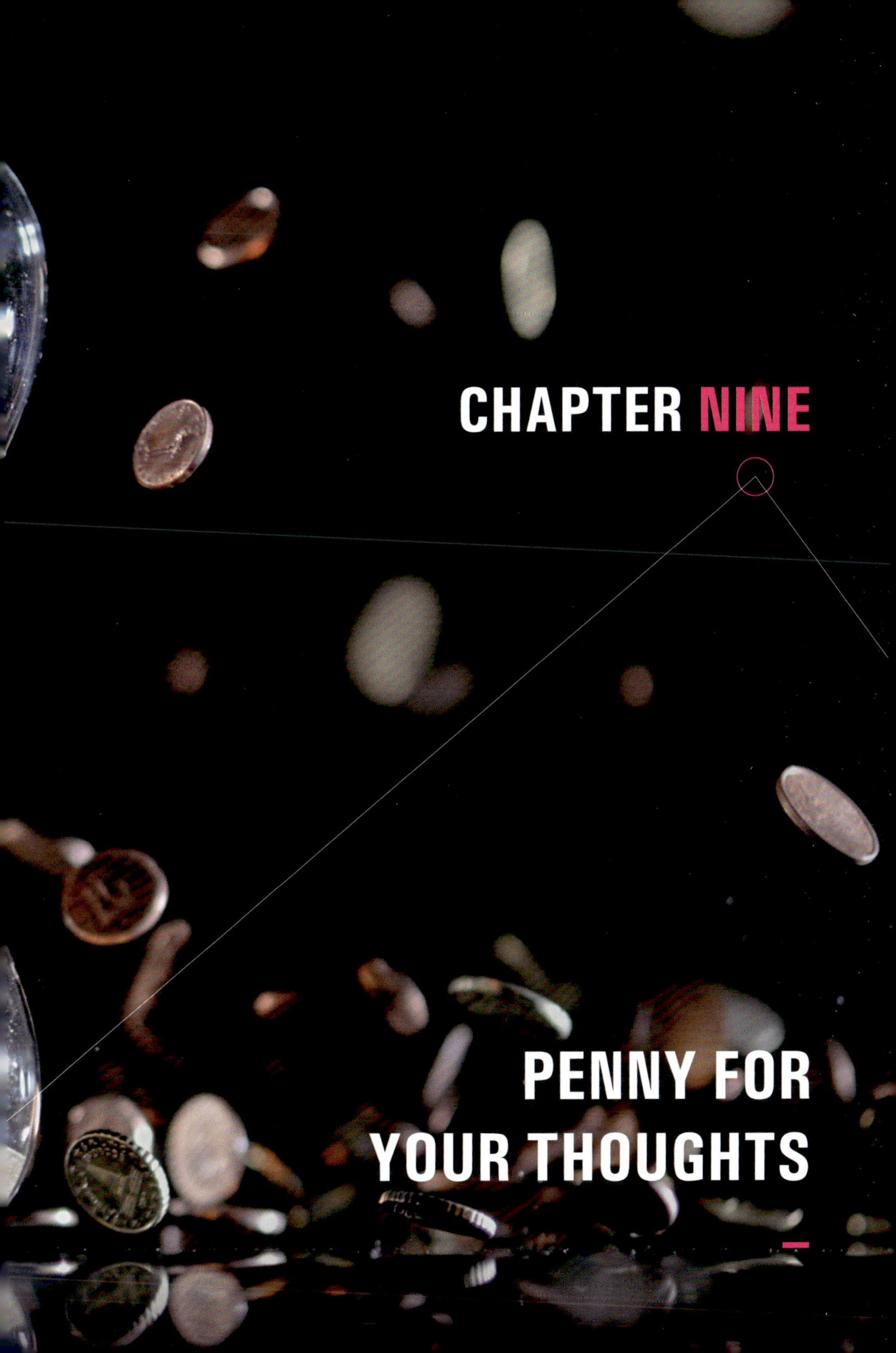

CHAPTER NINE

PENNY FOR YOUR THOUGHTS

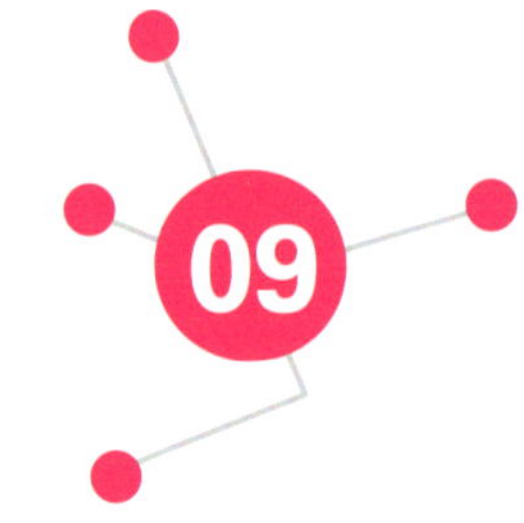

CHAPTER NINE

Penny for Your Thoughts:
The Critical Art of Business Planning

Think of business planning as the blueprint for your architectural firm's success. Without it, even a creative and innovative practice can crumble under the weight of financial mismanagement. This chapter provides an outline of how to navigate the business landscape—addressed in more detail in Sections Two and Three of this book.

9.1 // Setting Up: Business Planning, Benchmarking, and Marketing Plan

(Blueprints for Success: The Essentials of Planning)

As a business owner, you must take several important steps to ensure your business's success. These include creating a business plan, benchmarking your competitors, and developing a marketing plan. Creating a comprehensive business plan gives you a clear path forward, guiding your actions and decisions. By meticulously benchmarking your competitors, you gain insights into market trends and identify opportunities for differentiation. Developing a robust marketing plan enables you to effectively communicate the value you offer to captivate your target audience and establish a strong market presence.

Step 1 Business Planning:

A business plan outlines your goals, strategies, and tactics for achieving success, and as such should be regularly reviewed and updated as your business evolves. It will help you identify your target market, develop a pricing strategy, determine your expenses, and forecast your revenue. This helps you stay focused on your goals and make informed decisions about allocating your resources.[1]
A comprehensive business plan is also vital for securing financing from lenders or investors, demonstrating a solid understanding of your business's potential, and potential risks and opportunities.

[1] Drucker, P.F., 2011. The five most important questions you will ever ask about your organization. John Wiley & Sons..

The MOST Framework

The MOST framework (Mission, Objectives, Strategies, and Tactics) is a comprehensive tool for business and marketing planning, used to analyse an organisation's core components.
This framework helps businesses align their goals with actionable plans, ultimately reinforcing their overall purpose and capabilities. [2]

Comprehensive Business Plan Components

- **Executive Summary:** A brief overview of your business, mission, and vision.
- **Market Analysis:** Detailed research on your industry, target market, and competition.
- **Organisation and Management:** Outline your business structure, ownership, and management team.
- **Service Line or Product Line:** Describe your architectural services or products and their benefits.
- **Marketing and Sales Strategy:** Plan to reach and sell to your target market.
- **Funding Request:** Outline your funding requirements and future financial plans if seeking funding.
- **Financial Projections:** Provide income statements, cash flow statements, and balance sheets for the next 3-5 years.
- **Appendix:** Any additional information, such as resumes, permits, or legal documents.

9.2 // Benchmarking Competitors and Marketing Strategies

(Keeping Up with the Joneses: Staying Ahead in the Market)

Step 2 Benchmarking Competitors:

Benchmarking is the process of comparing your business's performance to that of your competitors. This helps you understand how your business stacks up against others in the industry, and allows you to identify areas for improvement to help you gain a competitive advantage.

- **Comparative Analysis:** Evaluate financial performance data and metrics against similar firms within the industry. This can include revenue, profit margins, and growth rates.

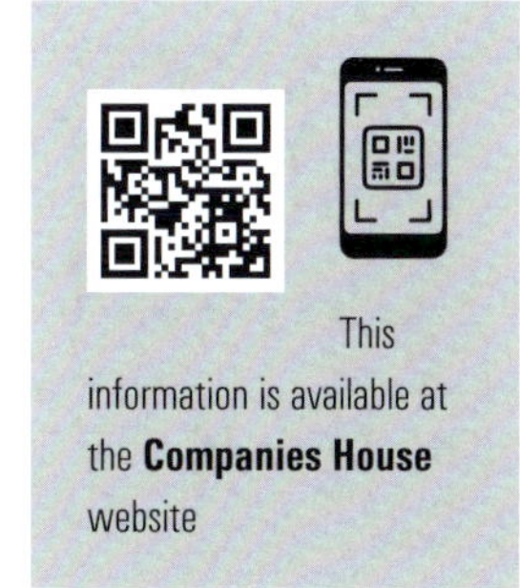

This information is available at the **Companies House** website

[2] Kaplan, R.S., 2009. Conceptual foundations of the balanced scorecard. Handbooks of management accounting research, 3, pp.1253-1269.

- **Industry Surveys and Reports:** Utilise surveys and reports from industry groups or consulting firms to gain insights into market trends and performance standards.
- **Peer Reviews and Networking:** Engage with peers through professional networks or associations to share knowledge and compare operational, financial, and project outcomes.
- **Software Tools:** Implement specialized software tools designed for firms to track and analyze key performance indicators (KPIs) over time.
- **Client Feedback:** Systematically gather and analyze client feedback to assess service quality, client satisfaction, and areas to enhance service.
- **RIBA Business Benchmarking Report:** The annual RIBA Business Benchmarking full report provides vital business knowledge about how your practice compares to others across a broad range of business metrics. It allows you to identify areas of strength, weakness and opportunity and make evidence-based business decisions. The full report offers an in-depth evaluation of how well your practice is performing in the following areas:
    - Staff salaries
    - Practice revenue, expenditure and profit
    - Charge out rates and billable hours
    - Work types and sectors
    - Business Policies
    - Sources of new commissions

  The findings also provide robust data about the business of architecture, informing and supporting RIBA's policy positions, and helping to shape the future of the profession. All RIBA Chartered Practices benefit from and are required to complete the RIBA Business Benchmarking survey.

Link to RIBA Business Benchmarking survey on **architecture.com**

[3] Collins, J., 2001. Good to Great: Why some companies make the leap...and others don't. HarperCollins

[4] Porter, M.E., 1992. Capital disadvantage: America's failing capital investment system. Harvard business review, 70(5), pp.65-82.

9.3 // Developing a Comprehensive Marketing Plan

(Plan to Prosper: Crafting Your Business Blueprint)

Step 3 Developing a Marketing Plan

Getting the Word Out

A marketing plan is a blueprint for promoting your business and attracting customers. It should include a clear understanding of your target market, your unique value proposition, and the channels you will use to reach your audience. A well-crafted marketing plan will help you build brand awareness, generate leads, and convert prospective clients into paying customers.

Let's break this down into its key stages:

1. **Identify Your Target Audience**
    - **Research and Analyse Competitors**: Understand who your competitors are targeting, and identify gaps or opportunities.
    - **Understand Your Market Position**: Tailor your efforts to your ideal clients, ensuring efficient use of time, money, and resources.
2. **Budgeting**

    Allocate your marketing budget wisely, considering both the scale of your operations and your strategic goals. A budget that reflects your business size and ambitions supports a balanced marketing strategy, incorporating digital presence, content creation, and community engagement. A practice should spend around 7-10% of its annual turnover on marketing activities.

    This will need to cover the following:

    - Marketing
    - Website
    - Blogs
    - Social media
    - Email marketing.
    - Marketing Staff Cost
3. **Costs of promoting your business:**
    - Local Networking
    - Public Relations
    - Industry Events
    - Industry Associations

4. **Setting Goals**

   Establish clear, measurable objectives for your marketing efforts. Utilising the Specific, Measurable, Attainable, Relevant, and Time-bound (SMART) framework helps set achievable targets and guide your budgeting decisions. A SMART goal could be to win 10 new clients and increase turnover by 30% whilst maintaining a gross margin of 20% by the end of your financial year.

In relation to your business plan, this is about developing a mix of strategies and tactics to meet your marketing goals. Strategies outline your approach and rationale, while tactics detail the specific actions and methods for achieving your goals. Consider a scenario where the objective is to enhance the firm's market share in eco-friendly design:

Mission: To be the leading sustainable architecture practice in the UK

Objective: Elevate market share in sustainable design by 25% within a year.

Strategy: Boost engagement and awareness around the firm's eco-friendly projects.

Tactics:

- Revamp the website to highlight sustainability projects, aiming for a 20% increase in project inquiries.
- Initiate a series of webinars on sustainable design practices to raise awareness and attract a 15% increase in web traffic.
- Partner with eco-friendly brands for joint marketing initiatives, aiming to enhance project inquiries by 20%.
- Apply for sustainability awards and leverage wins in marketing materials.
- Conduct targeted PR campaigns to feature your sustainable projects in green building magazines and websites.
- Host community events focused on sustainability, inviting both potential clients and collaborators, to foster new project leads.
- Amplify your presence on digital platforms through regular updates on sustainability projects, aiming for a 25% growth in online engagement.

This approach ensures a comprehensive strategy to attract new clients and solidifies the firm's reputation in the sustainable design sector.

Allocation:

Distribute your budget across various marketing activities, ensuring each is aligned with your strategic objectives and has a clear Return on Investment (ROI). For example:

Case Study: Developing an AI Designer Using GANs for Architectural Innovation

Introduction

ABC Architects Ltd. embarked on a strategic journey to develop an AI-powered designer using Generative Adversarial Networks (GANs). The goal was to leverage GANs to create innovative design solutions, enhance efficiency, and offer unique architectural services to clients.

Research and Development of GANs

The firm allocated significant resources to researching and developing GANs. This involved hiring AI specialists, collaborating with academic institutions, and investing in the necessary hardware and software infrastructure to support AI development.

Integration of AI into the Design Process

The firm integrated AI tools into their existing design workflows to enhance creativity and efficiency in the design process. The AI-powered designer, utilising GANs, was trained on a vast dataset of architectural designs to generate innovative and unique design concepts.

AI-Driven Content Marketing

To educate their audience and position the firm as an innovator in the field, they launched a new blog and podcast series focused on AI in architecture, sharing insights and trends in AI-driven design and construction.

Search Engine Optimization (SEO)

They invested in SEO strategies tailored to highlight their AI capabilities online. Keywords such as 'AI in architecture', 'AI design tools', and 'innovative architectural solutions' were targeted to elevate their website's search engine ranking.

Social Media Marketing

The firm implemented a comprehensive social media marketing strategy to reach a broader audience. This included regular posts on LinkedIn, Twitter, and Instagram showcasing their AI projects, behind-the-scenes looks at their development process, and thought-leadership articles.

Awards Submissions and Public Relations

They submitted their landmark AI-driven projects for prestigious industry awards to showcase their expertise and achievements, and used PR to highlight these accomplishments, gaining media coverage in industry publications and tech blogs.

Local and Industry Events

The firm leveraged local events and industry conferences as platforms to connect with the community, clients, and potential partners. They hosted workshops and presentations on the applications of AI in architecture, reinforcing their commitment to innovation and enhancing their professional network.

Budget Allocation

Marketing Activity	Allocation
R&D for GANs (Hardware, Software, and Specialists)	£150,000
AI-Driven Content Marketing (Blog Launch, 1 article/month)	£30,000
AI-Driven Content Marketing (Podcast Launch)	£25,000
Search Engine Optimization (SEO)	£20,000
Social Media Marketing (Post creation & Scheduling)	£25,000
Awards Submissions	£10,000
Media/Press Relations	£20,000
Local and Industry Events Sponsorship & Attendance	£30,000
Total	**£310,000**

Revised Annual Revenue and Budget

Given the increased scope and costs associated with developing AI capabilities using GANs, the total annual revenue (projected gross) was set at £5,000,000, and the total annual marketing budget was 6.2% of gross revenue.

Outcomes and Impact

- **Enhanced Online Presence** Integrating AI features and comprehensive content marketing resulted in a 50% increase in website traffic and a 30% increase in user engagement.
- **Thought Leadership and Brand Positioning** The AI-driven content marketing efforts positioned ABC Architects Ltd. as thought leaders in the industry. Their blog and podcast series gained significant traction, with a 60% increase in subscribers and high engagement rates on social media platforms.
- **Improved SEO Rankings** Targeted SEO strategies led to a 35% increase in organic search traffic, with several AI-related keywords ranking on the first page of search engine results.
- **Increased Social Media Reach** The social media marketing campaign significantly expanded their online presence, with a 40% increase in followers across platforms.
- **Recognition and Media Coverage** Submitting projects for awards and leveraging public relations gained them several accolades and extensive media coverage.
- **Networking and Collaboration** Participating in local and industry events fostered valuable connections and collaborations. Hosting workshops on AI applications in architecture positioned ABC Architects Ltd. as innovators and leaders.

Key Learning Points

- **Strategic Investment in Technology:** Integrating AI into architectural practices can significantly enhance efficiency and innovation.
- **Comprehensive Marketing Plan:** A well-rounded marketing plan, including content marketing, SEO, social media, and PR, is essential for establishing thought leadership and attracting clients.
- **Importance of Networking:** Participating in events and leveraging professional networks can open up new opportunities and collaborations.
- **Continuous Improvement:** Regularly reviewing and adjusting strategies based on performance data ensures sustained growth and success.

Execution

Set realistic goals, allocate resources wisely, and utilise project management tools like Asana or Slack to oversee progress, implement your strategy precisely, and break tactics into manageable tasks. Use visual aids or Gantt charts for a clear project overview. Prepare in advance, such as securing high-quality imagery for key projects before they feature on your website or award entries. Include a budget and metrics in your marketing plan to make data-driven decisions and remain agile.

Monitoring

Utilise analytics to assess the marketing effectiveness of your content, including tools like Google Analytics and Google Search Console for tracking website traffic. Monitor key metrics, and use custom URLs for precise campaign performance analysis.

Optimisation

Adjust strategies based on performance data. Refine your approach to enhance outcomes and respond to market changes. For example, revise content for relevance if it doesn't resonate with readers, but approach adjustments gradually, avoiding drastic actions. Stay agile in refining tactics as swiftly as possible to adapt to market changes.

Professional Guidance

Consider enlisting the help of professional marketing consultants who can offer insights and strategies tailored to your firm's needs, especially if you're short of time or expertise.

As we conclude this chapter, it's evident that effective business planning is integral to the success of any architectural practice. A well-structured business plan helps manage finances and guides strategic decisions, ensuring sustainable growth and long-term success. Understanding costs, managing overhead, and maintaining healthy profit margins are all crucial elements that contribute to the overall financial health of your firm. By incorporating these principles, you can build a solid foundation that allows your architectural creativity to flourish within a stable and sustainable business framework.

SECTION 1

AFTERWORD

From Foundations...
To The Real World

The journey you embarked upon in Section One has laid the foundation for a new understanding of the dynamic interplay between architecture and entrepreneurship. Sections Two and Three will explore the topics touched upon in this section in more detail, offering real-world examples of projects and innovative practices to act as inspiration—and as cautionary tales—to give you the knowledge and tools you will need to leverage your skills into a thriving career as an architect and entrepreneur.

CONCEPT
iDEAS
PRESENTATION
COST
diagrams
PC
SERVER
37%

SECTION TWO

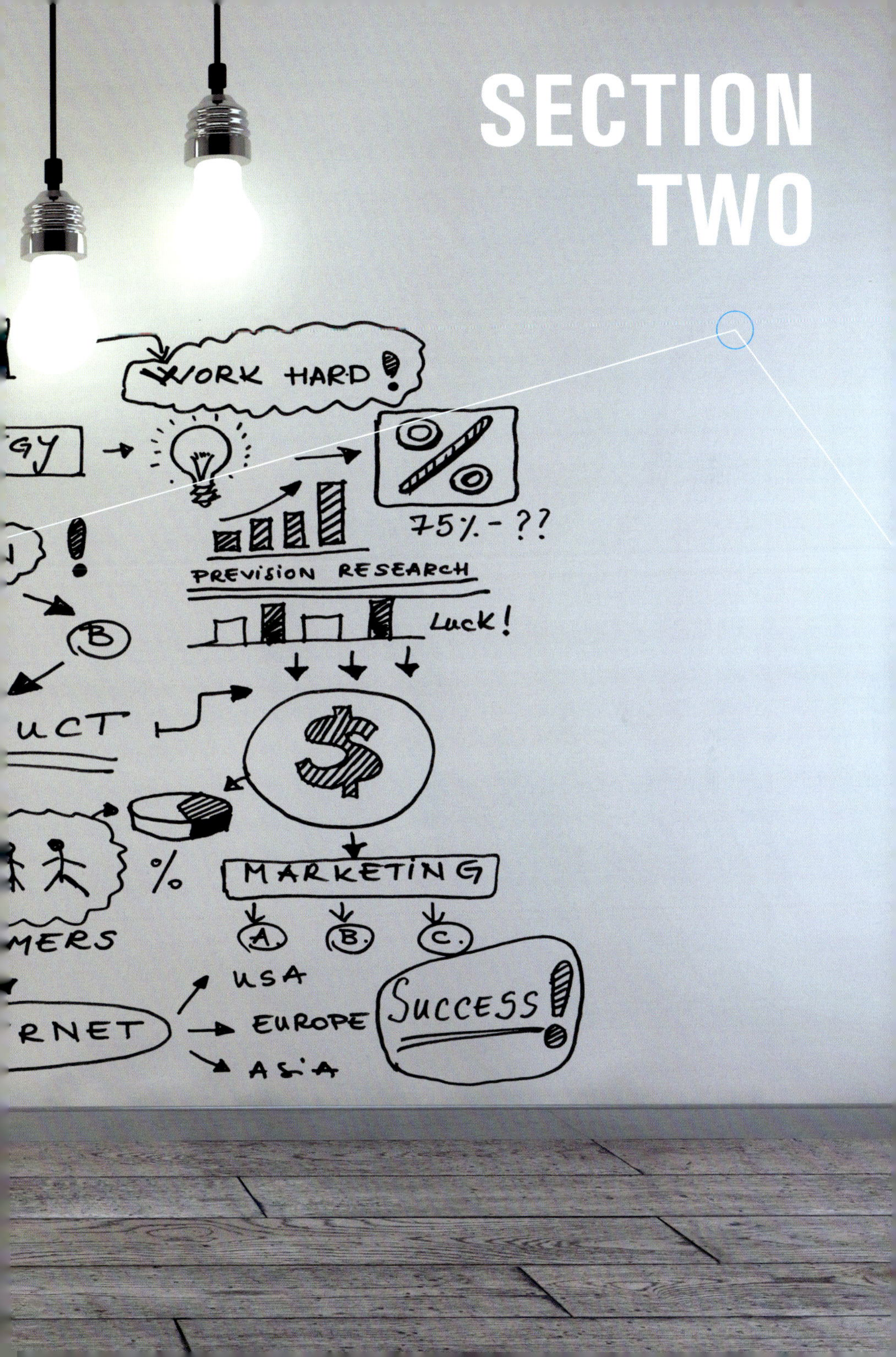

GET OUT THERE

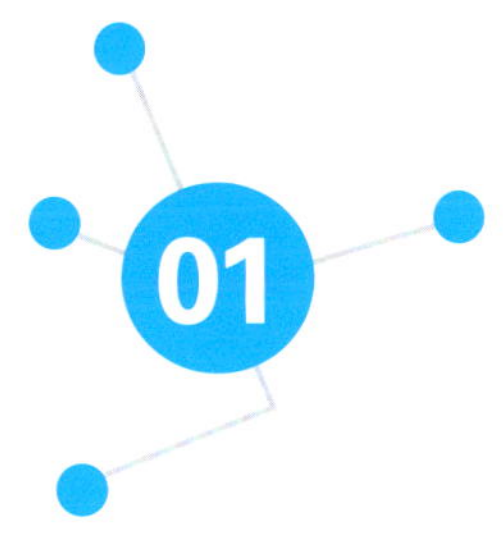

CHAPTER ONE

Get out there

Networking and building meaningful relationships are essential components of success in architecture, and building a solid network is a strategic investment in your career.1 In this chapter we will explore various strategies to enhance your networking efforts, showing how expanding one's network is not just about building a list of contacts but about cultivating meaningful relationships that inspire and challenge an architect's creative process. The exchange of ideas within diverse architectural communities can spark innovation, provide support during challenging projects, and open opportunities for collaboration on projects that might not be accessible otherwise.

1.1 // Network, Network and Network Some More .....

(Everyone Needs a Break Now and Again)

// Practical Advice on Expanding Networks

Attend Industry Events and Conferences

Events such the annual MIPIM Property Conference in Cannes, Regional RIBA events, and British Council of Offices (BCO) events offer platforms to meet industry leaders, potential clients, and collaborators, learn about new trends and technologies, and showcase your work and expertise. These can all lead to new business opportunities.

Join Professional Organizations

Professional organisations, including those allied to your core profession such as the Association for Project Management—an excellent adjunct to the RIBA—provide opportunities to meet other professionals in the field, keep up with industry news, and participate in events and activities. Many professional organisations also offer job boards and other resources to help architects find work and grow their careers.

[1] Pressman, A., 2014. Designing relationships: The art of collaboration in architecture. Routledge.

Collaborate with Other Professionals

Collaborating with other professionals is another effective way to network and build relationships. Interdisciplinary projects help architects better understand their colleagues' expertise and build trust and respect. Collaborations also provide unique learning experiences that allow architects to expand their skill sets, making them more versatile and attractive to potential clients.

Architectural Forums and Design Collectives

Seek out architectural forums, local design collectives, or online communities like Architizer or the Architectural Association's forums. Participating in these groups provides a platform for idea exchange and collaboration.

Design Competitions and Collaborative Projects:

Engage in design competitions or collaborative projects to build new connections and gain fresh perspectives. These activities can lead to new opportunities and enhance professional growth.

Workshops, Seminars, and Networking Events:

Set a schedule to attend workshops, seminars, and networking events hosted by architectural associations. These events provide valuable learning experiences and opportunities to connect with peers and industry leaders.

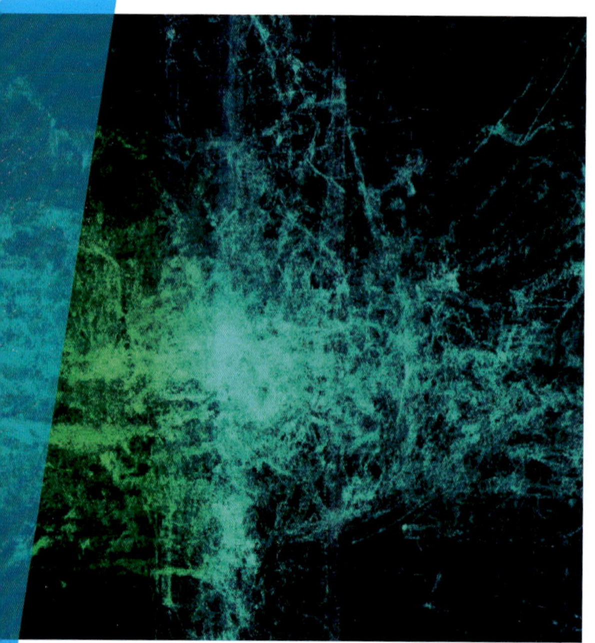

Build your network

Attend Networking Events

Networking events, such as happy hours and industry mixers, provide opportunities to meet new people in an informal setting, which can help break the ice and create more personal connections. Engaging in casual conversations can often lead to unexpected opportunities and collaborations, making these events invaluable for professional growth

Use Social Media Platforms

Social media and blogging have emerged as indispensable tools for architects. They offer unparalleled opportunities to showcase work, engage with communities, and build a brand. Embracing these digital platforms can amplify your reach, influence, and professional footprint, transforming how you connect with the world.

LinkedIn is the best-known social media platform for professionals, with over 740 million members worldwide. Boreal is a newer social media platform designed specifically for entrepreneurs and small business owners.

Instagram's visual-centric approach is ideal for showcasing architectural designs, progress shots, and completed projects. By curating a feed that reflects your design philosophy, you can attract a following that appreciates your work and vision. Posting regularly, using high-quality images, and leveraging features like Stories and IGTV can keep your audience engaged and invested in your projects. Young UK architects like George Bradley of Bradley Van Der Straeten and Eleni Soussoni of Eleni Interiors utilise Instagram to display their innovative designs, detail the design process, and highlight the human aspect of the spaces they create. Their authentic and visually appealing content helps them build a loyal following and connect with potential clients.

Blogs provide a space for storytelling that engages readers with the narrative behind projects. Unlike social media posts, blogs allow for in-depth exploration of design philosophies, project challenges, and creative processes. They are a platform to share insights, lessons learned, and detailed case studies that showcase your expertise and thought leadership. 'The Modern House' blog, for example, goes beyond merely presenting finished works; it delves into the architect's inspiration, the impact of architectural decisions on the living experience, and the integration of sustainability into design. This engages readers by offering them a deeper understanding of the architectural process.

Practical Steps for Engaging Through Social Media and Blogs

- **Consistent Branding:** Ensure that every post and content aligns with your brand's values and design philosophy. Adopt a specific colour scheme, typography, and style of imagery that reflects your architectural approach. Consistency creates a cohesive and memorable experience for your audience, enhancing brand loyalty and recognition.
- **Engaging Content:** Content that provides real value to your audience, such as behind-the-scenes looks at projects, detailed project breakdowns, and client testimonials, can captivate and build a more engaged following. Video walkthroughs, interactive Q&A sessions, and before-and-after comparisons are particularly effective.
- **Interactive Engagement:** Host live sessions where you discuss architectural trends and sustainability practices or conduct virtual tours of ongoing projects. Interactive elements like polls, surveys, and live Q&A sessions foster a sense of community and provide valuable insights into your audience's preferences and interests.
- **Collaborations:** Partner strategically with other professionals or brands to highlight the collaborative nature of architecture in joint projects, guest blog posts, and co-hosted events. Collaborating with interior designers, landscape architects, or even artists can provide a multidisciplinary perspective to your content.

- **Analytics:** Utilise advanced analytics tools to track engagement and gain insights into audience behaviour. Analysing which types of content generate the most interaction, the times of day your audience is most active, and the demographics of your followers can inform your content strategy and improve your project pitches and proposals.

Emerging Trends in Networking - Virtual Reality Meetups

The rise of virtual reality (VR) technology has revolutionised how architects network. VR meetups allow professionals to work together, share feedback and brainstorm ideas in a shared virtual space without having to travel.

A significant advantage of VR meetups[2] is the ability to showcase projects in 3D, allowing participants to walk through interactive virtual models, examine design details up close, and manipulate design elements in real-time. This makes presentations more engaging and accessible, and provides deeper insights into the architect's vision and thought processes. As VR technology evolves, and these meetups become more accessible and user-friendly,[3] VR meetups are likely to become a standard tool for architectural networking.

Online Networking Platforms for Architects

Several online platforms have emerged designed to meet the unique needs of architectural professionals, providing spaces to share work, discuss industry trends, and find potential collaborators. Websites like Archinect, Dezeen Jobs, and LinkedIn's architecture groups provide dedicated forums where architects can interact. Archinect, for example, is a comprehensive platform that combines job listings, news, and community features. Architects can create profiles to showcase their portfolios, connect with other professionals, and participate in discussions about the latest industry trends. The platform also hosts competitions and events, providing additional opportunities for exposure and networking.

1.2 // ......And Wear Out Your Shoe Leather

(you can always get another pair)

To succeed at networking, you must be proactive, persistent, and genuine, and approach it as a long-term investment in your career or business. Be willing to take the initiative to reach out to people you admire or want to work with rather than waiting for them to come to you, even if you still lack a specific need to do so. Ask for help from others and offer help and support to others in return, even if that doesn't immediately benefit your business. Take the time to listen and learn from others, even if you think you already know everything there is to know about your industry. Building meaningful relationships requires effort and a willingness to invest in the success of others, creating a reciprocal environment of growth and support.

[2] Rheingold, H., 1993. The virtual community: Homesteading on the electronic frontier. Addison-Wesley.
[3] Lanier, J., 2017. Dawn of the new everything: Encounters with reality and virtual reality. Henry Holt and Company.

It is also important to be strategic about your approach: identify your goals and priorities and focus on connecting with people who can help you achieve them. For example, if you're looking to expand your business into a specific region or industry sector, target networking efforts on events and people with connections in those areas.

Wear out your shoe leather.

Networking Etiquette

Effective networking also requires good etiquette. Here are some guidelines to help you make a positive impression and build lasting relationships:

- **Be Punctual:** Always be on time. Punctuality shows respect for others' time and professionalism. Arriving late can leave a negative impression and disrupt the flow of the event or meeting.
- **Dress Appropriately:** Your appearance can influence first impressions. Dressing appropriately shows you understand and respect the event's culture and context.
- **Prepare Your Introduction:** Know how to summarise who you are, what you do, and what you seek. A well-prepared introduction helps you make a solid first impression and sets the stage for meaningful conversations.
- **Active Listening:** Listen actively, ask thoughtful questions, and avoid interrupting. Active listening helps build rapport and shows that you value the other person's perspective.
- **Exchange Contact Information:** Always carry business cards or have a digital way to share your contact information. Ensure you follow up after the initial meeting. Exchanging contact information facilitates future communication and helps keep the connection alive.

- **Respect Boundaries:** Be mindful of personal space and avoid dominating conversations. Networking is about mutual exchange, so conversations should be balanced and respectful.
- **Express Gratitude:** Always thank people for their time and any assistance they provide. A simple thank-you can go a long way in building rapport. Showing gratitude helps foster positive relationships and leaves a lasting impression.
- **Follow-Up Etiquette:** Always follow up with a personalised message after meeting someone new. To make it personal, express your pleasure in meeting them and reference something specific from your conversation. This demonstrates your professionalism and genuine interest.

Additional Tips for Maintaining and Nurturing Professional Relationships

Building a network is just the beginning; maintaining and nurturing these relationships is crucial for long-term success. Here are some additional tips to help you maintain and nurture your network:

- **Regular Check-Ins:** Keep in touch with your contacts periodically to strengthen the relationship. Send updates about your work, share relevant articles, or check in to see how they are doing.
- **Offer Value:** Look for ways to provide value to your network. Share insights, offer assistance with their projects, or connect them with others in your network who might benefit them.
- **Be Genuine:** Be sincere in your interactions and show genuine interest in your contacts' work and well-being.
- **Celebrate Milestones:** Acknowledge and celebrate your network's achievements and milestones. Showing that you care about their success helps strengthen your connection.
- **Seek Feedback and Give Feedback:** Ask for feedback on your work and be willing to provide constructive feedback when asked. This helps build mutual respect and can improve both parties' work.

1.3 // That First Win

(Celebrating Success and Building Community)

By recognising and celebrating milestones we can inspire and motivate each other to achieve great things in our careers and create a supportive and collaborative environment that benefits us all. Winning your first architectural project is a moment to be cherished and celebrated—savour the moment and recognise the hard work and dedication that went into achieving the win. And as you move forward, remember that every interaction is an opportunity to build your network and create new avenues for growth and collaboration.

Help others up the ladder of success

STAND UP SPEAK UP

Stavros Niarchos Foundation Cultural Center

CHAPTER TWO

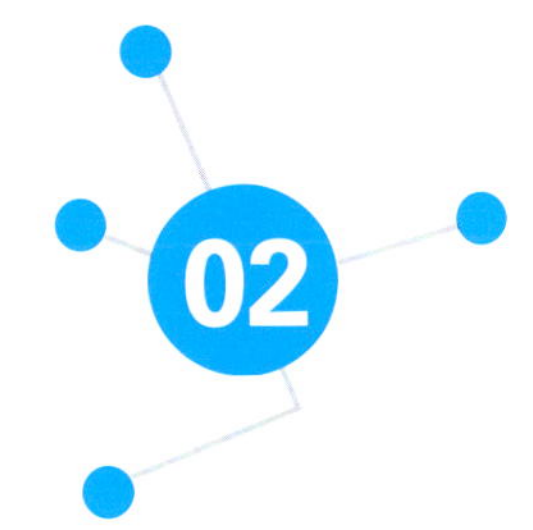

Stand Up, Speak Up

Effective communication is a cornerstone of successful architectural practice. While this chapter focuses primarily on public speaking, it is important to remember that architects must also excel in interpersonal, written, and digital communication to convey their ideas clearly and persuasively.

For architects, effective public speaking goes beyond eloquence. This chapter will endeavour to help you elevate your public speaking to an art form. Using examples of iconic speakers, we explore the nuances of engaging delivery, the magic of storytelling, and the power of connecting with your audience personally, using stories, emotions, and visuals to convey your message and make it unforgettable.

2.1 // Effective Communication

(Get straight to the point!)

Interpersonal communication involves the direct, face-to-face exchange of information and ideas. It includes verbal communication and non-verbal cues such as body language, facial expressions, and eye contact. Mastering interpersonal communication is essential when collaborating with clients, colleagues, and stakeholders, and helps architects build strong relationships, facilitate teamwork, and resolve conflicts effectively.

Written communication is equally important, as architects often need to create detailed reports, proposals, emails, and other documents. Clear and concise writing ensures that ideas are understood and project details are conveyed accurately. Well-crafted written communication can help persuade clients and stakeholders, secure funding, and manage projects efficiently.

Digital communication encompasses using digital tools and platforms to share information. This includes creating and presenting digital models, using project management software, and engaging in online collaboration. As the architectural industry embraces technology, proficiency in digital communication is becoming indispensable. Architects must continuously improve their communication skills to convey their vision, collaborate effectively, and achieve their professional goals.

Pitches and Presentations

Whether advocating for visionary urban development, engaging stakeholders in a community project, or making client presentations, the ability to publicly and compellingly communicate your vision can make the difference between project approval and rejection. This section explores how architects can use public speaking effectively, leverage visual aids to bring their designs to life and tailor messages for diverse audiences, drawing inspiration from communicators like former President Obama

2.2 // Overcoming Public Speaking Challenges

(Strategies for Confidence and Resilience)

Public speaking can be daunting, even for experienced professionals. Two of the most common challenges are stage fright and dealing with difficult audiences. Stage fright, or glossophobia, often stems from concerns about judgment, failure, or embarrassment in front of an audience. It can cause intense physical symptoms such as sweating, trembling, and a racing heart. On the other hand, difficult audiences can disrupt the flow of a presentation, posing questions or making comments that can unsettle even the most seasoned speakers. Successfully navigating these challenges requires a blend of preparation, emotional intelligence, and strategic techniques.

1. Overcoming Stage Fright:

Several techniques can help mitigate this common anxiety:

- **Preparation and Practice:** Thorough preparation is one of the best ways to combat stage fright. Know your material inside and out, and practice your presentation multiple times. Rehearsing in front of friends or colleagues can also help build confidence.
- **Visualisation:** Visualisation is a powerful tool. Imagine yourself delivering a successful presentation. Visualising positive outcomes can help reduce anxiety and boost confidence.
- **Breathing Exercises:** Deep breathing can help calm nerves. Practice breathing exercises before taking the stage to help control your physiological response to anxiety.
- **Starting Strong:** Begin with a strong opening to capture your audience's attention and set the tone for the rest of the presentation. A compelling story or an interesting fact can be effective openers.

2. Dealing with Difficult Audiences:

Here are some effective strategies to handle difficult audiences effectively:

- **Engage Early:** Engage with your audience early in the presentation. Ask questions, encourage participation, and show that you value their input. This can help create a more collaborative atmosphere.

- **Maintain Composure:** Stay calm and composed, even if faced with challenging questions or interruptions. Take a moment to breathe and respond thoughtfully rather than reacting emotionally.
- **Use Humour:** Appropriate humour can diffuse tension and help build rapport with your audience. Be cautious with humour, ensuring it is relevant and inoffensive.
- **Acknowledge and Redirect:** If faced with a difficult question or comment, acknowledge the person's concern and then redirect the conversation back to your main points. This shows that you respect their input but intend to keep the presentation on track.

2.3 // Architectural Storytelling and Visual Aids

(Crafting Memorable Narratives and Engaging Visuals)

Narratives have a unique ability to engage, persuade, and leave a lasting impression on an audience. This section explores the psychological impact of stories on memory and persuasion, emphasising why architects should integrate storytelling into their presentations.

1. The Psychological Impact of Stories on Memory

Research shows that stories have a profound effect on human memory because they activate multiple areas of the brain, including those responsible for emotions, sensory experiences, and motor functions, making them more memorable than plain facts and figures. When people listen to a story, they often visualise the events, making the information more vivid and easier to recall. Incorporating storytelling into your presentations means that the audience is more likely to remember the key points and the essence of the project.

2. The Persuasive Power of Stories

Stories are persuasive as well as memorable. They can influence beliefs, attitudes, and behaviours by creating emotional connections with the audience. For architects, a well-crafted story can make their designs more compelling and their arguments more convincing.

3. Crafting an Effective Architectural Story

To craft an effective architectural story, architects should focus on the following elements:

- **Identifying the Core Message:** Begin by distilling the essence of your project into a singular, impactful message that encapsulates the uniqueness of your design and sets the foundation for your narrative. Ensure every element aligns with and reinforces this central theme.
- **Problem-Solution Dynamic:** Architectural narratives are most compelling when they present a clear arc from challenge to resolution. Start by outlining the specific issue your project addresses, then guide your audience through how your design approaches

and resolves these challenges, detailing the research, innovation, and creative problem-solving involved.

- **Humanising Your Story:** To truly connect with your audience, incorporate elements that highlight the human impact of your design. Share stories or testimonials of individuals or communities who will benefit from the project. Discuss how the space will be used and how it will enhance daily life or work. By anchoring your project in human experiences, you create an emotional resonance that facts and figures alone cannot achieve.
- **Strategic Visual Storytelling:** Visual aids should be chosen to illuminate and amplify your narrative. Each visual should serve a specific illustrative purpose. Opt for clarity and simplicity to ensure your audience can easily grasp complex architectural concepts.

Guidelines for Crafting Effective Visual Aids

Visual storytelling is a crucial component of effective architectural presentations. The principles of design thinking can make complex concepts more accessible and engaging for the audience. This section discusses how these principles can be applied to create effective visual aids.

1. Principles of Design Thinking in Visual Storytelling:

Design thinking is a human-centred approach to innovation that integrates people's needs, technology's possibilities, and business success requirements. In the context of visual storytelling; by applying the principles of design thinking and incorporating insights from various sources, architects can create visual aids that inform, engage, and inspire their audience and transform complex architectural concepts into compelling narratives that resonate with stakeholders.

2. Applying Design Thinking to Create Effective Visual Aids:

- **Tailored Communication Strategies:** Understand your audience's needs, preferences, and expectations by conducting research, gathering feedback, and practicing empathy. For example, avoid complex diagrams for non-technical audiences, opting for simple, intuitive visuals that effectively convey the core message.
- **Define the Core Message:** Ensure all visuals support the main message. This keeps the presentation focused and prevents cognitive overload.
- **Ideate and Prototype:** Brainstorm to test multiple visual ideas and create prototypes. Experiment with sketches, creating mock-ups, or using digital tools to refine and test the most effective representations.
- **Iterate Based on Feedback:** Design thinking is iterative. Continuously refine visuals based on feedback to ensure their clarity and effectiveness and that they resonate well with the audience to significantly enhance the quality of your visual storytelling.

3. Types of Effective Visual Aids:

- **Diagrams and Infographics:** Use diagrams and infographics to break down complex ideas into easily understandable components. These visuals can simplify architectural processes, sustainability features, or spatial relationships, making them accessible to all audience members.
- **3D Models and Renderings:** 3D models and renderings of your architectural designs help the audience visualise the project in a realistic context, enhancing their understanding and engagement.
- **Interactive Elements:** Incorporate interactive elements such as virtual reality (VR) tours or augmented reality (AR) experiences. These technologies can provide an immersive experience, allowing the audience to explore the architectural space in an engaging and memorable way.

Tailored Communication Strategies

By tailoring your message to your audience, you can make your presentation more engaging and relatable. For instance, former President Barack Obama, known for his exceptional public speaking skills, researches his audience before delivering a speech. In his famous 'A More Perfect Union' speech on racial inequality, he used his insight into the racially diverse audience to make his message more impactful.

Recognise and adapt to your audience's knowledge level and interests. For technical audiences, emphasise architectural and engineering aspects, focusing on innovation and technical challenges. For community stakeholders, highlight how the project benefits the environment and the local community, focusing on sustainability, beauty, and functionality.

Case Study

Brené Brown.

Before diving into the case study, watch **Brene Brown's** TED Talk.

In Brené Brown's TED Talk, 'The Power of Vulnerability', she explores the profound connection between vulnerability and human experiences, emphasising its critical role in fostering empathy, belonging, and love. Brown's effective communication style is notable for several reasons, and architects and professionals in other fields can learn from it to enhance their presentations.

Enhanced Engagement and Persuasion

First, Brown uses body language masterfully to reinforce her message. Her gestures align with her words, adding emphasis and clarity to her points. This non-verbal communication helps to keep the audience engaged and underscores the importance of her message.

Deliberate Pacing

Second, her pacing is deliberate and impactful. Brown modulates her speech to build tension and create anticipation. She pauses at critical moments, allowing the audience to absorb and reflect on her words. This technique not only maintains interest but also highlights the significance of the information being conveyed.

Emotional Resonance and Memorability

Third, the narrative structure and emotional engagement in Brown's talk make her message resonate long after the presentation. For architects, incorporating storytelling into presentations can be particularly effective in competitive pitches or when seeking project approval.

Motivation and Call to Action

Ending with a strong call to action motivates the audience to embrace new ideas and take specific actions. For architects, a powerful conclusion is crucial in inspiring clients to support bold designs or innovative solutions with enthusiasm and confidence.

Incorporating Brown's communication techniques—effective body language, strategic pacing, relatable storytelling, and a powerful conclusion—enables architects to present their ideas more effectively. These skills enhance understanding and engagement, and also build trust and motivate action—essential for driving successful creative projects.

The following case studies are examples where public speaking was critical in securing funding and project support. The architects used their visual aids and their rhetorical skills to communicate the vision and benefits of their projects to a range of stakeholders, build trust and enthusiasm, and ultimately secure the necessary investment to turn their ideas into reality.

Case Study The High Line, New York City

The High Line in New York City is a public park built on a long-abandoned elevated freight rail line. Designed to preserve the historical structure of the rail line while creating a new green space in the city's heart, it was a unique and challenging undertaking requiring much public support and investment. In their pitch for the project, architects James Corner and Diller Scofidio + Renfro used 3D models, detailed renderings, and diagrams that showed how the park would look and function. They also created an animated video to provide a virtual park tour and showcase its unique features. These visuals demonstrated the park's potential to transform the neighbourhood, create opportunities for public recreation, and promote sustainable urban development. One of the key challenges of the

High Line New York

High Line project was gaining public support and funding. The architects' public speaking skills played a vital role in gaining support and funding from stakeholders, including community groups, city officials, and potential donors. By making it more tangible and easier to understand, they built trust and enthusiasm for the project.

Case Study **Stavros Niarchos Foundation Cultural Centre, Athens, Greece**

Figure 3: Stavros Niarchos Foundation Cultural Centre

Similarly, when pitching for the Stavros Niarchos Foundation Cultural Centre in Athens, Greece, architect Renzo Piano and his team used visual aids and their public speaking skills to communicate the vision and benefits of the project to a range of stakeholders, including government officials, philanthropists, and the public. The visual aids illustrated its unique features and potential and made the project more comprehensible and easier to envisage. Detailed 3D models and renderings showed the scale and design of the cultural centre and the integration of the park and green roof. Diagrams and animations demonstrated the project's environmental and social benefits.

Stavros Niarchos Foundation Cultural Centre

The Tablecloth!

Authors lunchtime sketch of the Ai Weiwei Serpentine Pavilion Under Construction

Other Ways to Persuade Clients and Win Work

It is important not to forget the importance of creativity and spontaneity in the design process and the value of communicating one's vision effectively regardless of circumstances.

There are several legendary examples of architects winning work by drawing on tablecloths. One is Frank Gehry, who recounted that while dining with the Guggenheim's director, Thomas Krens, in 1991, Krens asked him to sketch a design for the Guggenheim's new museum in Bilbao. Gehry sketched his vision for the building on a tablecloth, using a pen and a wine cork as tools. Krens was impressed, and immediately commissioned Gehry to build the museum.

Remember the importance of a tablecloth!

Similarly, Renzo Piano is reported to have drawn the initial design for the Pompidou Center in Paris on a tablecloth using a pen and some salt and pepper shakers as his tools while dining with his collaborators, the engineer Peter Rice and the designer Richard Rogers, when they asked him to sketch his idea for the building.

In both cases, the architects won major commissions by using simple tools and materials to convey their ideas compellingly and persuasively.

STAND UP, SPEAK UP

4 Key Learning Points //

1. **Understand your audience:** tailor your message to their concerns and desires by researching your audience's demographics and interests, and adjusting your message accordingly.
2. **Use models and visuals such as diagrams, charts, and infographics:** Provide a tangible representation of your ideas and communicate complex ideas simply, making them easier to understand and remember.
3. **Use storytelling techniques** Capture your audience's attention and connect with your message emotionally. Start with a compelling opening that grabs your audience's attention, and then use anecdotes and stories to illustrate your points.
4. **Practice your delivery and body language:** Rehearse your presentation several times, paying attention to your tone of voice, pacing, and body language. Stand tall, make eye contact with your audience, and use gestures to emphasise your points

Finally,

End your presentation with a strong call to action that inspires your audience to respond and act.

LEAD FROM THE FRONT

CHAPTER THREE

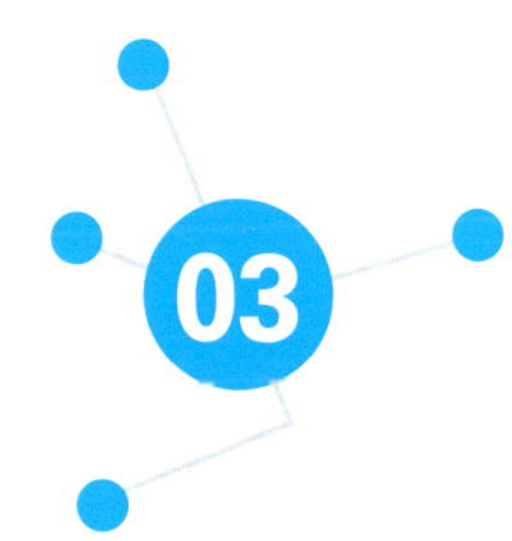

Lead from The Front

In the world of architectural practice, good leadership combines visionary design with organisational efficiency. This chapter discusses how architects can cultivate a thriving organisational culture to foster innovation, sustainability, and growth. Leading by example is key, and this chapter explores how a firm's organisational culture can be shaped through theoretical models such as Social Learning Theory and Hofstede's Cultural Dimensions Theory to support creativity, collaboration, and ethical practice.

It also explores various organisational structures, from matrix management to team-based and market sector models, highlighting their practical use in creating a dynamic, flexible organisational model that balances efficiency, creativity, and responsiveness to market demands.

3.1 // Leading by Example

(Organisational Culture)

Leading by example is a crucial aspect of leadership in any organisation. An architect who models desired behaviours and values sets the tone, inspiring others and shaping the organisation's culture to align with shared goals. This leadership style goes beyond personal integrity and professionalism; it influences not only the immediate team but also sets industry benchmarks for excellence and responsibility. This section will explore the importance of leading by example by looking at theoretical propositions and models architects can use to define their firm's culture.

Lead by example.

[1] Walters, R.H., 1963. *Social learning and personality development.* New York; Toronto: Holt, Rinehart and Winston.
[2] Hofstede, G., 1984. *Culture's consequences: International differences in work-related values (Vol. 5).* Sage.
[3] Quinn, R.E. and Rohrbaugh, J., 1983. *A spatial model of effectiveness criteria: Towards a competing values approach to organizational analysis.* Management Science, 29(3), pp.363-377.

Social Learning Theory

Bandura and Walters's social learning theory, one of the theoretical propositions that can be used to understand the importance of leading by example, suggests that individuals learn by observing and modelling others' behaviour. Leaders who demonstrate positive behaviours, such as integrity and honesty, can inspire their followers to emulate them. This theory emphasises the importance of role models and their influence.[1]

In architectural firms, when leaders actively engage in sustainable practices, promote innovation and demonstrate ethical client interactions, they set a powerful example for their team. This can also be applied through structured mentorship programs.

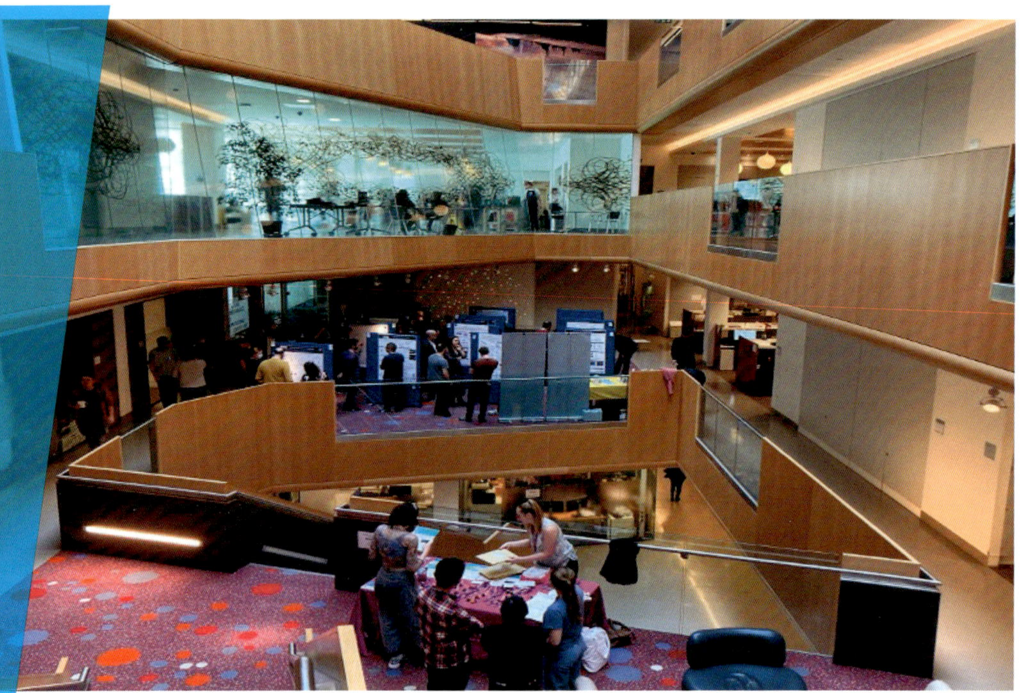

Organisational culture - Biochemistry , Oxford University, Hawkins Brown

Cultural Dimensions Theory

Hofstede's cultural dimensions theory proposes to define organisational structure by dimensions like power distance, individualism vs. collectivism, masculinity vs. femininity, uncertainty avoidance, and long-term vs. short-term orientation. Architects can use these dimensions to define their firm's culture. For instance, an organisation's focus on individualism may foster independence and self-reliance, while valuing collectivism may promote teamwork and collaboration.

[4] Denison, D., 1990. *Corporate culture and organizational effectiveness*. New York: Wiley. Dike, P. (2013).

By applying this framework, leaders can create a workplace that supports individual creativity and team collaboration. Practical steps include conducting workshops to assess the current culture and identify desired shifts to enhance the firm's collective ethos and adaptability.2

Competing Values Framework

Quinn's Competing Values Framework (CVF) identifies four different organisational cultures: clan, adhocracy, market, and hierarchy. Each culture represents different values and behaviours prevalent in the organisation. Clan culture emphasises collaboration and teamwork and a family like environment; adhocracy encourages innovation and risk-taking; market culture focuses on competition and achievement, and hierarchy culture is characterised by structure and stability, where rules and procedures are strictly followed.[3]

The CVF helps architecture firms shape their culture by identifying which type they align with. For example, leaders can use this information to promote innovation (adhocracy) or improve efficiency (hierarchy) through regular team discussions and reflections on the firm's operational and strategic goals, and aligning them with the firm's cultural attributes.

Denison Organizational Culture Model

The Denison Organizational Culture Model identifies four dimensions of organisational culture: involvement, consistency, adaptability, and mission. Involvement refers to employee participation in decision-making; consistency to employees' shared understanding of the organisation's goals and objectives; adaptability refers to how well the organisation responds to changes, and mission to the clarity of its vision and values. Architects can use these to define their own firm's organisational culture.

Practical application of the Denison Model includes encouraging employee involvement in decision-making, clearly communicating goals and objectives for consistency, promoting adaptability through flexible project management, and regularly revisiting the firm's mission to keep it aligned with internal values and external market demands.4

Practical Tips:

Regardless of the models and frameworks that characterise a practice, the following tips will help create an environment where creativity can thrive and employees feel empowered.

- **Vision and Communication:** An architecture leader must model desired behaviours and values to set the tone, and embody a compelling vision that should guide every project and decision within the practice. Communication is key to making your vision resonate, ensuring all stakeholders understand and embrace it.

- **Avoid Micromanagement:** While detail-oriented leadership is valuable, micromanagement can diminish trust and stifle initiative among your team. Recognise the fine line between providing guidance and controlling every aspect of the work. Trust your team's expertise and empower them to make decisions.
- **Build a Culture of Trust:** Encourage a culture where trust is paramount. Empower your team by delegating responsibilities and providing the support they need to succeed. This empowerment boosts morale, fosters accountability, and enhances creativity.

What's yours?

Matrix Management

3.2 // Frame It

(Organisational Structure)

Architects can ensure their organisations are aligned by defining their organisational culture.

The structure of an organisation determines how tasks are divided, how communication flows, and how decisions are made, and each type of structure has its advantages and disadvantages. Here, we will explore some of the hierarchical structures that can work in architectural practice.

Matrix Management

Matrix management is an organisational structure often used in architectural practices, where individuals from various disciplines, such as design, engineering, and project management, are organised into teams that work on specific projects.66 A project manager oversees each team, ensuring timely and on-budget project completion, while reporting to both the functional manager (who oversees their expertise) and the project sponsor or client.

In architectural firms, matrix management facilitates interdisciplinary collaboration, which is essential for addressing the complex challenges of modern architectural projects, and provides opportunities for employees to develop new skills. However, it requires strong communication skills and teamwork. Regular cross-functional meetings and the use of advanced project management software can improve communication and conflict resolution.

Team based Structure

Team-Based Structure

A team-based structure organises employees into teams focused on specific business areas like design, engineering or project management, each led by a team leader responsible for overseeing its work and ensuring it meets its objectives. This structure promotes collaboration and teamwork, ownership and responsibility, as team members work closely together and are accountable for their team's success. However, team-based structures require strong team leadership and skilled conflict management. In architectural firms, this structure fosters creativity and responsibility by encouraging cohesive teamwork and leveraging each individual's skills to drive innovative design solutions. To maximise its benefits, architectural firms can establish teams with complementary skill sets and promote leadership development within teams, enabling decentralised decision-making and greater responsiveness to market changes.

Market Sector Structure

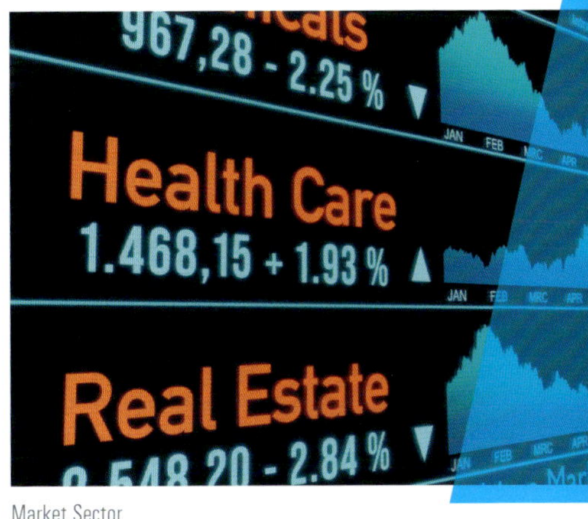

Market Sector

A market sector structure organises employees by specific market sectors, such as residential, commercial, or institutional architecture. Each sector is led by a manager responsible for meeting objectives and overseeing the work. This allows firms to specialise, focusing on specific market segments and developing expertise in those areas. Firms can become leaders in their chosen sectors, offering tailored design solutions that meet specific market demands and build strong client relationships within those niches. This structure also provides employees with clear career paths, as they can develop their skills within a specific market sector. However, market sector structures can create silos and face challenges when projects span multiple sectors.[5] To capitalise on this structure, firms should actively market their sector-specific expertise and highlight their ability to address unique sector-specific challenges.

[5] Den Otter, A. and Emmitt, S., 2007. *Exploring effectiveness of team communication: Balancing synchronous and asynchronous communication in design teams. Engineering, Construction and Architectural Management, 14* (5), pp.408-419.

[6] Wakkary, R., Desjardins, A., Hauser, S. and Maestri, L., 2013. A sustainable design fiction: Green practices. *ACM Transactions on Computer-Human Interaction (TOCHI), 20* (4), pp.1-34.

Architectural practices can adopt various hierarchical structures, including matrix management, team-based, or market sector structures, each with its own advantages. The choice of structure will depend on the organisation's needs and objectives. Matrix management draws on individuals' expertise from different functional areas, team-based structures promote collaboration and teamwork, and market sector structures focus on specific market segments.

A hybrid model combining elements of these structures can create a dynamic, flexible organisational model, leveraging the interdisciplinary collaboration of matrix management, the innovation of team-based structures, and the focused expertise of market sector structures. Leaders can balance efficiency, creativity, and market responsiveness by adapting the structure to the firm's evolving needs, ensuring it supports their goals and objectives.

Challenges and Solutions

Each organisational structure also presents its own challenges. To address these, firms can implement comprehensive onboarding to familiarise employees with the organisational model, continuous training programs to improve skills and teamwork, and adopt technology to facilitate collaboration and knowledge sharing across projects and sectors.6

Pitfalls:

- **Ignoring Team Dynamics:** Overlooking the impact of team interactions and relationships can lead to conflicts and a toxic work environment. It's crucial to monitor and nurture the social fabric of your workplace.
- **Lack of Shared Values:** Without a strong set of shared values, your organisation may struggle with identity and cohesion, making it hard to unite the team towards common objectives.
- **Overworking and Underappreciating:** Failing to acknowledge and reward your team's hard work and achievements can lead to burnout and high turnover rates

Solutions:

- Foster a positive team environment by regularly engaging in team-building activities and open discussions about workplace culture. Address conflicts promptly and constructively to maintain a healthy work environment.
- Clearly define and communicate your practice's core values and ensure they are reflected in every aspect of your work.
- Recognise and reward contributions by establishing a recognition program to celebrate individual and team achievements. Offer competitive salaries, benefits, and opportunities for professional growth to show appreciation for your team's hard work.

LEAD FROM THE FRONT
9 Key Learning Points //

1. **Apply Social Learning Theory to Lead by Example:** Model desirable behaviours and values to influence your team. By demonstrating integrity, professionalism, and a commitment to sustainable design and innovation, leaders can foster a culture of ethical practice and inspire their teams to align with shared goals and values.
2. **Utilise Hofstede's Cultural Dimensions:** Understand concepts like power distance and individualism vs. collectivism to define and enhance your firm's organisational culture. Promote a collaborative and adaptable work environment tailored to your architectural practice.
3. **Implement the Competing Values Framework (CVF):** Identify whether your firm aligns with clan, adhocracy, market, or hierarchy cultures. Use this understanding to balance innovation with operational efficiency and make strategic decisions that support your architectural goals.
4. **Adopt the Denison Organizational Culture Model:** Focus on involvement, consistency, adaptability, and mission within your firm. Develop policies that align with your firm's mission, encourage employee participation in decision-making, communicate goals clearly and practice flexibility in project management.
5. **Utilise Matrix Management:** Organise teams around projects to facilitate interdisciplinary collaboration. Ensure effective project management to bridge functional areas, aligning projects with client expectations and budgets.
6. **Implement a Team-Based Structure:** Organize employees into dedicated teams focusing on specific architectural areas. Promote collaboration and innovation and instill a sense of ownership and responsibility within your teams.
7. **Specialise with a Market Sector Structure:** Develop deep expertise in specific market sectors like residential, commercial, or institutional architecture. Build strong client relationships and offer tailored design solutions that meet sector-specific demands.
8. **Overcome Structural Challenges:** Address communication barriers and potential silos by implementing comprehensive onboarding, continuous training, and technology solutions. Facilitate collaboration and knowledge sharing across projects and sectors within your architectural firm.
9. **Cultivate Innovation and Inclusivity:** Encourage a workplace where new architectural ideas are welcomed and explored. Foster diversity within your teams to fuel creativity and promote work-life balance to maintain a healthy and productive work environment.

Finally, Lead from the Front, Eat Last

As entrepreneurs, it is easy to get caught up in the excitement of building a business, creating new products, and making money. However, entrepreneurs have a unique opportunity to positively impact the world by embodying the principles of servant leadership and the concept that 'leaders eat last'. This philosophy, popularised by author and speaker Simon Sinek, emphasises the importance of leaders putting the needs of their team members before their own. This means making sacrifices, taking responsibility for the well-being of others, and creating a sense of belonging and purpose that inspires everyone to work together towards a common goal.

At its core, servant leadership is about recognising that your success is tied to the success of those around you and creating a culture that supports and empowers others to achieve their full potential. This is particularly important for architects as entrepreneurs, who have the power to shape the culture of their companies and the communities they serve.

To be influential servant leaders, architects can put this principle into practice by developing a deep understanding of the needs and aspirations of their employees, customers, and other stakeholders. This means taking the time to listen and learn from others, building trust and mutual respect relationships, and creating an environment where everyone feels valued and supported. This approach may seem counterintuitive in a business world that often values competition and individual achievement above all else. However, by leading by example and demonstrating the value of putting others first, entrepreneurs can help create a more collaborative and compassionate business world.

APPLE MARKET
Hand-made Art & Design
APPLE MARKET

LIFTING THE BONNET

CHAPTER FOUR

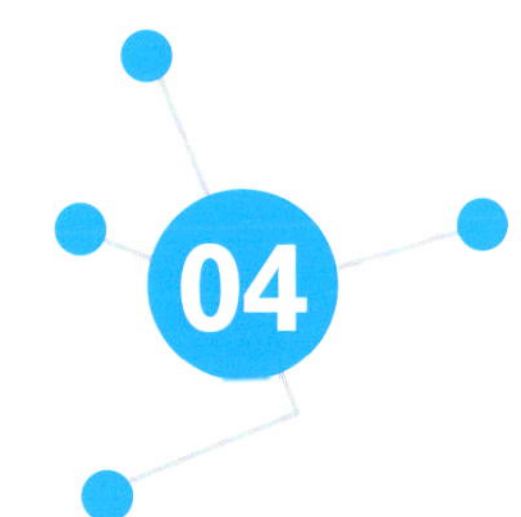

Lifting the Bonnet

Understanding and effectively managing the less glamorous aspects of entrepreneurship—such as legal considerations, financial management, and administrative duties—can significantly aid an entrepreneur's ability to innovate and compete. Mastering these tasks creates a robust framework that supports innovation and drives sustained growth and competitive advantage. A business's administrative backbone encompasses various activities, from human resources to supply chain management. Effective HR practices, particularly, are pivotal in attracting and retaining top talent, fostering a positive workplace culture, and ensuring compliance with labour laws.

4.1 // Lifting the Bonnet

(HR and things that make a business work)

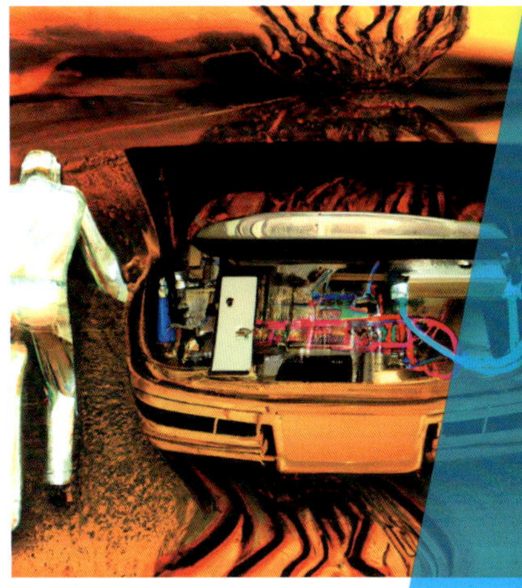

Lifting The Bonnet

This section addresses the significance of HR concerns for architects, accentuating how integrating HR best practice into a firm's administrative structure can facilitate elevated productivity, efficiency, and innovation. Notably, this integration underscores the importance of ethical practices. It's self-evident that all architects should be equal opportunities employers, ensuring unbiased treatment of all job candidates regardless of race, ethnicity, gender, sexual orientation, marital status, age, disability, or religion. The push for diversity in various fields, including architecture, is rooted in recognising the profound benefits it brings to the profession and society. The Stephen Lawrence Trust and the Royal Institute of British Architects (RIBA) have aptly highlighted the crucial connection between the profession's survival and relevance and its ability to reflect the diversity of the society it serves.

4.2 // Diversity and Inclusion

(Enhancing Creativity and Problem-Solving in Architecture)

Diversity within professions like architecture contributes to a richer and more well-rounded approach to problem-solving and innovation by introducing a wide range of backgrounds, experiences, and perspectives. This variety opens doors to creative ideas and solutions that might not have been considered otherwise, and fosters a dynamic environment that can lead to more innovative designs that address a diverse population's evolving needs and aspirations.

Promoting diversity also signals a commitment to inclusivity and social equity. When underrepresented groups thrive within a profession, it sends a powerful message that talent and potential are not confined to specific backgrounds, and enables aspiring professionals from all walks of life to pursue careers that may have previously seemed inaccessible to them.

Diversity's impact extends beyond the profession, as architectural decisions shape communities and influence their quality of life. When professionals with varied backgrounds contribute to these decisions, the resulting designs are more inclusive and culturally sensitive, enhancing societal well-being as a whole.

In essence, 'More is More' when it comes to diversity. As the world becomes increasingly interconnected and culturally diverse, fostering diversity within professions like architecture becomes a necessity for continued relevance, growth, and positive impact.

Gender Pay Gap

Gender Pay Gap

The introduction of Gender Pay Gap reporting on April 5, 2017 represented a significant advance in addressing gender inequality in the workplace. The legislation requires UK organisations with over 250 employees to disclose their gender pay gap results annually, promoting transparency in corporate practices. By establishing guidelines for calculating and reporting the gender pay gap, the regulations facilitate comparisons across various industries, encouraging a deeper analysis of gender-based pay disparities.

Although initially focused on large corporations, the principles of fair pay and transparency should apply to businesses of all sizes. Accepting gender pay gap reporting enables companies to address and rectify gender-based wage disparities and demonstrate their commitment to diversity and inclusion as responsible employers.

Smaller architectural firms, though not legally required to do so, can benefit from adopting these practices. As indicated in research conducted by the Chartered Institute of Personnel and Development (CIPD), this proactive approach fosters fairness and trust, attracting and retaining top talent and improving employee engagement and performance.

Living Wage

The Living Wage represents a shift in how societies perceive the connection between work, compensation, and overall well-being. It surpasses the legally mandated minimum wage, being set at a level that enables workers to cover essential living expenses like housing, food, transportation, and healthcare. This approach recognises that fair remuneration isn't solely about financial stability, but is also a foundation for social justice and economic advancement.

Implementing the Living Wage demonstrates a company's recognition that employees are its most prized possessions, and that their well-being directly contributes to overall business prosperity. Data from the Living Wage Foundation indicates that this approach increases employee motivation, engagement, and loyalty, leading to higher productivity and lower rates of turnover, as well as reduced absenteeism.

Paying a Living Wage has broader implications for social equality and economic development. It helps reduce financial distress, dependence on governmental aid, and income disparity while improving. physical and mental well-being. Workers paid fairly have more disposable income, which stimulates local economies and supports growth. In essence, by acknowledging that workers aren't merely participants in production processes but individuals with livelihoods to earn to sustain themselves and their families, companies actively help create a more just, sustainable, and prosperous world.

4.3 // Employee Ownership and Sustainable Practices

(Fostering Participation and Innovation)

The number of businesses owned by their employees is growing in the UK, with increasing interest from businesses and individuals. Transitioning to employee ownership can be made relatively straightforward with the right guidance, focusing on choosing the best model for your business rather than getting bogged down in legal and financial detail. The key is to focus on the broader perspective and envision the long-term impact on both your employees and customers.

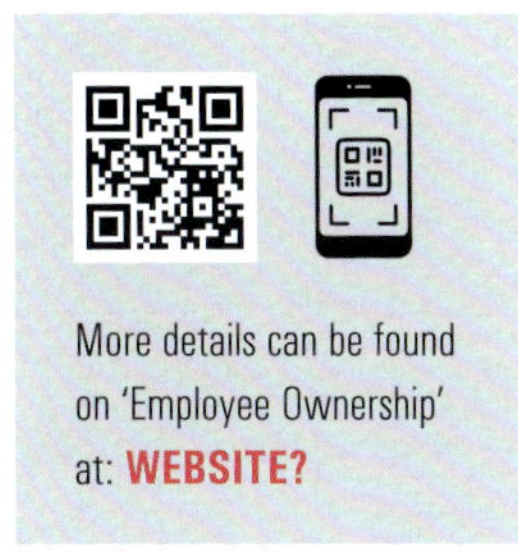
More details can be found on 'Employee Ownership' at: **WEBSITE?**

The decision to become or start as an employee-owned company reflects the belief that a company's success comes from a participative team, where every individual is invested in their work. This model has proven benefits for productivity and profitability, as seen with companies like Make, Hawkins Brown, AHMM and Feilden Clegg Bradley Studios.

Case Study Useful Studio and the Useful Simple Trust

We are a BCorp, a Social Enterprise and have been an Employee Benefit Trust since 2008. 'Useful' and 'Simple' describe the work we want to do. 'Trust' describes both our business model and our ethos: we trust ourselves and aspire to earn the trust of others.

Our ethos was originally written by the founders when they gave away their multi-million-pound shareholdings to create the Trust. The ethos is periodically reviewed by the beneficiaries but hasn't really changed in 15 years. In the traditional sense, we are an anti-ownership business, because no one owns or retains any financial stake, but we do share a mission stake: to trail-blaze and make a positive impact on society and the environment through our work. The Trust describes employee 'Benefit' as taking responsibility, having a voice, contributing to wellbeing, education and sustainable projects. The Trust deed gives everyone a voice in business strategy. There are many perks rooted in the Trust, with strong agency in our direction of travel, and we share the consequences of our decisions.

As beneficiaries, we expect to be empowered: there are strong and sometimes conflicting opinions about who we work for, and where we should practice. We have responsibility for our choices, and we strive for consensus but don't often achieve it.

How does this benefit us?

Our model supports internal investment and innovation—a sort of pro-social entrepreneurial start-up fund. The start-ups mostly spring from our passions, using our profits to get established. Useful Studio began this way, as did ThinkUp (education); Useful Projects (sustainability); MustRD (R&D); and Construction Innovation. At one point we nearly joined up with a sub-Saharan batik co-operative. The climate emergency is a good fit for the Trust because it maps to our nature: enquiring, radical, collaborative, equitable, and practical.

Everyone shares resource, administrative, technical and physical space. We are highly transparent with our performance, our pipeline and our risks and this helps us share in the evolution of the practice by sharing the load across the Trust. When people leave the Trust, they do so with our support, and we often continue to collaborate.

We have collectively navigated difficult times, including 2008 and COVID, showing great resilience and adaptability, and are busy and growing in this current lean economic phase.

Pitfalls

The right to internal consultation and ensuring transparency can be time- and energy-consuming, overcomplicate matters, and may not always lead to a clear conclusion. We consistently face the challenge of getting the best out of outliers and wild cards, whose voices are sometimes diluted in the search for consensus. For the founders who established the Trust, developing their successors isn't easy, and they sometimes agonise about their chosen direction of travel.

Chiswick Bridge

Clove Office Fit-out

Foundry Office

University Reception

St Mary's University Master Plan

Overall

We try to be inspired and empowered, to learn enough about ethical business without being steamrolled into outdated models, to trust our pioneering spirit, and to challenge norms.

4.4 // Looking for a job or setting up a Company

(The Significance of Human Resources)

Human Resources has evolved from a mere administrative function to a strategic cornerstone in architectural firms. This section addresses the multifaceted significance of HR within architectural firms, exploring its pivotal influence on talent acquisition, professional development, employee well-being, and the synergistic convergence of HR with technology.

Recognising HR's role is particularly important for individuals entering the architectural field or starting their own architectural business. For job seekers, an architectural firm with a robust HR department signals a commitment to employee growth, fostering learning and development. Effective HR practices demonstrate a firm's dedication to attracting, nurturing, and retaining top talent, and a well-structured HR function streamlines recruitment processes, ensuring that the best-suited candidates are hired. Additionally, HR initiatives focused on employee well-being create a supportive workplace culture that appeals to prospective employees and fosters loyalty among existing ones.

For entrepreneurs establishing their architectural practice, HR plays a vital role in laying the foundation for future growth and scalability. It ensures compliance with employment regulations, mitigates risks and sets ethical standards that resonate with potential clients and partners. A robust HR framework also contributes to effective team management and client interactions, crucial for success in the competitive architectural landscape.

As technology reshapes industries, including architecture, integrating HR with technological advancements becomes crucial. HR technology, such as applicant tracking systems and performance management platforms, streamlines operations and makes HR more effective. For individuals seeking to join progressive architectural firms or establish tech-driven architectural businesses, this integration both improves HR operations and supports strategic decision-making. It also fosters engagement through digital platforms, demonstrating an innovative approach to talent management in an increasingly technology-focussed professional landscape.

LIFTING THE BONNET
4 Key Learning Points //

1. **Talent Acquisition and Retention: Building a Diverse and Expert Team:** An architectural firm's success relies on assembling a team of diverse and skilled professionals. HR plays a strategic role in talent acquisition by identifying and recruiting top-tier talent and cultivating an environment where individual strengths harmonise into a creative collective. By recognising the distinct contributions of architects from various backgrounds, HR enhances collaboration and broadens perspectives, enriching design solutions.
2. **Professional Development and Skill Enhancement:** Nurturing Lifelong Learning: Staying current with industry trends and technological advancements is paramount. In collaboration with architectural leaders, HR can drive initiatives that encourage continuous learning. By providing opportunities for skill development, HR ensures architects remain agile in addressing new challenges and contributing their best to projects.
3. **Harmonising HR and Technology: Crafting a Bright Architectural Future:** By harnessing the synergistic integration of technology and HR, architects unlock the potential for a future where efficiency, innovation, and team expertise converge. Leveraging technology in HR strategies helps firms streamline processes, enhance collaboration, and amplify their impact.
4. **Employee Well-Being and Work-Life Balance: Fostering Motivation and Retention:** The architectural profession is notoriously demanding, with intense schedules and high-stakes projects. By acknowledging and mitigating stressors unique to the field, HR fosters resilience, minimises burnout, and supports architects in delivering their best work. HR initiatives prioritising employee wellness and work-life balance create an environment where a balance between professional aspirations and personal life nurtures a sustainable and harmonious work culture

THE WORLD OF THE ENTREPRENEUR

Antwerp Port · Zaha Hadid Architects

CHAPTER FIVE

The World of the Entrepreneur
It's Lonely out there

The entrepreneurial journey, particularly in creative fields like architecture, is inherently stressful. Balancing the demands of creative output with business management can often lead to significant stress and burnout. The pressure to innovate constantly, meet client expectations, manage finances, and handle administrative tasks can be overwhelming. Prolonged exposure to such stressors without adequate coping mechanisms can lead to physical and mental health issues, including anxiety, depression, and burnout.

This chapter focuses on the importance of wellness in architectural practice and offers practical strategies for maintaining creativity and productivity. From ergonomic workspace design and regular physical activity to mindfulness practices and healthy eating, we offer actionable advice backed by expert insights and real-world examples. By embracing these wellness strategies, architects can enhance their well-being, boost performance, and create a healthier work environment.

5.1 // Balancing Creativity and Well-Being

(Strategies for Maintaining Mental and Physical Health)

The demands of managing both the creative and business aspects of entrepreneurial ventures often lead to feelings of loneliness, which can negatively impact mental health and overall well-being.[1] This isolation often stems from the intense focus required for creative work, long hours, and constant pressure to produce high-quality results. Entrepreneurial ventures also require enormous self-reliance, leaving little room for external support or collaboration.

[1] Cameron, J. (2019). The Artist's Way: A Spiritual Path to Higher Creativity. New York: TarcherPerigee.

[2] Fortino, A. and Nayak, A., 2010, May. An architecture for applying social networking to business. In 2010 IEEE Long Island Systems, Applications and Technology Conference (pp. 1-6). IEEE.

Wellness

The psychological impact of isolation is well-documented, with research indicating it can lead to anxiety and depression. In creative entrepreneurship, this can lead to lack of motivation, creative blockages, and burnout. Without a support network, managing the emotional highs and lows of running a business becomes harder. The competitive nature of the industry compounds these feelings, as creative professionals may hesitate to share their struggles for fear of appearing weak or less competent.[2]

Practical Solutions:

- **Join Professional Communities:** Being part of a community provides emotional support, as members can share their experiences, challenges, and successes. This camaraderie can significantly improve mental health and well-being by creating a sense of belonging, crucial for mental wellness. For example, the Royal Institute of British Architects (RIBA) offers various Knowledge Communities that focus on different aspects of architecture, providing valuable resources and networking opportunities. Online platforms like Architizer offer opportunities to participate in competitions and collaborative projects, which can be both professionally rewarding and personally fulfilling.

architizer.com

- **Collaborate on Projects:** Engaging in collaborative projects can help break the monotony of solitary work and reduce feelings of isolation.
- **Local Meet-Up Groups:** Form or join local meet-up groups for creative professionals to discuss challenges, share knowledge, and offer mutual support. In-person networking and professional development helps create a supportive local community.
- **Virtual Communities and Social Media:** Virtual communities and social media platforms such as LinkedIn groups, Twitter chats, and Facebook communities can connect you with a broader network of professionals and provide instant access to discussions and resources.
- **Attend Industry Events:** Industry conferences, workshops, and seminars are excellent ways to meet new people, learn from experts, and stay updated on industry trends. These events also often provide networking opportunities that can lead to long-term professional relationships

[3] Wellbeing and Resilience Committee, 2019. World health organisation recognises burnout-but do you?. Bulletin (Law Society of South Australia), 41(7), p.41.

5.2 // Mental Wellness: Managing Stress and Burnout

(Techniques for Sustaining Creativity and Productivity)

Understanding Burnout

Burnout is a state of chronic physical and emotional exhaustion that can significantly impact one's professional and personal life. It is marked by energy depletion, increased mental detachment from one's work, and reduced professional efficacy. In creative professions like architecture, burnout can severely hinder creativity and productivity. A World Health Organization (WHO) study identifies burnout as a result of unsuccessfully managed chronic workplace stress.[3]

Signs of Burnout:

- **Exhaustion:** Feeling physically and emotionally drained.
- **Detachment:** Developing a cynical attitude towards work and feeling detached from job responsibilities.
- **Inefficiency:** Reduced performance and productivity at work.

The Salk Institute Exterior Office Building Louis Kahn

National Assembly Building, Sher-e-Bangla Nagar, Dhaka: view across the lake

Consequences of Neglecting Self-Care

Louis Kahn's relentless pursuit of perfection and dedication to his work often led to long hours and neglect of his well-being. He faced significant health issues, including heart problems, which were exacerbated by his intense schedule and personal struggles. Financial difficulties and a complex personal life added to his stress, ultimately contributing to his untimely death from a heart attack in 1974. Despite his brilliance, Kahn's struggles highlight the need for architects to manage stress effectively by balancing creativity with self-care to maintain a healthy and sustainable career.

Salk Institute Louis Khan

In contrast, a prominent example of the positive effect of self-care for creative entrepreneurs is the story of Arianna Huffington, the co-founder and former editor-in-chief of The Huffington Post. In her journey as a media entrepreneur, she experienced burnout due to her relentless pursuit of success, which prompted her to prioritise her well-being. She adopted a self-care routine that included getting adequate sleep, engaging in meditation and mindfulness practices, and setting boundaries to prevent overworking.

This transformation significantly impacted her creativity and decision-making abilities, and she became a strong advocate for the importance of self-care in entrepreneurial success.

Mindfulness Practices

Regular mindfulness practices such as meditation, yoga, and mindful walking can significantly reduce stress levels by helping to calm the mind, improve concentration, and foster a sense of well-being. When performed regularly, they improve emotional regulation, reduce symptoms of anxiety and depression, and increase overall life satisfaction.[4] For architects, incorporating mindfulness into daily routines can enhance creativity and productivity by providing a mental break from the constant pressures of work.[5]

Specific Mindfulness Practices Tailored to the Architectural Profession:

- **Design-Focused Meditation:** Engage in meditation sessions that focus on visualizing design solutions or architectural spaces to help reduce stress and stimulate creative thinking.
- **Architectural Sketching:** Use sketching as a form of mindfulness. Spending time on freehand sketches can be a relaxing activity and also enhances creativity.
- **Mindful Walking:** Take breaks to walk mindfully, with awareness of your surroundings, which can be inspiring and mentally relaxing.

Professional Counselling: Counselling services that specialise in supporting creative professionals provide tailored advice and strategies to manage stress and avoid burnout. Counsellors can offer coping mechanisms specific to the challenges of creative entrepreneurs and also provide a safe space to discuss professional and personal challenges. Regular counselling sessions can improve mental health, and according to the American Psychological Association, therapy can help individuals develop resilience and effective stress management techniques.

Workshops and Webinars: Workshops and webinars on mental wellness in the creative industry offer tools and community support that provide practical techniques for stress management and opportunities to connect with others facing similar challenges. For example, the Royal Institute of British Architects (RIBA) hosts regular webinars and runs the Well Architect Program, both aimed at supporting architects in managing stress and preventing burnout, and providing industry-specific insights and support. The program includes workshops, webinars, and counselling services specifically designed for architectural professionals, emphasising the importance of mental health and offering practical tools for maintaining well-being.

Practical Solutions for Managing Stress:

- **Mindfulness Practices:** Incorporate mindfulness practices such as meditation or yoga into your daily routine to help manage stress and maintain focus. Apps like Headspace and Calm offer guided meditations specifically designed for stress reduction.

[4] Kabat-Zinn, J. (2015). Mindfulness for Beginners: Reclaiming the Present Moment—and Your Life. Boulder: Sounds True.

[5] Shapiro, S.L., Carlson, L.E., Astin, J.A. and Freedman, B., 2006. Mechanisms of mindfulness. Journal of clinical psychology, 62(3), pp.373-386.

- **Professional Counseling:** Engage with counselling services that specialise in supporting creative professionals that can provide tailored strategies for managing stress and avoiding burnout. Platforms like BetterHelp and Talkspace offer online therapy sessions, making it easier to access mental health support.
- **Workshops and Webinars:** Attend workshops and webinars focused on mental wellness in the creative industry. These offer tools and community support to navigate stress effectively. The Well-Architect Program by RIBA is an excellent resource for architects.
- **Regular Breaks and Time Management:** Implement regular breaks and effective time management strategies. Tools like the Pomodoro Technique can help manage workload by breaking work into manageable intervals with short breaks in between.
- **Physical Activity:** Exercise has been shown to reduce stress, improve mood, and boost overall health. Integrate regular physical activity such as walking, running or cycling into daily routines.
- **Healthy Work Environment:** Create a healthy work environment. Ensure your workspace is ergonomically designed to reduce physical strain and encourage a positive working atmosphere. Incorporate elements like natural light and plants to enhance the workspace.

5.3 // Physical Wellness: Staying Active and Healthy

(Ergonomic Workspaces, Regular Exercise, and Healthy Eating)

Physical and mental wellness are equally important for creative entrepreneurs. The sedentary nature of architectural work, with long hours spent at desks or drafting tables, can lead to physical health issues like back pain, eye strain, and fatigue. Incorporating physical activity into one's daily routine is essential to maintaining overall health and well-being. Much of what follows is stating the obvious, but sometimes it's useful to see it written down as an aide memoire.

Ergonomics

[6] Wright, T.A., Adkins, J.A., Nelson, D.L. and Quick Jonathan, D., 2013. Preventive stress management in organizations. American Psychological Association.
[7] Royal Institute of British Architects (RIBA). (2020). RIBA Knowledge Communities. London: RIBA.
[8] Royal Institute of British Architects (RIBA). (2020). RIBA Knowledge Communities. London: RIBA.
[9] Kabat-Zinn, J. (2015). Mindfulness for Beginners: Reclaiming the Present Moment—and Your Life. Boulder: Sounds True.
[10] Cirillo, F., 2018. The Pomodoro technique: The acclaimed time-management system that has transformed how we work. Currency.
[11] JJ, R., 2008. Spark: The revolutionary new science of exercise and the brain. Hachette Digital, Inc.
[12] Eilouti, B., 2023. A framework for integrating ergonomics into architectural design. Ergonomics in design, 31(1), pp.4-12.

Ergonomic Workspaces

According to Hedge, incorporating ergonomic principles into workspace design can reduce the risk of musculoskeletal disorders and improve productivity. This includes using adjustable chairs and desks, ensuring proper lighting, and positioning computer screens at eye level to reduce strain.

Benefits of Ergonomics:

- **Reduced Physical Strain:** Proper ergonomic setups help reduce strain on the body, particularly the back, neck, and shoulders.
- **Enhanced Comfort:** Ergonomic furniture and equipment can enhance overall comfort, making it easier to maintain focus and productivity.
- **Increased Productivity:** Comfortable and well-designed workspaces lead to increased productivity and efficiency, as employees are less likely to experience discomfort and fatigue.

Peter Zumthor Thermal Baths at 7132, Vals, Switzerland

Regular Exercise

Exercise not only improves physical health but also boosts mental well-being by releasing endorphins, which help in reducing stress and improving mood. Incorporating regular exercise into daily routines has been shown to improve concentration, enhance creativity, and reduce the risk of chronic diseases.

Exercise Recommendations:

- **Daily Physical Activity:** Aim for at least 30 minutes of moderate exercise each day. This can include brisk walking, jogging, or cycling.
- **Strength Training:** Incorporate strength training exercises at least twice a week to build muscle strength and endurance.
- **Flexibility Exercises:** Activities like yoga or stretching can improve flexibility, reduce muscle tension, and promote relaxation.

Connection Between Physical Health and Creativity

Physical health is also deeply connected to sustained creativity and effective decision-making. When architects maintain their physical health through regular exercise and ergonomic practices, they are better equipped to handle the mental demands of their work. Physical activity also increases blood flow to the brain, enhancing cognitive function and creativity. Don't just design gyms and wellness centres—use them!

[13] Seim, R. and Broberg, O., 2010. Participatory workspace design: A new approach for ergonomists?. International Journal of Industrial Ergonomics, 40(1), pp.25-33.
[14] Eilouti, B., 2023. A framework for integrating ergonomics into architectural design. Ergonomics in design, 31(1), pp.4-12.

Healthy Eating

Proper nutrition supports brain function, enhances mood, and provides the necessary fuel for creative work. Creative professionals should focus on consuming a balanced diet rich in fruits, vegetables, whole grains, and lean proteins to maintain energy levels and overall health. Staying hydrated and limiting the intake of caffeine and sugary foods can also improve concentration and productivity.

Dietary Tips:

- **Balanced Meals:** Ensure that each meal includes a balance of macronutrients—carbohydrates, proteins, and fats—to maintain energy levels throughout the day.
- **Hydration:** Drink plenty of water to stay hydrated. Dehydration can lead to fatigue and impaired cognitive function.
- **Healthy Snacks:** Opt for healthy snacks like fruits, nuts, and yoghurt to keep energy levels stable and avoid sugar crashes.

5.4 // Building Emotional Resilience in Architectural Practice

(Developing Self-Awareness and Coping Strategies)

An architectural career comes with challenges, from managing client feedback to adapting to changing industry standards and technologies. Building emotional resilience is critical for architects to navigate these challenges without losing motivation or confidence. Resilient individuals handle setbacks better and are more likely to view challenges as opportunities for growth rather than obstacles. Emotional resilience is not an innate trait but a skill that can be developed through intentional practices.

Strategies for Building Emotional Resilience

- **Self-Awareness:** Developing self-awareness involves recognising and understanding one's emotions to help identify stress triggers and understand how different situations impact emotional well-being. Practices such as journaling and mindfulness meditation can enhance self-awareness.
- **Positive Thinking:** Maintaining a positive outlook is crucial for emotional resilience. This involves focusing on strengths, celebrating small successes, and reframing negative thoughts. Positive thinking can be cultivated through practices such as gratitude journaling and positive affirmations.
- **Coping Strategies:** Effective coping strategies are essential for managing stress. These can include problem-solving techniques, relaxation exercises, and seeking social support. Regularly practicing these strategies can help manage stress effectively and reduce its negative impact.

[15] JJ, R., 2008. Spark: The revolutionary new science of exercise and the brain. Hachette Digital, Inc.
[16] Nash, C., 2021. Design your life: An architect's guide to achieving a work/life balance. RIBA Publishing.

Galaxy Soho and Hudson Yards New York by ZHA

Case Study Emotional Resilience in Practice
The Experience of Zaha Hadid Architects

Zaha Hadid Architects (ZHA), one of the world's most renowned architectural firms, has demonstrated the importance of emotional resilience in practice. The firm, known for its innovative and often controversial designs, has faced numerous challenges, including public criticism, financial constraints, and the sudden passing of its founder, Zaha Hadid, in 2016.

Following Hadid's death, the firm had to navigate the immense pressure of maintaining its legacy while continuing to innovate. The resilience of the team was put to the test as they dealt with emotional grief and professional challenges. The leadership at ZHA emphasised the importance of emotional resilience by encouraging open communication, providing support systems, and fostering a collaborative environment.

Practical Solutions Implemented by ZHA:

- **Open Communication:** The firm established regular check-ins and open forums for employees to express their concerns and emotions. This practice helped address issues promptly and maintain a supportive work environment.
- **Support Systems:** ZHA provided access to professional counselling services and encouraged employees to seek help when needed. This support was crucial in helping the team cope with stress and emotional challenges.
- **Collaborative Environment:** By fostering a collaborative environment, ZHA ensured that employees felt valued and supported. Team projects and collaborative problem-solving sessions were regularly organised to promote a sense of community and shared purpose.

[17] Hadid, Z., 2017. Zaha Hadid architects: redefining architecture & design. The Images Publishing Group

THE WORLD OF THE ENTREPRENEUR
7 Key Learning Points //

1. **Balancing Dual Demands:** Architects must juggle creative and business responsibilities, which can lead to significant stress and burnout. Prioritising self-care is essential for maintaining mental and physical health.
2. **Integrating Wellness:** Integrating wellness into daily routines enhances well-being, boosts professional performance, and creates a sustainable work routine. Strategies include ergonomic workspace design, regular physical activity, mindfulness practices, and healthy eating.
3. **Isolation and Mental Health:** The solitary nature of creative entrepreneurship can lead to feelings of loneliness and stress, negatively impacting mental health. Joining communities like the AIA's Knowledge Communities or online platforms like Architizer helps reduce isolation, provides emotional support, and fosters collaboration, which are all crucial for mental wellness.
4. **Managing Stress and Burnout:** Architects experience high levels of stress due to the demands of the profession. Strategies to manage stress and prevent burnout include mindfulness practices, professional counseling, attending wellness workshops, regular breaks, and effective time management.
5. **Physical Wellness:** Physical wellness is as important as mental wellness. Designing ergonomic workspaces, engaging in regular exercise, and maintaining a healthy diet are crucial for overall health and productivity.
6. **Emotional Resilience:** Building emotional resilience helps architects handle professional challenges without losing motivation or confidence. The skill involves developing self-awareness, maintaining a positive outlook, and employing effective coping strategies.
7. **Holistic Approach to Wellness:** A holistic approach to wellness and self-care addresses both physical and mental health. Architects can enhance their professional performance and personal health by integrating ergonomic workspaces, regular exercise, healthy eating, and mindfulness practices, leading to a more balanced and fulfilling professional life.

Keep back.
This door is
unpredictable.

THE POWER OF SAYING NO

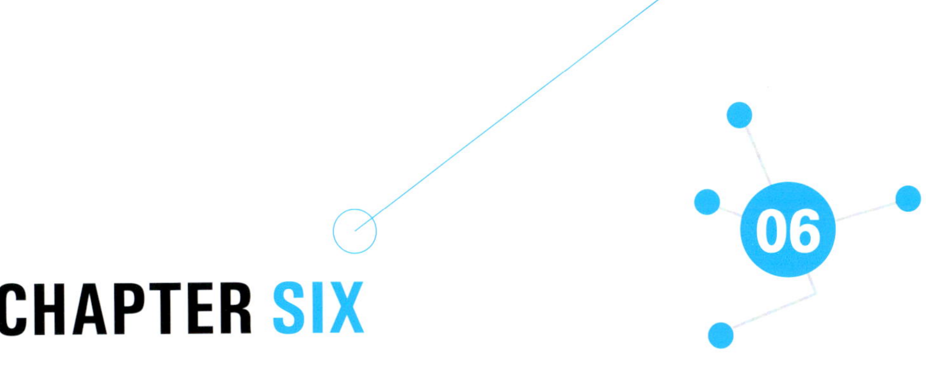

CHAPTER SIX

The Power of Saying No!

The ability to say 'No' is about making strategic choices that align with one's professional and personal goals. Mastering the strategic use of 'No', empowers architects to navigate the complexities of their profession with confidence and clarity, ultimately leading to greater success and satisfaction in their careers. This chapter explores the value of saying 'No', and through practical strategies demonstrates how mastering this crucial skill can lead to greater innovation, productivity, and professional fulfilment.

6.1 // The Strategic Value of 'No' in Architecture

(Maintaining Integrity and Managing Workload)

In architecture, every project comes with its unique set of challenges, constraints, and budgetary limitations.

Saying 'No' strategically means carefully assessing each opportunity to evaluate whether it aligns with one's professional goals and values. By focusing on projects that resonate with their passion and expertise, architects can invest the necessary time and effort to produce their best work and make a lasting impact on the world.

The strategic use of 'No' is crucial in maintaining high standards in architectural practice. An architectural firm's integrity and identity are based on the quality of their work. When architects decline projects that do not align with their expertise or values, they prevent the dilution of their brand and reputation. Clients and peers come to recognise the firm for its specific strengths and high standards, which can lead to more aligned and high-quality project opportunities in the future.

Saying 'No' helps architects manage their workload more effectively. Overcommitment can lead to rushed work and mediocre results and eventually to burnout, which is detrimental to both the architect's well-being and the quality of their work. By strategically declining projects, architects can

[1] Nickerson, C.A., 2018. There is no empirical evidence for critical positivity ratios: Comment on Fredrickson (2013). Journal of Humanistic Psychology, 58(3), pp.284-312

The power of No

maintain a manageable workload, ensuring they have the time and energy to dedicate to each project fully. This focus also fosters a healthier work-life balance.[1]

The strategic use of 'No' also helps innovation. Architects who can focus on fewer projects have the mental and creative bandwidth to explore new ideas and approaches; they can delve deeper into research, experiment with new materials, and explore unconventional design methodologies, leading to more innovative and impactful outcomes.

6.2 // Fostering Creativity through Selective Engagement

(Enhancing Quality and Innovation)

Refusing to compromise by saying 'No' to certain projects, demands, or conditions amplifies rather than limits an architect's creative expression. Selective engagement in projects that resonate with their creative ethos ensures their creative energies are not dispersed across too many fronts, enabling a deeper and more focused exploration of innovative architectural solutions.

For architecture students and early-career professionals, saying 'No' can be particularly empowering. Declining extracurricular activities or projects that do not contribute to their growth enables them to focus on academic and professional opportunities that align with their career goals. By concentrating on developing skills and knowledge in the chosen areas, they can achieve higher-quality outcomes and gain deeper insights into their work. This leads to greater understanding and expertise, which is invaluable for building a strong foundation for their future careers.[2]

6.3 // Navigating Constraints with Creative Resilience

(Turning Limitations into Opportunities)

Constraints are often viewed as obstacles to creativity, but by setting clear boundaries around what is feasible and what aligns with their vision, architects can leverage constraints as catalysts for innovation, encouraging the exploration of alternative materials, sustainable practices, and novel design methodologies that might not have been considered otherwise.[3]

For example, budget constraints may lead to the exploration of cost-effective and sustainable alternatives. Saying 'No' to expensive materials or overly complex designs can result in more innovative and environmentally friendly solutions, such as utilising recycled or locally sourced materials to reduce costs and environmental impact, or adopting modular construction techniques for flexibility and efficiency without compromising on quality or aesthetics.[4]

[2] Neff, K. and Germer, C., 2018. The mindful self-compassion workbook: A proven way to accept yourself, build inner strength, and thrive. Guilford Publications.
[3] Neff, K. and Germer, C., 2018. The mindful self-compassion workbook: A proven way to accept yourself, build inner strength, and thrive. Guilford Publications.
[4] Nickerson, C.A., 2018. There is no empirical evidence for critical positivity ratios: Comment on Fredrickson (2013). Journal of Humanistic Psychology, 58(3), pp.284-312
[5] Seligman, M.E., 2011. Flourish: A visionary new understanding of happiness and well-being. Simon and Schuster.

Similarly, time constraints can push architects to adopt new technologies and work more efficiently. This might involve using advanced software for rapid prototyping, virtual reality for immersive design reviews, or AI for optimising space and energy use. These can enhance productivity and allow for quicker iterations, leading to more refined and effective designs.[5]

Overcoming constraints with creativity also demonstrates an ability to innovate under pressure and adapt to changing circumstances—qualities highly valued by both clients and colleagues. Projects that overcome significant constraints often earn attention and acclaim because they showcase the architect's ingenuity and problem-solving abilities. For example, the use of innovative materials or construction techniques to meet strict environmental regulations can highlight an architect's commitment to sustainability and excellence.[6]

In academia, constraints can be a learning tool. By understanding a project's limitations—whether in time, budget, or scope—students develop problem-solving skills and learn to innovate within given parameters, which prepares them for the realities of professional practice, where constraints are a constant. Students who learn to view constraints as opportunities develop resilience and adaptability—crucial skills for any successful architect[7]— and are better equipped to handle the complexities of real-world projects.

6.4 // Incorporating Psychological Insights

(Improving Decision-Making and Stress Management)

Saying 'No' effectively in a professional context requires an understanding of decision-making and stress management. Insights from psychology can illuminate the cognitive and emotional benefits of this practice. The human brain has a limited capacity for decision-making, known as cognitive load. Research in psychology has also shown that reducing cognitive load improves problem-solving skills and creativity.[8] Limiting commitments by strategically saying 'No' frees up mental resources for innovative design and strategic thinking, leading to higher quality work and more fulfilling professional experiences. Additionally, reducing cognitive load can reduce stress. As discussed in the previous chapter, chronic stress—linked to various health issues—is a common issue in high-pressure professions like architecture.[9]

In practical terms, reducing cognitive load means being selective about the projects and commitments one accepts. Using decision-making frameworks like the Eisenhower Matrix helps architects prioritise tasks and decline non-essential commitments to help focus remain on high-impact activities and maintain a healthier work-life balance to reduce the risk of burnout.[10 11]

The reflection prompts below may help you gain clarity about challenges you might have with saying 'No', and help develop strategies to improve your ability to manage commitments effectively.

[6] Den Otter, A. and Emmitt, S., 2007. Exploring effectiveness of team communication: Balancing synchronous and asynchronous communication in design teams. Engineering, Construction and Architectural Management, 14(5), pp.408-419.

[7] Hendrickson, C. and Au, T., 1989. Project management for construction: Fundamental concepts for owners, engineers, architects, and builders. Chris Hendrickson.

Reflection Prompts:

1. **Identify Your Triggers:** Reflect on specific situations where you find it hardest to say 'No.' What patterns do you notice? Is it certain types of projects, specific people, or particular times of the year?

   Action Step: Write down these triggers and think of alternative responses you could use next time.

2. **Assess Your Priorities:** List your top five professional and personal priorities. Are you dedicating enough time to each?

   Action Step: Consider how accepting or declining requests impacts these priorities and adjust your responses accordingly.

3. **Evaluate Past Experiences:** Recall a recent instance when you said 'No.' How did it make you feel? What was the outcome?

   Action Step: Reflect on the positive outcomes of saying 'No' and how it benefited your work or well-being.

4. **Develop a Strategy:** Think about strategies that could help you say 'No' more effectively, such as using softer language, providing alternatives, or setting clearer boundaries.

   Action Step: Choose one strategy to implement over the next month and observe its impact on your stress levels and productivity.

5. **Seek Support:** Consider who in your professional network can support you in this endeavour. Is there a mentor, colleague, or friend who models good boundary-setting?

   Action Step: Talk to this person about their strategies for saying 'No' and ask for advice or support.

6. **Practice Saying 'No':** Practice different ways of saying 'No' in low-stakes situations. This could involve declining small requests or practicing with a trusted friend.

   Action Step: Gradually apply these techniques to more significant requests and monitor how your confidence grows.

Practical Applications

- **Prioritise Tasks:** Use decision-making frameworks like the Eisenhower Matrix to prioritise tasks based on their urgency and importance.
- **Mindfulness Practices:** Incorporate mindfulness techniques such as meditation and deep-breathing exercises into daily routines. These practices can reduce stress, enhance emotional regulation, and improve overall well-being.

[8] Sweller, J., 1988. Cognitive load during problem solving: Effects on learning. Cognitive science, 12(2), pp.257-285.
[9] BS, M., 1995. Stress and cognitive function. Curr Opin Neurobiol., 5, pp.205-216. [10] Maslach, C. and Leiter, M.P., 2016. Burnout: A brief history and how to measure it. Understanding the burnout experience: Recent research and its implications for psychiatry, pp.105-128. [11] Burke, R.J. and Richardsen, A.M., 2000. Psychological burnout in organizations: Research and intervention. In Handbook of Organizational Behavior, Revised and Expanded (pp. 349-386). Routledge.

- **Reflective Journaling:** Maintain a journal to reflect on daily experiences and decisions. This can help recognise patterns of overcommitment and provide insights into managing responsibilities more effectively.
- **Seek Professional Support:** Engage with counselling services or professional coaches who can provide strategies for managing stress and improving decision-making skills.

6.5 // Exploring Ethical and Social Implications

(Promoting Integrity and Sustainability)

Architects have a duty to uphold ethical standards in their work. Saying 'No' to projects that compromise these values is essential for maintaining professional integrity,[12] builds trust and respect among clients and colleagues, and encourages the industry to prioritise sustainability and ethical considerations.[13]

Ethical responsibility also involves considering the long-term impact of projects on communities and the environment. Declining projects that contribute to environmental degradation or social injustice reflects a commitment to creating positive change, enhancing a firm's credibility and attracting clients who also value ethical integrity and sustainability.

Ethical responsibility includes being transparent with clients about the feasibility and implications of their requests within given constraints, and ensuring that their projects do not harm the environment or the community. Clear communication about challenges, limitations, and ethical concerns helps manage client expectations and fosters a collaborative relationship based on mutual respect and understanding. This approach ensures that projects align with a shared commitment to ethical standards and sustainable outcomes.[14]

Promoting a Positive Workplace Culture

A workplace culture that respects the power of 'No' is healthier and more productive. When employees can set boundaries, they experience greater job satisfaction and are less likely to suffer from burnout, improving morale and team cohesion.[15]

Leaders in architecture firms can model this behaviour by setting clear boundaries and encouraging their teams to do the same. This creates an environment where employees feel valued and supported, enhancing creativity and collaboration. Policies like flexible working hours or remote work options promote a work-life balance, while showing trust in employees' ability to manage their workloads effectively.[16]

Encouraging open communication about workloads and stress levels can help prevent burnout. Regular check-ins and team meetings can allow employees to express concerns and request support before issues escalate. This proactive approach ensures team members are not overwhelmed.[17]

[12] Fisher, C.M. and Lovell, A., 2009. Business ethics and values: Individual, corporate and international perspectives. Pearson Education.
[13] Harriss, H. and Widder, L. eds., 2014. Architecture live projects: Pedagogy into practice. Routledge.

Empowering employees to say 'No' also fosters a culture of mutual respect. When employees see their leaders and peers respecting boundaries, they are more likely to do the same. A more harmonious and cooperative workplace develops, where individuals can contribute meaningfully without sacrificing their well-being.[18]

Practical Application

- **Ethical Guidelines:** Develop and adhere to a set of ethical guidelines that outline the principles and standards of the firm to help make informed decisions about which projects to accept or decline.
- **Sustainability Practices:** Commit to sustainability by saying 'No' to projects that do not meet environmental standards. Implement practices that prioritize the use of sustainable materials and methods.
- **Supportive Policies:** Establish workplace policies that support employees' ability to say 'No'. This includes flexible work arrangements, reasonable workload expectations, and open communication channels.
- **Training Programs:** Offer training programs on ethics and stress management to help employees navigate complex decisions and maintain their well-being.

6.6 // Addressing Cultural Differences

(Adapting Communication and Building Relationships)

Effective communication is a cornerstone of successful project management and client relations, and being culturally aware can significantly enhance these interactions. In some cultures, direct communication is valued, and saying 'No' is seen as a straightforward and honest response. In other cultures, indirect communication is preferred, and saying 'No' can be perceived as rude or confrontational. Understanding these cultural differences is crucial for architects who work on global projects or with international clients.[19]

Adapting to Cultural Contexts

Cultural competence involves understanding verbal communication, nonverbal cues, decision-making processes, and business customs. To navigate complex interactions more effectively and foster more productive collaborations, architects should invest time in learning about different cultures' communication styles and business etiquette.

For instance, in many Asian cultures, maintaining harmony and avoiding direct confrontation is important. This approach helps maintain positive working relationships while setting clear boundaries.[20] When working on a project in Japan, for example, an architect might use indirect language such as 'I will consider it' or 'Let me think about it' to communicate a refusal without

[14] Edwards, B., 2013. Sustainability and education in the built environment. In The Sustainability Curriculum (pp. 129-140). Routledge [15] Cooper, C.L. and Cartwright, S., 1994. Healthy mind; healthy organization—A proactive approach to occupational stress. Human relations, 47(4), pp.455-471..[16] Edwards, J.R., 2008. 4 person-environment fit in organizations: An assessment of theoretical progress. The Academy of Management Annals, 2(1), pp.167-230. [17] Burke, R.J. and Richardsen, A.M., 2000. Psychological burnout in organizations: Research and intervention. In Handbook of Organizational Behavior, Revised and Expanded (pp. 349-386). Routledge.

causing offence. This approach respects cultural norms and maintains a positive working relationship while still setting boundaries.[6]

Similarly, in Middle Eastern cultures, where hospitality and personal relationships are highly valued, building rapport through social interactions might be beneficial before discussing business matters. This relational approach can make it easier to navigate difficult conversations, including saying 'No' when necessary.[21]

Strategies for Cultural Adaptation

- **Cultural Training:** Participate in cultural competency training to understand the communication styles and business practices of different cultures to improve interactions with international clients and colleagues. Cultural training programs can provide valuable insights into the dos and don'ts of professional conduct across various cultures.[22]
- **Flexible Communication:** Adapt communication strategies to align with cultural norms. Use indirect language or provide alternative solutions when working with cultures that value harmony over directness. For instance, instead of outright declining a project scope change, an architect might say, 'We need to evaluate this further to ensure it aligns with our overall objectives'.[23]
- **Cultural Advisors:** Engage cultural advisors or consultants to provide insights and guidance on navigating cultural differences in professional settings. These experts can offer tailored advice and strategies for specific regions or client bases, enhancing the architect's ability to manage international projects successfully.
- **Building Relationships:** Invest time in building relationships with international clients and partners. Understanding their cultural context can help in making informed and respectful decisions. This includes participating in local customs, understanding holiday schedules, and respecting cultural norms regarding hierarchy and decision-making processes. [24]

6.7 // Economic and Market Factors

(Strategies for Maintaining Focus during Downturns)

Economic and market factors significantly influence an architect's ability to say 'No.' During economic downturns, the construction and real estate sectors often suffer. This impacts architectural firms, as fewer projects are available and competition for existing ones becomes fierce. Architects may feel compelled to accept projects that don't align with their values or expertise to ensure the firm's survival. Understanding and navigating these economic dynamics is crucial for sustaining a successful practice. This scenario aligns with Porter's theory of competitive strategy, which emphasises the need for businesses to adapt to external economic pressures while maintaining their core strategic focus.

[18] Harter, J.K., Schmidt, F.L. and Hayes, T.L., 2002. Business-unit-level relationship between employee satisfaction, employee engagement, and business outcomes: a meta-analysis. Journal of Applied Psychology, 87(2), p.268. [19] Hall, E. T. (1976). Beyond Culture. Garden City [20] Ting-Toomey, S. (1999). Communicating Across Cultures. Guilford Press .[21] Gesteland, R. R. (2012). Cross-Cultural Business Behavior: Negotiating, Selling, Sourcing and Managing Across Cultures. Copenhagen Business School Press [22] Livermore, D. and Soon, A.N.G., 2015. Leading with Cultural Intelligence 3rd Edition: The Real Secret to Success. AMACOM.

Strategies for Maintaining Integrity

- **Diversification of Services:** By expanding into related areas such as urban planning, interior design, or sustainability consulting, architects can create multiple revenue streams that cushion the impact of economic downturns. Diversification allows firms to remain selective about the projects they accept.
- **Building Strong Client Relationships:** Developing and maintaining strong client relationships can help provide a steady stream of work even during economic slowdowns. Long-term clients are more likely to provide repeat business and refer new clients, reducing the pressure to accept less-desirable projects. Architects should focus on delivering exceptional service and maintaining open, honest communication with their clients to build trust and loyalty.
- **Financial Planning and Reserves:** By building financial reserves during prosperous times, firms won't operate from a position of financial desperation during downturns, and can maintain the flexibility to be selective about the projects they accept.
- **Emphasising Quality Over Quantity:** Maintaining a reputation for high-quality work differentiates a firm in a competitive market. Even during downturns, clients seeking exceptional design and reliability will prioritise firms known for their integrity and excellence. Architects should focus on maintaining their standards and delivering high-quality outcomes, even by accepting fewer projects.
- **Adapting Business Models:** Flexibility in business models helps firms navigate economic challenges. For instance, adopting a lean operational model reduces overheads, making it easier to maintain profitability with fewer projects. Exploring collaborative ventures or strategic partnerships can provide new opportunities and share project risks and rewards.

[23] Meyer, E., 2014. The culture map: Breaking through the invisible boundaries of global business. Public Affairs.
[24] Thomas, D.C., 2010. Cultural intelligence: Living and working globally. ReadHowYouWant.com.
[25] Porter, M.E. and Strategy, C., 1980. Competitive Strategy: Techniques for analyzing industries and competitors. Free Press, New York.

THE POWER OF SAYING NO

5 Key Strategies for Saying 'No' //

1. **Prioritise and Focus:** Architects should prioritise their commitments and projects based on their goals and values. This focus improves productivity and aligns actions with long-term objectives. For students, this means focusing on coursework and projects aligned with their career goals. For practitioners, it involves evaluating each project for its impact and alignment with personal and firm-wide objectives.

2. **Assertive Communication:** Communicate 'No' clearly and directly to avoid misunderstandings and leave no room for ambiguity. A confident stance establishes boundaries and sets expectations, fostering efficient interactions. In client interactions, explaining why a particular design element or approach is not feasible can help clients understand the architect's perspective and build trust. It also ensures that projects proceed smoothly without unrealistic expectations.

3. **Guilt-Free Approach:** Recognise that saying 'No' is a natural part of managing workloads and commitments. By letting go of guilt, architects can focus on chosen projects without unnecessary emotional burden, promoting mental clarity and effective decision-making.[26]

   Students and professionals alike need to understand that prioritising their well-being and work quality over sheer quantity of commitments is not only acceptable but essential for long-term success.

   Respectful Declination Be respectful when declining opportunities. Acknowledging the other's time and effort demonstrates professionalism and maintains positive relationships. Expressing gratitude while politely declining leaves a favorable impression, upholds interpersonal rapport and cultivates supportive professional relationships.[27]

4. **Honesty and Transparency:** Effective use of 'No' involves honesty. When appropriate, provide transparent reasons for decisions, helping others understand your perspective and fostering open communication. However, balance honesty with maintaining confidentiality, building trust, and encouraging collaborative understanding.[28]

5. **Practice and Rehearsal:** Saying 'No' effectively can be challenging, especially when it's not a familiar response, so practice and rehearse your approach to build confidence. This preparation reduces apprehension and ensures a polished communication style.[29]

[26] Seligman, M.E., 2011. Flourish: A visionary new understanding of happiness and well-being. Simon and Schuster.
[27] Neff, K., 2011. Self-compassion: The proven power of being kind to yourself. Hachette UK.
[28] Nickerson, C.A., 2018. There is no empirical evidence for critical positivity ratios: Comment on Fredrickson (2013). Journal of Humanistic Psychology, 58(3), pp.284-312.
[29] Brown, B., 2018. Dare to lead: Brave work. Tough conversations. Whole hearts. Random House.

WE CAN DO IT DIFFERENTLY

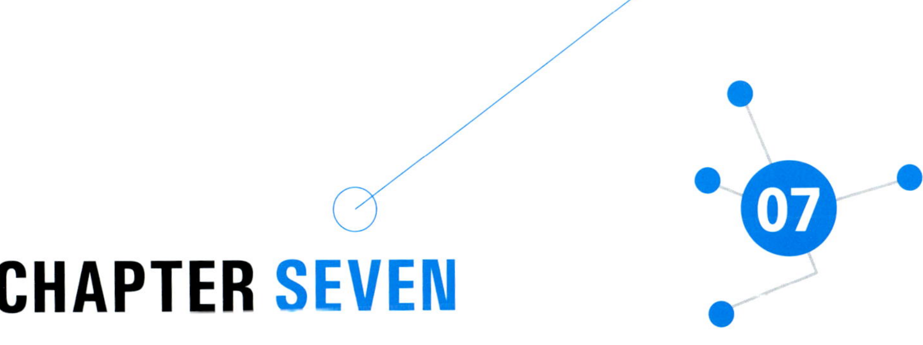

CHAPTER SEVEN

We Can Do It Differently

In a rapidly changing industry landscape characterised by evolving client demands, technological advancements, and heightened competition, architectural firms must look beyond traditional business models to thrive. This chapter explores various entrepreneurial strategies such as diversification of services, strategic partnerships, and leveraging technology to help architectural firms enhance their market presence, financial stability and innovative capabilities.

7.1 // Understanding and Implementing Business Models

(Enhancing Employee Motivation and Firm Success)

The following sections detail several innovative business models that can help architectural firms distinguish themselves in the market and enhance their financial stability while fostering a culture of innovation and adaptability, ensuring long-term success.

Profit Sharing Models

Profit-sharing models, which involve distributing a portion of the firm's profits to employees, can significantly influence workplace dynamics and overall firm performance. Rooted in theories of employee participation and motivation such as Maslow's Hierarchy of Needs and Herzberg's Two-Factor Theory, the concept suggests that giving employees a stake in the firm's financial success will make them more committed to achieving its goals.

Beyond financial gains, these models improve job satisfaction, reduce turnover, and align individual and organizational goals. According to Social Exchange Theory, which posits that relationships are built on the expectation of mutual benefit, profit-sharing fosters a reciprocal relationship where employees see it as a gesture of goodwill and are more likely to reciprocate with increased effort and loyalty.

In the architectural profession, profit-sharing encourages teams to work toward shared financial goals, leveraging their collective skills to improve project outcomes. It also promotes a culture of

[1] Herzberg, F., 1968. One more time: How do you motivate employees?. Harvard Business Review (Vol. 65).
[2] Maslow, A.H., 1943. A theory of human motivation. Psychological Review Google Scholar, 2, pp.21-28.
[3] Oyer, P., 2004. Why do firms use incentives that have no incentive effects?. The Journal of Finance, 59(4), pp.1619-1650.

transparency and shared responsibility, where employees are likelier to take ownership of their work and strive for excellence. Additionally, profit-sharing enables smaller firms to compete with larger firms by offering competitive compensation packages that attract and retain top talent.

Profit-sharing can take various forms, from cash bonuses to retirement-linked benefits, each with unique advantages and challenges. However, successfully implementing profit-sharing models requires understanding the firm's financial health, clear communication with employees, and regular plan reviews and adjustments.

7.2 // Types of Profit-Sharing Models

(Direct, Deferred, and Combination Plans)

- **Direct Profit-Sharing:** Based on predefined criteria, employees receive a share of the firm's profits directly.

  Example: A percentage of the firm's net profits is distributed to employees annually.

  Detailed Explanation: If an architectural firm sets aside 10% of its annual net profits for profit-sharing, this amount is divided among eligible employees based on predetermined criteria such as seniority, role, or performance. This model creates a direct link between the firm's success and employee compensation, fostering a sense of ownership and accountability.

- **Deferred Profit-Sharing:** Profits are allocated to employees but paid out later, often tied to retirement plans.

  Example: Contributions to a pension fund or a retirement savings plan.

  Detailed Explanation: A firm might contribute some of its profits to employees' retirement accounts, which are only accessible upon retirement. This model provides financial security and tax benefits for employees, and tax benefits for the firm. The deferred nature of these benefits helps retain employees, as they have a vested interest in the firm's long-term success.

- **Combination Plans:** Combines elements of direct and deferred profit-sharing.

  Example: Immediate cash bonuses plus contributions to long-term savings plans.

  Detailed Explanation: An architectural firm might provide an annual cash bonus based on the firm's profits and simultaneously contribute to employees' retirement plans, rewarding employees for their contributions while also securing their financial future. This approach can benefit firms with a diverse workforce with varying financial needs and preferences.

[4] FitzRoy, F.R. and Kraft, K., 1987. Cooperation, productivity, and profit sharing. The Quarterly Journal of Economics, 102(1), pp.23-35.
[5] Blau, P., 2017. Exchange and power in social life. Routledge.

7.3 // Benefits of Profit-Sharing

(Motivation, Retention, and Alignment of Goals)

- **Enhanced Motivation:** Research shows profit-sharing significantly increases employee engagement and motivation, as employees see a direct link between their efforts and financial rewards. This can lead to better performance, more innovative solutions, and a stronger commitment to the firm's goals.
- **Attraction and Retention:** Firms with attractive profit-sharing plans are more likely to attract highly skilled professionals looking for more than just a salary. Additionally, these plans can help retain employees, reducing the costs and disruptions associated with high turnover rates.
- **Alignment of Goals:** When employees understand that their financial rewards are tied to the firm's success, they are more likely to align their efforts with its strategic objectives, leading to more cohesive teamwork, better decision-making, and a unified approach to achieving the firm's goals.
- **Increased Productivity:** Profit-sharing can encourage employees to find more efficient working methods, reduce waste, and improve project delivery times. This can enhance the firm's competitive edge, allowing it to take on more projects and improve profitability.

7.4 // Implementation Steps

(Defining Metrics, Communication, and Review)

1. **Define Profit-Sharing Metrics:** Determine the criteria for profit-sharing, such as overall firm profitability, individual project success, or department performance.

   Detailed Explanation: Metrics could include net profit margins, project completion rates, and client satisfaction scores. For example, a firm might allocate a portion of its profits based on the firm's overall profitability and another portion based on the successful completion of key projects. It's crucial to ensure the metrics used are transparent and measurable, building employee trust and clarity.

2. **Establish Communication Channels:** Communicate the profit-sharing plan to all employees.

   Detailed Explanation: Transparency is key to the success of any profit-sharing plan. Employees must understand how their contributions impact profitability and how the profit-sharing model works. Regular communication helps build trust and ensures employees fully engage with the plan.

3. **Regular Review and Adjustment:** Continuously monitor the effectiveness of the profit-sharing plan.

   Detailed Explanation: Annual reviews and feedback surveys provide insights into how the plan is perceived and its impact on employee morale and performance. Regular reviews help identify any issues with the plan and allow for adjustments to ensure it remains effective and fair. Gather employee feedback to highlight areas for improvement and ensure that the plan continues to meet their needs.

7.5 // Challenges and Solutions

(Addressing Fluctuating Profits and Perception Issues)

- **Fluctuating Profits:**

  Challenge: Architectural firms often face profitability fluctuations due to the cyclical construction industry and project-based work.

  Solution: Set a base salary and use profit-sharing as a bonus. This hybrid approach ensures a stable income during lean periods and provides additional incentives during profitable times.

- **Employee Perception:**

  Challenge: Employees may perceive profit-sharing as unfair or complicated, causing dissatisfaction and disengagement.

  Solution: Maintain transparency in how profits are calculated and shared. Educate employees on how their contributions impact profitability through clear explanations and regular financial updates to build trust.

- **Administrative Burden:**

  Challenge: Managing a profit-sharing plan can be administratively burdensome, especially for smaller firms with limited HR resources.

  Solution: Utilise professional services and HR software solutions to reduce the administrative burden and ensure accuracy and efficiency by simplifying or automating this process.

[6] Oyer, P., 2004. Why do firms use incentives that have no incentive effects?. The Journal of Finance, 59(4), pp.1619-1650.
[7] Kruse, D., 1993. Profit sharing: does it make a difference?: the productivity and stability effects of employee profit-sharing plans. Upjohn Institute for Employment Research
[8] Blasi, J.R., Freeman, R.B. and Kruse, D., 2014. The citizen's share: Reducing inequality in the 21st century. Yale University Press.
[9] FitzRoy, F.R. and Kraft, K., 1987. Cooperation, productivity, and profit sharing. The Quarterly Journal of Economics, 102(1), pp.23-35.

Case Study Feilden Clegg Bradley Studios

Overview

Founded in 1978, Feilden Clegg Bradley Studios (FCBS) is one of the UK's leading architectural practices, known for its innovative approach to sustainable design and social responsibility. The firm is committed to fostering a collaborative and motivated workforce and has successfully implemented a profit-sharing model to enhance morale and align employee efforts with the firm's goals.

Implementation

FCBS uses a combination of direct profit-sharing and deferred benefits in their approach to employee compensation. This approach balances immediate financial rewards with future stability, catering to diverse employee needs.

Detailed Implementation:

- **Direct Profit-Sharing:** Each year, a percentage of the firm's net profits is set aside for employee distribution. The criteria for distribution include factors such as seniority, role, and performance, ensuring that contributions to the firm's success are recognized and rewarded.
- **Deferred Profit-Sharing:** Contributions to employees' retirement plans are based on the firm's profitability, ensuring that employees benefit from the firm's long-term success. This provides financial security for employees and helps retain talent by aligning their future financial well-being with the firm's success.

Outcome:

The implementation of the profit-sharing model at FCBS has led to several positive outcomes:[11]

- **Higher Employee Satisfaction:** According to the firm's internal surveys, employee satisfaction ratings have significantly improved since the implementation of the profit-sharing model.
- **Reduced Turnover:** Higher employee retention has created stability, which has allowed FCBS to maintain a consistent and experienced workforce, crucial for delivering its high-quality projects.
- **Improved Performance:** The alignment of employee efforts with the firm's financial goals has resulted in higher productivity, better project outcomes and delivery times, and overall client satisfaction.
- **Enhanced Collaboration and Innovation:** The profit-sharing model fosters a sense of ownership that has encouraged greater collaboration and innovation among employees. This cultural shift has been instrumental in maintaining FCBS's reputation for pioneering work in sustainable design.

[10] Feilden Clegg Bradley Studios LLP. (2022). Annual Report 2022. Retrieved from Companies House.

Financial Performance:

- **Revenue Growth:** According to its annual reports, FCBS has seen steady revenue growth. For instance, the firm's revenue for the financial year ending March 2022 was £25.6 million, up from £22.3 million the previous year.[12 13]
- **Profit Margins:** Profit margins have also improved, a portion of which is redistributed to employees through the scheme. This financial success has reinforced the profit-sharing model's positive impact on the firm's overall performance.

Practical Steps for Implementing Profit-Sharing Models

1. **Assess Your Firm's Financial Health:** Understand your firm's profitability and cash flow to determine the feasibility of implementing a profit-sharing plan. Conduct a thorough financial analysis to ensure the firm can sustain the plan over the long term.
2. **Set Clear Objectives:** Define what you aim to achieve, whether it's improved productivity, higher retention, or better financial performance. Clear objectives will guide the design and implementation of the plan.
3. **Engage Employees:** Involve employees in the design of the plan to ensure it meets their needs and expectations. Solicit employee input and feedback to ensure the plan is well-received and effective.
4. **Communicate Transparently:** Ensure transparent and regular communication with employees about the plan. Use multiple communication channels to ensure all employees understand the plan, how it works, and what employees can expect.
5. **Monitor and Adjust:** Regularly review the plan's effectiveness and adjust based on employee feedback and financial performance. Continuous monitoring and adjustment will ensure that the plan remains fair and effective.
6. **Define Profit-Sharing Metrics:** Identify and clearly define the criteria for profit-sharing.
7. **Utilise Technology:** Use software solutions to manage the distribution and tracking of profit-sharing.
8. **Educate Employees:** Provide training and information sessions to help employees understand how the plan works and its benefits.

7.6 // Diversification of Services

(Expanding Entrepreneurial Horizons in Architecture)

Vertical Integration

Vertical integration for architectural firms involves expanding operations into different stages of production or service delivery within the same industry, such as offering construction management services alongside design. According to Michael Porter's value chain model, controlling multiple

[11] Feilden Clegg Bradley Studios LLP. (2022). Annual Report 2022. Retrieved from Companies House.
[12] Companies House. (2023). Feilden Clegg Bradley Studios LLP Filing History. Retrieved from Companies House
[13] Reporting Accounts. (2023). Feilden Clegg Bradley Studios LLP. Retrieved from Reporting Accounts

production stages can provide a competitive advantage[14] by reducing transaction costs, enhancing coordination, and securing supply chains, ultimately improving project outcomes and leading to higher profitability.

Vertical integration can enhance a firm's control over projects from initial design to final construction, leading to more consistent quality and reduced outsourcing risks. Additionally, it can open new revenue streams and improve client satisfaction by providing a seamless service experience. Acquiring or partnering with construction firms, for example, can create a more cohesive workflow, reducing miscommunication and errors often caused when separate entities handle design and construction, while improving resource allocation and risk management. By having a stake in the construction phase, architectural firms can ensure that work quality aligns with their standards, enhancing client satisfaction and trust.

Vertical integration also allows firms to experiment with innovative construction techniques, new methods, and technologies without being constrained by the limitations of external contractors. This can lead to more efficient building processes and higher-quality outcomes, distinguishing firms from competitors reliant on traditional methods.

Horizontal Integration

Horizontal integration involves expanding a firm's operations into related fields that complement its existing services, such as interior design, landscape architecture, or urban planning services. Igor Ansoff's growth matrix suggests that diversifying services mitigates risks from market fluctuations and creates synergies between service areas, enhancing competitiveness.[15] For example, an architectural firm that expands into landscape architecture can offer more integrated design solutions that consider both the building and its environment. Adding interior design services allows a firm to remain involved during the fit-out phase, ensuring the interiors align perfectly with the architectural vision.

Because horizontal integration allows firms to offer comprehensive design services from initial concept to final execution, it enhances the firm's reputation as a one-stop provider for all design needs, appealing to clients seeking comprehensive, streamlined service offerings.

Furthermore, horizontal integration drives innovation within the firm by bringing together professionals from various disciplines. Collaboration between architects, interior designers, and landscape architects encourages more creative and holistic design solutions that address a broader range of client needs and preferences.

// Strategic Partnerships

Joint Ventures with Developers

Rosabeth Moss Kanter's research emphasises the value of strategic alliances in collaboration and resource sharing between firms. For example, an architectural firm partnering with a developer on an urban regeneration project benefits from the developer's local market knowledge and financial resources, while contributing their design expertise. Joint ventures with real estate developers also can allow architectural firms to access new markets and undertake large-scale or ambitious projects they might not be able to handle alone.

International joint ventures enable firms to expand into new geographic markets by collaborating with local developers, helping them navigate regulations more effectively and understand regional market dynamics. Such partnerships often result in culturally and contextually sensitive designs that are also economically viable, socially inclusive, and environmentally sustainable, enhancing both partners' reputations and market positions.

Joint ventures also allow firms to share best practices and innovative solutions. By working closely with developers, architectural firms can gain insights into construction efficiencies, market trends, and client preferences to inform future projects and business strategies. This collaborative approach can lead to more resilient and adaptable business models.

The Fusion of Design and Real Estate

Venturing into property development enables architects to seamlessly integrate their design philosophies and expertise with the practical aspects of construction and business acumen. Unlike conventional projects, where architects work within the constraints set by developers, this approach gives architects both creative control and the opportunity to realise and monetise their design concepts in the built environment.

How to Be an Architect Developer by Amanda Baillieu and Gus Zogolovitch, available from RIBA Books
ribabooks.com

Getting Started

For those interested in exploring this model, *How to Be an Architect Developer* by Amanda Baillieu and Gus Zogolovitch, available from RIBA Books, is a comprehensive guide. Covering every stage of the development process—from finding land and raising capital to understanding risk, marketing, and selling—the book highlights projects across building types ranging from commercial, co-housing, cultural and residential buildings to new builds and conversions. It emphasises the architect's unique advantage in identifying promising sites and crafting creative solutions, while stressing the importance of development appraisal and managing risk as primary skills. A key takeaway is that architects must adopt a commercial mindset and embrace the profit motive to succeed as developers. The book also offers valuable insights into market demands and the financial implications of design decisions, filling a crucial gap in traditional architectural education.

[14] Porter, M.E., 2008. Competitive advantage: Creating and sustaining superior performance. Simon & Schuster.
[15] Ansoff, H.I., 1957. Strategies for diversification. Harvard business review, 35(5), pp.113-124.

Case Study Playbuildings by Hawkins Brown

Both Roger Hawkins and Russell Brown trained at Rock Townsend, where David Rock campaigned actively to promote architects as entrepreneurs in their own right. In the early eighties, Rock converted the historic Sanderson wallpaper factory in Chiswick into the Barley Mow Centre, acting as both developer and operator of the shared workspace—the first of its kind in the UK. Both Russell and Roger were architects for phases of this project, where they gained first-hand experience of how architects might act as entrepreneurs.

Hawkins Brown's first design project was a system of modular play buildings. The London Borough of Newham were keen to appoint them, but the public sector procurement system required them to have filed three years of accounts, which as a new company they were unable to do. So, they formed Interplace Ltd. as a joint company with the contractors, Jarvis, and Interplay, playground designers and producers of play equipment.

Hawkins Brown and Interplay ventured their time, intellectual capital, and salesmanship. Jarvis supplied the contracting framework, costings and programming to offer the buildings as a 'product' rather than a service. Newham Council bought two Playbuildings of different sizes, including the play equipment and a training programme, as 'turnkey' operations.

Playbarn by Hawkins Brown Architects (HBA)

As the client, the architects had control of the quality of construction on site, so that both buildings were finished to a sufficiently high standard to win design awards and be featured in the 'Architects Journal'. The outcome might have been more remunerative for Hawkins Brown had not the contractor absorbed the profit, but the collaboration allowed HB to complete the project within ten months of starting. This project marked the start of a lasting relationship with LB Newham and Community Links, the charity that now operates the Playbuildings. Hawkins Brown continues to collaborate work with Community Links in designing community buildings, conversions and refurbishments, and later adaptations of various Playbuildings.

Playbarn - HBA

Collaborations with Technology Firms

Clayton Christensen's theory of disruptive innovation shows how partnering with technology firms can provide architectural firms with access to advanced tools and expertise, allowing them to integrate cutting-edge technology into their design processes to create competitive advantages.[16] For example, collaborating with a software company to develop custom Building Information Modeling (BIM) tools can significantly enhance a firm's design capabilities and project delivery. An architectural firm that co-develops a unique software solution for sustainable design can offer specialised services that competitors cannot match, attracting new clients and expanding market opportunities.

Technology partnerships can also integrate artificial intelligence (AI) and machine learning (ML) tools to optimise design processes. ML algorithms analyse past project data to improve future outcomes, enhancing efficiency and creativity. AI generates design options based on specific parameters, enabling architects to quickly generate multiple design iterations, leading to more innovative solutions within tight timelines.

// Leveraging Technology

Building Information Modeling (BIM)

Building Information Modeling (BIM) is a digital representation of a building's physical and functional characteristics. Integrating BIM into architectural practices can significantly reduce project costs and timelines by improving efficiency. BIM's collaborative platform allows architects, engineers, contractors, and clients to work seamlessly together, and provides a single source of truth for project data, reducing the likelihood of discrepancies and miscommunications. BIM's capabilities also

16 Christensen, C.M., 2015. The innovator's dilemma: when new technologies cause great firms to fail. Harvard Business Review Press

17 Royal Opera House. (n.d.). Open Up Project. Retrieved from Royal Opera House..

support facility management and lifecycle analysis for more sustainable and cost-effective buildings and can facilitate regulatory compliance by providing a detailed and accurate documentation trail. Furthermore, BIM can help manage and maintain buildings over their lifecycle by providing detailed information that supports maintenance and operational decisions.

Virtual Reality (VR) and Augmented Reality (AR)

VR and AR can enhance client engagement, improve design communication, and reduce revisions by improving stakeholder communication and decision-making. By providing immersive experiences that allow clients to experience a space before it is built, the technologies enable them to visualise outcomes more effectively. AR also can be used during construction to overlay digital models onto physical spaces, assisting builders in visualising complex structures and ensuring accuracy in execution, thus reducing errors.

Conclusion

Architectural firms can expand their entrepreneurial horizons by embracing innovative business strategies such as diversification, strategic partnerships, and leveraging technology. Architectural firms willing to explore and implement these strategies will be better positioned to thrive in the competitive business landscape of the 21st century.

Practical Learning Points:

1. **Assess Opportunities for Vertical Integration:** Evaluate the feasibility of offering additional services, such as construction management, to gain better control over project outcomes and open new revenue streams.
2. **Explore Horizontal Integration:** Consider expanding into interior design and landscape architecture to provide comprehensive services and diversify your portfolio.
3. **Form Strategic Partnerships:** Collaborate with technology firms and real estate developers to leverage their expertise and resources, enhancing your firm's capabilities and market reach.
4. **Leverage Advanced Technologies:** Implement tools like BIM, VR, and AR to improve design accuracy, client engagement, and project delivery efficiency.
5. **Stay Adaptable and Innovative:** Continuously monitor industry trends and be willing to adapt your business model to stay competitive and meet evolving client needs.

Case Study Vertical Integration in Action – Royal Opera House

Leveraging my qualifications and background as a Chartered Architect, Project Manager, and Management Consultant, we integrated these roles to deliver a seamless project experience by vertically diversifying our services into a construction management company through our brand, Rise. In 2015 we won the Open Up Project at the Royal Opera House in Covent Garden, which was completed in autumn 2018 in collaboration with Stanton Williams. The case study highlights the cross-over of skills, design management, and the synergy between design and construction that contributed to the project's success.[17]

Project Overview

The Open Up Project aimed to transform the Royal Opera House into a more accessible and engaging public space. The project included the redesign of public areas, improved accessibility, and enhanced visitor experiences. Assemble Creative, in collaboration with Stanton Williams, was responsible for the architectural design, while Rise handled the construction management, ensuring seamless integration between design and execution.

Open Up - Royal Opera House (ROH)

Implementation

Design and Collaboration: We worked closely with Stanton Williams to develop innovative solutions that met the client's vision and functional requirements. The collaboration involved regular design workshops, joint meetings, and shared digital platforms to ensure alignment and integration of ideas. Our team bridged the design and execution phases, ensuring the architectural vision was preserved throughout the project.

Construction Management: Rise employed an agency-style construction management approach with an open-book staff costs and fees policy. This transparency differentiated us from major competitors like Mace, ISG, Bovis, McAlpine, and Knight Harwood. By adopting this model, we built trust with the client and other stakeholders, ensuring all costs were visible and controlled.

As construction and project managers, our teams' skills in managing complex projects and coordinating multidisciplinary teams were crucial in maintaining project timelines and budgets.

ROH - New Linbury theatre Foyer

Procurement and Build: Understanding the intricacies of design and construction, Rise streamlined procurement processes, selecting materials and contractors aligned with the project's quality and sustainability goals. This comprehensive approach ensured all project elements were executed to the highest standards. The integration of construction management allowed for real-time adjustments and quick decision-making, enhancing overall project efficiency.

Challenges and Solutions

Design and Construction Coordination: One of the main challenges was ensuring seamless coordination between the design and construction teams. Regular coordination meetings and an integrated project management system helped mitigate potential conflicts, ensuring that design intents were accurately translated into the final build. Our dual roles facilitated clear communication and swift resolution of issues, maintaining project momentum.

Complex Site Conditions: Working within an operational cultural landmark posed significant challenges. Detailed planning and flexible scheduling allowed the team to work around live performances and public visits, minimising disruptions. Rise's expertise in managing complex construction environments was crucial in navigating these challenges effectively. We implemented innovative construction techniques and staged work schedules to ensure minimal impact on the Royal Opera House's operations.

Linbury Studio Theatre at ROH

Stakeholder Engagement: Engaging with multiple stakeholders, including the Royal Opera House management, cultural advisors, and the public, required careful communication and negotiation. Rise facilitated stakeholder meetings and public consultations to gather feedback and ensure the project met diverse expectations. This inclusive approach fostered a collaborative environment where all voices were heard and project goals were aligned.

Outcomes

The Open Up Project was completed on time and within budget, receiving acclaim for its design and execution. The successful vertical integration of design and construction management resulted in a cohesive and high-quality outcome. The project won several awards, including the RIBA London Award, showcasing the effectiveness of the integrated approach.

Awards: 2020 RIBA London Award [18] / Civic Trust Award [19]

Key Achievements:

- Enhanced accessibility and visitor experience at the Royal Opera House.
- Seamless integration of contemporary design within a historic building. Successful collaboration between Rise and Stanton Williams.[20]

Conclusion

The vertical integration of skills on the Open Up Project at the Royal Opera House exemplifies the benefits of combining architectural design with construction management. The cross-over of skills and close collaboration between the teams ensured a successful project that met high standards of design and execution.

Practical Learning Points:

- **Foster Strong Collaboration:** Regular workshops and meetings between design and construction teams ensure alignment and efficient problem-solving.
- **Integrate Project Management Tools:** Use shared digital platforms for seamless communication and coordination.
- **Engage Stakeholders:** Facilitate continuous stakeholder engagement to gather feedback and align project goals.
- **Plan for Complex Environments:** Develop flexible schedules to navigate operational challenges in complex sites.
- **Leverage Vertical Integration:** Utilise the synergy between design and construction management to streamline processes and enhance project outcomes.

[18] RIBA Awards. (n.d.). 2020 RIBA London Award Winners. Retrieved from RIBA.
[19] Civic Trust Awards. (2020). Winners of the 2020 Civic Trust Awards. Retrieved from Civic Trust Awards
[20] Stanton Williams. (n.d.). Project Portfolio. Retrieved from Stanton Williams.

RESILIENCE AND RENEWAL

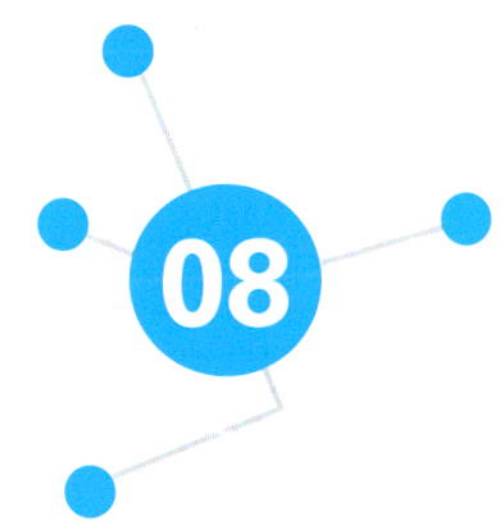

CHAPTER EIGHT

Resilience and Renewal: A Vision for Tomorrow

The journey towards innovation in architecture is complex and multifaceted, requiring a blend of creativity, resilience, and strategic thinking. This chapter explains the dynamic interplay between failure and breakthroughs, the importance of psychological safety, and the iterative nature of prototyping with both theoretical insights and practical strategies. Understanding these critical aspects of innovation helps architects better navigate the challenges and opportunities that arise throughout their careers.

8.1 // Understanding the Role of Failure in Innovation

(Redefining Setbacks as Stepping Stones)

The complex interplay between failures and breakthroughs defines the innovation journey, where cultivating a culture of psychological safety, and engaging in iterative prototyping are vital elements of the innovation process.

To fully understand the role of failure in innovation, it is essential to redefine setbacks as learning opportunities rather than roadblocks. In the creative industries, failure is a catalyst for learning and growth. Embracing failure makes it possible to gain wisdom from mistakes, refine concepts through iterative processes, and chart new courses toward success.

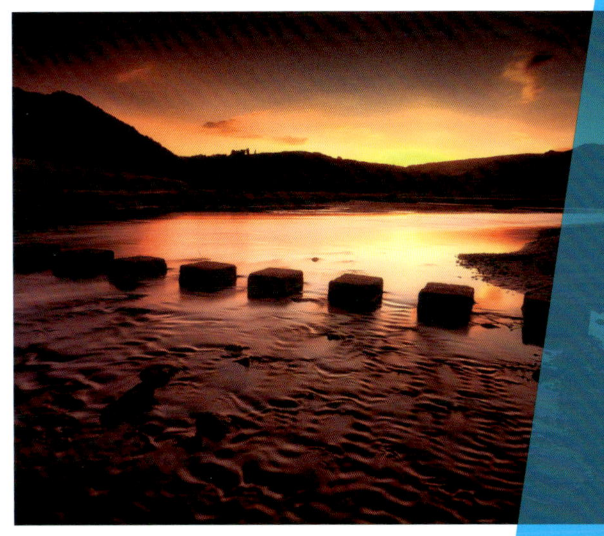

Steppingstones

8.2 // Cultivating a Culture of Psychological Safety

(Fostering Creativity and Bold Experimentation)

The concept of psychological safety forms the bedrock of successful creative environments. When individuals feel free from fear of judgment or punishment, they feel liberated to experiment and test unconventional theories. The sense of safety encourages bold thinking, leading to novel solutions and breakthroughs as the bounds of conventional thinking are stretched to yield remarkable outcomes.

Defining Psychological Safety

At its core, psychological safety means that team members feel they can be open and vulnerable. They trust their colleagues will not criticise or ridicule them for speaking up with ideas, questions, or doubts. It's about creating an environment where people are comfortable being themselves, fully engaging in collaborative processes, and contributing to their maximum potential.[1] Creating a culture of psychological safety within your practice unlocks the full potential of individuals and teams, leading to higher levels of engagement, increased motivation, better decision-making, and, ultimately, superior innovation and performance.

Implementing Psychological Safety

Implementing psychological safety starts with leadership, but requires consistent effort and a genuine commitment from all levels of a team or organisation. Training sessions on communication, emotional intelligence, and conflict resolution can equip team members with the skills to contribute to a psychologically safe environment where creativity is nurtured and everyone feels empowered to contribute their best work.

Cultivating Psychological Safety as a Practice

- **Leadership Vulnerability:** Leaders must model the behavior they wish to see by being open about their own failures and uncertainties. Admitting one's mistakes and not knowing all the answers encourages others to do the same.
- **Encourage Participation:** Create forums and opportunities for sharing ideas and opinions. Regularly invite input and show genuine interest in team members' contributions to reinforce the value of diverse perspectives.
- **Active Listening:** Practice active listening, where responses are heard, acknowledged, and considered. This demonstrates respect for the contributor and encourages further participation.
- **Foster an Environment of Mutual Respect:** Ensure that all interactions, even during disagreements, are conducted with respect. This involves setting clear communication norms that reject behaviors like interrupting or dismissing others.

[1] Edmondson, A., 1999. Psychological safety and learning behavior in work teams. Administrative science quarterly, 44(2), pp.350-383.

- **Celebrate Experimentation and Learning from Failure:** Encourage a mindset where failures are not seen as setbacks but as vital steps in the learning process. Celebrate and share the lessons from these experiences.
- **Feedback Mechanisms:** Develop and maintain open channels for constructive feedback focused on growth. Feedback should be timely, specific, and delivered to reflect a commitment to individual and collective improvement.
- **Safety Checks:** Regularly assess psychological safety within the team or organization using surveys, one-on-one meetings, and open forums where team members can express how safe they feel to take risks and contribute ideas.
- **Conflict Resolution:** Address conflicts openly and constructively, ensuring that differences in opinion do not lead to personal attacks. A healthy conflict resolution process explores diverse viewpoints and enhances the team's creative solutions.

8.3 // Iteration and Prototyping: The Heartbeat of Innovation

(Refining Ideas Through Continuous Improvement)

Iteration and prototyping are the tools that drive innovation. The cycle of repeated refining, testing, and improving ideas, allows creatives to identify weak links, optimise designs, and recalibrate their strategies to transform creativity into innovation.

The process works because the focus is on continuous improvement, not perfection. Prototyping allows creatives to turn abstract ideas into tangible solutions, and the iterative process paves the way for transformative breakthroughs which, when leveraged, propel continued success and sustained innovation.

8.4 // Pick Yourself Up and Dust Yourself Down

(Strategies for Resilience When Things Don't Quite Work Out)

Setbacks inevitably happen along the path to success, which can be disheartening. Resilience is the ability to rise above disappointment and embrace new challenges with determination and optimism. ......

Bouncing Back

Strategies for Bouncing Back Stronger

Building resilience in response to challenges is key to thriving in the creative industries. Such resilience is rooted in cultivating a supportive network, self-reflection, and compassion. The following tips can help you lay the groundwork for a resilient creative process.

Tips for Practising Resilience in the Creative Journey

- **Cultivate a Supportive Network:** Surround yourself with positive, understanding individuals who appreciate the nuances of the creative process and can provide emotional support. Engage with peers who share your passion and vision to expand your perspective and open new doors to collaboration and inspiration.
- **Embrace Self-Reflection and Compassion:** Shift your perspective to view setbacks as opportunities for growth rather than personal failure. Practice self-compassion to nurture your well-being and foster a resilient mindset that views obstacles as part of your development as a creative individual.
- **Set Realistic Goals:** Break down larger projects into manageable tasks to regain a sense of control and maintain momentum and confidence. This helps create a sense of progress and achievement, fueling continued creativity.
- **Seek Diverse Perspectives:** Collaboration opens up new perspectives and opportunities. Embracing diverse perspectives challenges conventional thinking and sparks innovation by introducing fresh ideas and solutions.
- **Maintain a Positive Inner Dialogue:** Treat yourself with kindness and understanding, just as you would a close friend, to help yourself navigate difficult times with grace and resilience.
- **Celebrate Small Wins:** Amid setbacks, allow yourself to enjoy your victories and triumphs. Acknowledge and appreciate your progress, no matter how incremental. Each achievement contributes to your growth as a creative individual over setbacks. Celebrating small victories builds confidence and maintains momentum, making the creative journey more structured and less daunting.

In the creative industries, setbacks are inevitable, but success is measured in how we handle them. Resilience is the key to bouncing back stronger, embracing failures, and using them as stepping stones to greater achievements. By adopting a growth mindset, reframing setbacks, and learning from mistakes, creatives can transform setbacks into catalysts for growth and innovation.

Practising resilience involves cultivating a support network, self-reflection, self-compassion, and setting realistic goals to regain momentum. Many examples demonstrate the power of resilience in achieving remarkable success despite numerous setbacks. In pursuing creativity, embracing resilience is a skill and a way of life. By picking ourselves up and dusting ourselves down after setbacks, we fortify our creative spirit and rise stronger than ever, ready to face the ever-changing landscape of the creative industries.

Case Study Carmody Groarke – Design Museum Gent

In early 2019, the Design Museum Gent and urban development company Sogent appointed Carmody Groarke, ATAMA, and RE-ST to renovate and extend their museum, including a new five-storey extension known as DING (Design-in-Gent).

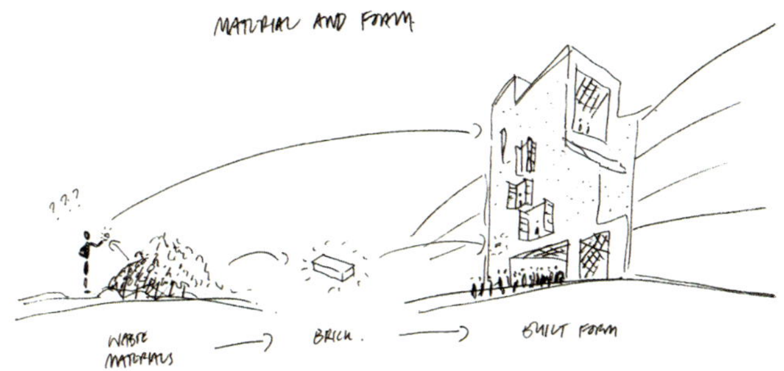

Design Museum Concept Sketch

The existing buildings will be sensitively refurbished and optimised to display internationally significant collections of design objects. The new museum wing will host temporary events and exhibitions, enabling the museum's expanded and enriched programme of design culture.

The team envisioned the new wing as a brick-faced building infilling the fourth corner of the existing museum masterplan. Brick construction is synonymous with the local vernacular of Flanders, therefore a light-toned brick building felt contextually and culturally appropriate for the city. However, we were also conscious of the significant environmental impact of using traditional clay-fired bricks, typically made with virgin materials extracted from the ground and fired at high temperatures.

Design Museum Front elevation

Design Museum Front Model

As part of the project, the design team developed a bespoke low-carbon, recycled brick—now known as the 'Gent Waste Brick'—for use on the façade. The Gent Waste Brick is made from 63 per cent locally sourced municipal waste streams, including crushed concrete and white glass, with hydraulic lime (NHL 3.5) as the primary binding agent.

Unlike conventional clay bricks, the Gent Waste Brick is cured rather than fired, gaining strength through carbonation with atmospheric CO2. This process, coupled with the recycled composites, results in a brick with one-third of the embodied carbon of a typical Belgian clay-fired brick when measured over a 60-year life cycle. The bricks will be coursed with a bespoke lime mortar also made from recycled content.

The development of the Gent Waste Brick was catalysed by 100,000 in funding from Circular Flanders very early in the project stage. Early prototypes were developed by Local Works Studio based in Sussex, whose team are experts in lime and localised low-carbon construction. As the project evolved, further research, development and production of the 100,000+ bricks was carried out by BC Materials, based in Brussels.

The bricks have undergone a robust development process. Over two years, some 30 different prototypes were tested and developed for aesthetics and performance against European Norms, and certification for use was achieved through lengthy consultation with the Belgian Construction Certification Association Belgian (BCCA) for the construction sector.

Brick making process begins

Gent Waste Brick production copy for captions

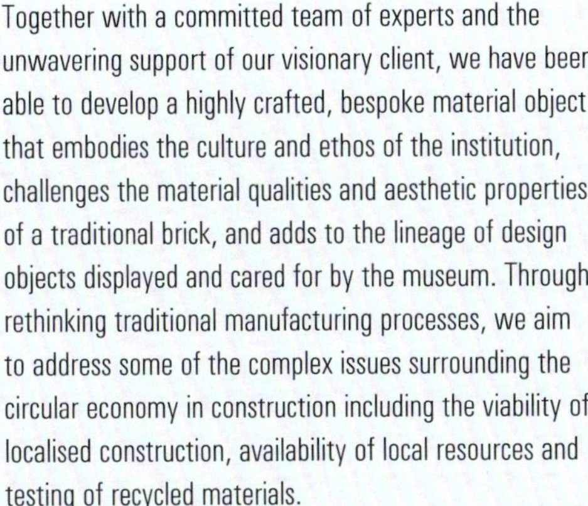

Together with a committed team of experts and the unwavering support of our visionary client, we have been able to develop a highly crafted, bespoke material object that embodies the culture and ethos of the institution, challenges the material qualities and aesthetic properties of a traditional brick, and adds to the lineage of design objects displayed and cared for by the museum. Through rethinking traditional manufacturing processes, we aim to address some of the complex issues surrounding the circular economy in construction including the viability of localised construction, availability of local resources and testing of recycled materials.

Brick production is now underway in the new museum wing, set to reopen in 2026.

Reflection on the Carmody Groarke Case Study

The Carmody Groarke case study is an excellent example of the power of innovative thinking and sustainability in modern architecture. In renovating and extending the Design Museum Gent, the team enhanced the functionality and aesthetic appeal of the museum while prioritising environmental sustainability and cultural resonance. The Gent Waste Brick, made from 63% locally sourced municipal waste streams and hydraulic lime, reduced environmental impact by creating a low-carbon alternative to traditional clay-fired bricks.

The finished 'Gent Brick'

This project highlights the importance of rethinking traditional construction methods and materials to address environmental challenges. The rigorous testing and development process of the Ghent Waste Brick, including creating over 30 prototypes, underscores the iterative nature of innovation. This dedication to refining and perfecting the brick design until it met aesthetic and performance standards, demonstrates the value of perseverance and meticulous attention to detail in achieving breakthrough results.

The Carmody Groarke case study shows how the spirit of innovation is fueled by creativity, resilience, and a deep commitment to sustainability. This project is an inspiring example for architects and designers worldwide, demonstrating that with the right blend of vision, collaboration, and perseverance, it is possible to achieve remarkable advancements that benefit both the environment and the community.

RESILIENCE AND RENEWAL
10 Key Learning Points //

1. **Redefine Failures as Stepping Stones:** Actively reflect on past projects to identify failures. Analyse these setbacks to extract valuable lessons that can guide future work. Use these insights to refine processes and improve outcomes.
2. **Embrace a Culture of Psychological Safety:** Foster an environment where team members feel safe to express ideas, questions, and concerns without fear of ridicule. Implement regular training sessions on communication and emotional intelligence to support this culture.
3. **Implement Iteration and Prototyping:** Develop a structured approach to iteration and prototyping in your projects. Set up regular review cycles to test and refine ideas, ensuring continuous improvement and innovation.
4. **Cultivate Resilience and Adaptability:** Build personal and team resilience by setting realistic goals and celebrating small wins. Encourage a growth mindset that views setbacks as opportunities for development and innovation.
5. **Leverage Diverse Perspectives:** Actively seek diverse viewpoints by involving different team members and external experts in the brainstorming and design processes. This can lead to richer, more innovative solutions.
6. **Foster Entrepreneurial Spirit:** Encourage entrepreneurial thinking within your team. Promote character, effort, and integrity as core values. Provide opportunities for team members to take ownership of projects and drive them to completion.
7. **Commit to Sustainable Practices:** Integrate sustainable materials and practices into your projects. Use local resources and innovative techniques to reduce environmental impact, as exemplified by the Gent Waste Brick in the Carmody Groarke case study.

SECTION 2

AFTERWORD

I've Had an idea...
Now Go and Realise It

Architects, with their revolutionary concepts and inventive ideas, play a key role in shaping our spatial environments, our interaction with our surroundings, and ways of life. Moreover, with their unorthodox ideation and panoramic vision, architects are ideal candidates for thriving as entrepreneurs; they understand how ethereal visions can be transformed into tangible structures, fully recognizing the potency embedded within ideas.

Architects are also uniquely positioned to promote the use of renewable materials, green buildings and eco-friendly designs. Their problem-solving abilities contribute to creating a more sustainable future, extending into the broader domains of urban planning and development, where their role is pivotal in addressing systemic challenges such as urban congestion, environmental degradation, and socio-spatial inequalities. The ability to conceptualise and implement efficient urban layouts is both a technical skill and a strategic intervention that intersects with public policy, sustainability imperatives, and human well-being. Well-designed urban spaces can mitigate the adverse effects of overpopulation and pollution, fostering healthier and more inclusive environments. Architects' holistic perspective enables them to transcend traditional boundaries, offering innovative approaches in adjacent sectors. In healthcare, architectural design is increasingly seen as a determinant of patient recovery and well-being, where spatial arrangements and material choices align with evidence-based practices to enhance comfort and reduce stress. Similarly, in workplace design, architects contribute to reshaping organisational dynamics by prioritising layouts that encourage collaboration, adaptability, and productivity, reflecting a deeper understanding of how built environments influence human behaviour and performance.

Architects' strong leadership skills, developed while acting as project managers during intricate construction projects, translate seamlessly into entrepreneurial ventures where effective resource allocation, team management, and strict adherence to timelines are key elements for success. Their empathy enables them to relate to users and stakeholders alike, allowing them to design inclusive solutions and lead social entrepreneurship in areas such as affordable housing or disaster relief through innovative design solutions.

Architects are more than simply designers of buildings—they are visionaries and innovators, at the forefront of driving change and positively impacting our world. As they continue to embrace their entrepreneurial spirit, the possibilities for their contributions are endless.

So, pay attention the next time an architect says, 'I've had an idea', for it might just be the beginning of something rather special.

Railroad station at dusk, Liege, Guillemins, Belgium - Calatrava

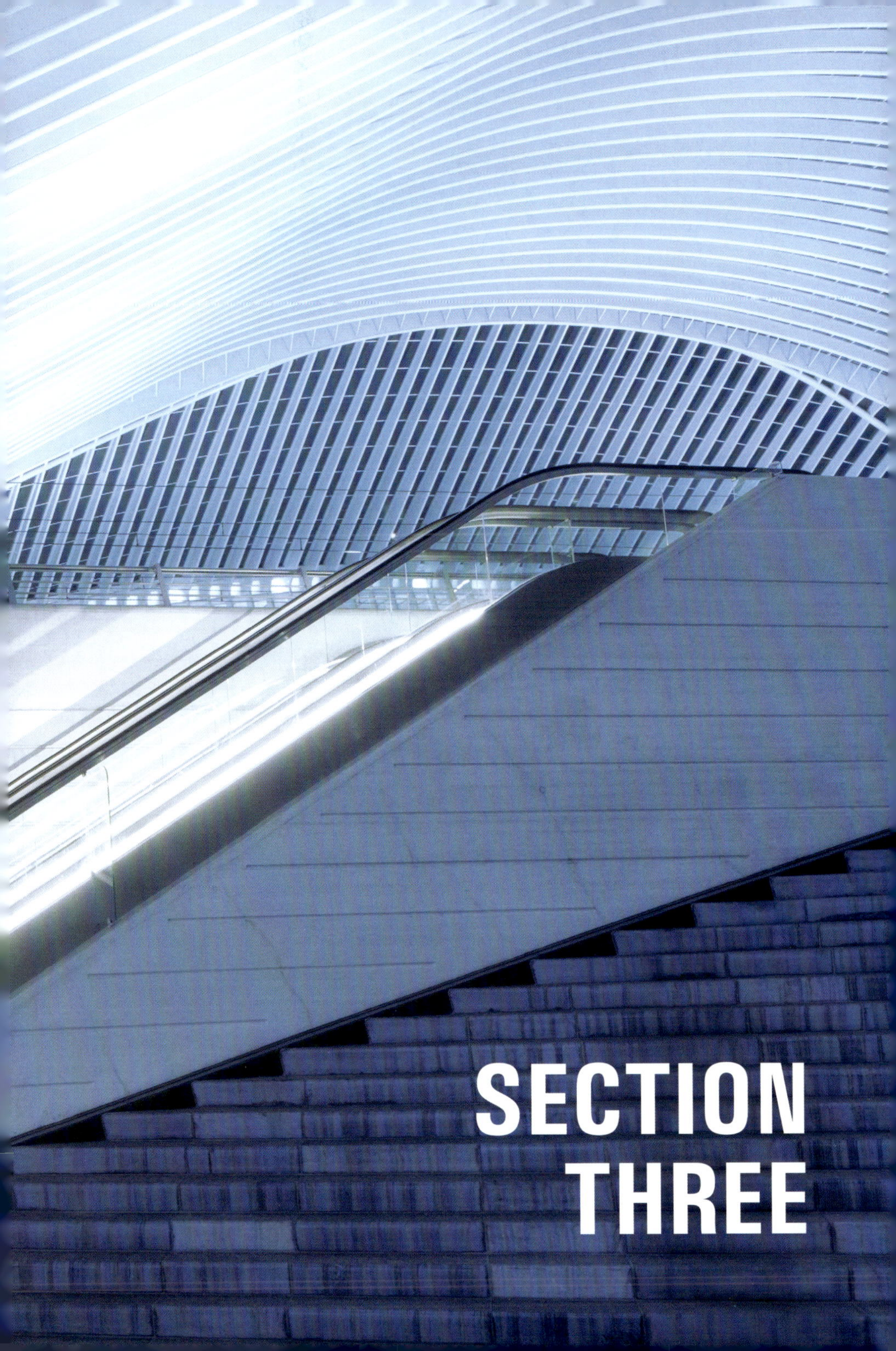

SECTION THREE

THE BUSINESS OF ARCHITECTURE

Schwartz Reisman Innovation Centre by Weiss/Manfredi and [illegible] Architects

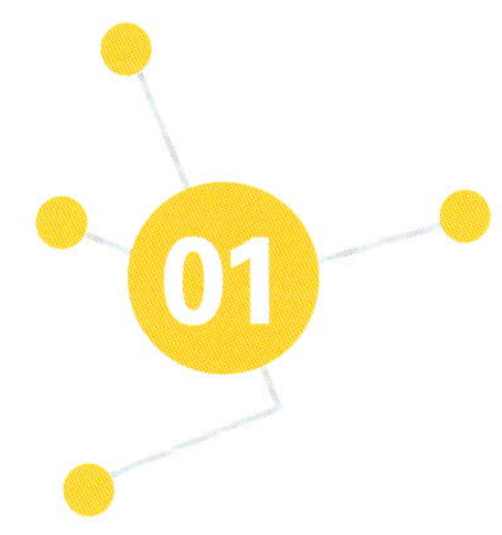

CHAPTER ONE

The Business of Architecture

The world of business planning is where the creativity of architecture meets the practicality of finance. In architecture, success hinges on more than creativity and technical skill. It's about recognising the value of your expertise and the myriad underlying costs that come with running a practice. Although discussing financial management might not have the allure of designing a skyscraper, even the most visionary designs need a solid foundation, and in the business world that foundation depends on understanding costs, managing budgets, and ensuring profitability. This chapter will guide you through the essential principles of financial management tailored to the unique needs of architects, helping you ensure that your creative endeavours are also profitable.

1.1 // Show Me the Money!

(Business Planning for Architects)

For architects (or any service provider), understanding the full cost of doing business is essential. This extends beyond material and labour costs to include the unique expenses tied to selling knowledge and expertise. Unlike businesses that sell tangible products, an architect's cost model requires a different approach and must reflect both the direct and indirect costs of running their business and the value of their expertise. This includes ongoing investments in education and professional development to stay abreast of new technologies, building codes, and design trends. Additionally, architects must communicate their ideas effectively to clients, contractors, and other stakeholders, which requires strong interpersonal and communication skills.

Business Planning

1.2 // Selling Knowledge and Expertise

(Core Principles)

Principle 1 Understand the Mission of Your Business

Clearly understanding your business's core mission is essential before structuring its finances. Reflect on what drives your architectural practice, as this will shape strategic decisions, guiding resource allocation and financial planning. For instance, a commitment to sustainable design might require a higher investment in R & D, impacting your budget and operational focus.

Principle 2 Identify All Direct and Indirect Costs.

Direct costs are expenses directly tied to a project, such as labour, materials, and equipment. Indirect costs are expenses not directly tied to a project, such as rent, utilities, insurance, and administrative expenses. Both must be factored into your cost model to understand your expenses and ensure you appropriately price your services. For UK-based ABC Architects Ltd., accurately understanding and managing these costs is crucial for accurate pricing and financial health

Example Project // Direct Costs	Total
Labour: Architect and designer time at £100/hour, totalling £30,000 for a 300-hour project.	**£30,000**
Equipment: Specialized software and hardware directly used for the project, leasing costs amounting to £2,000.	**£2,000**
	£32,000

Indirect Costs Allocation

While indirect costs like rent, utilities, insurance, and administrative salaries have been detailed previously (£124,666 annually), these need to be proportionately allocated to each project based on duration or resource usage. For example, if ABC Architects Ltd. handles 20 projects a year, an equal distribution would allocate £6,233 of indirect costs per project. However, more accurate allocation might consider project scale or complexity, affecting resource usage differently.

Integrating Costs into Pricing

By adding direct costs (£32,000) and allocating indirect costs (£6,233), the total cost for the sample project is £38,233. ABC Architects Ltd. must apply its desired profit margin to this total cost to ensure profitability when pricing its services. This detailed approach enables ABC Architects Ltd. to price its services more accurately, ensuring all costs are covered while maintaining competitiveness and profitability in the UK market.

Principle 3 Track Your Time and Expenses

For ABC Architects Ltd., tracking time and expenses on each project is integral for financial accuracy and operational efficiency. This requires a robust time-tracking system that allows architects and designers to log hours spent on project tasks. Additionally, recording all project-related expenses—from materials to outsourced services—ensures a comprehensive financial overview. This approach clarifies the firm's hourly rates and project costs and reveals potential cost-saving and optimisation opportunities. By analysing this data, ABC Architects Ltd. can adjust pricing, streamline workflows, and improve profitability and service quality in the competitive UK architecture market.

Example **ABC Architects Ltd. //** PROJECT ALPHA

To illustrate Principle 3 with data for ABC Architects Ltd.:

Time Tracking:	**Total**
Architect Hours: 150 hours at £50/hour = £7,500	
Designer Hours: 100 hours at £40/hour = £4,000	**£11,500**
Expenses Tracking:	
Materials: £15,000	
Software Licenses for Project Duration: £500	
Printing and Presentation Materials: £300	**£15,800**
	£27,300

By tracking time and expenses, ABC Architects Ltd. finds the actual cost of Project Alpha is £27,300. This data helps the firm refine its pricing model and identify efficiency improvements, such as negotiating better rates for materials or optimising design time.

Principle 4 Determine Your Overhead Costs.

Overhead costs are essential expenses necessary to keep your business running but are not directly tied to a specific project. Examples of overhead costs include rent, utilities, insurance, taxes, and administrative salaries. Understanding your overhead costs is critical, as they can significantly impact profit margins. By accurately assessing overhead, you can make informed decisions about pricing your services and allocating resources.

Impact on Pricing and Resource Allocation

To maintain a healthy profit margin, ABC Architects Ltd. must ensure that their service pricing covers

Understanding Overhead Costs for ABC Architects Ltd.		
		ANNUAL TOTAL
Office Rent	Location: Cardiff Monthly Rent: £3,500	**£42,000**
Utilities	Electricity, Heating, Water: £250/month Internet and Phone: £150/month	**£4,800**
Insurance	Professional Indemnity Insurance: £2,000/year Public Liability Insurance: £1,200/year Contents and Equipment Insurance: £800/year	**£4,000**
Salaries for Administrative Staff	Office Manager: £30,000/year Receptionist/Secretary: £22,000/year	**£52,000**
Taxes	Business Rates (Non-Domestic Rates): £8,000/year	**£8,000**
Computer Hardware and Software	Workstations and Laptops: £5,000 (renewed every 3 years, £1,666/year) Software Licenses (AutoCAD, Revit, Adobe Suite): £2,400/year	**£4,066**
General Expenses	Office Supplies: £1,200/year Professional Memberships (RIBA, ARB): £600/year Travel and Entertainment: £3,000/year Marketing and Website Maintenance: £5,000/year	**£9,800**
Total Annual Overhead Costs		**£124,666**

both overhead costs and direct project costs. For instance, pricing strategies might be adjusted for a 20% profit margin above all expenses. A detailed understanding of these costs enables the firm to identify potential savings, such as switching to more energy-efficient utilities or renegotiating rent. By meticulously analysing and managing overhead, ABC Architects Ltd. can more accurately forecast their financial health, set competitive yet profitable pricing, and strategically allocate resources to ensure the firm's sustainability and growth in the competitive UK architecture market.

Principle 5 **Determine Your Profit Margin.**

Understanding your profit margin offers a critical insight into your business's financial health and operational efficiency. It requires a meticulous breakdown of all costs associated with your services, including direct costs of labour, materials, and equipment and indirect costs like rent, utilities, and administrative support. This comprehensive understanding enables strategic pricing that not only covers costs but generates a sustainable profit. Such profit fuels business growth, enabling reinvestment in innovation, technology, and talent development. A well-managed profit margin reflects your business acumen, directly influencing your competitive edge and long-term success.

Example **ABC Architects Ltd. //** PROJECT ALPHA

For ABC Architects Ltd., determining profit margin involves subtracting total costs (both direct and indirect) from service charges.:

Service Charge – Total Costs = Profit

If Project Alpha is billed at £40,000, with costs of £27,300:
Service Charge: £40,000
Total Cost: £27,300

Profit

£12,700

Profit Margin Calculation:

Profit (£12,700) / Service Charge (£40,000) x 100 = **31.75%**

This 31.75% profit margin reveals the firm's financial health and guides pricing and investment decisions, ensuring sustainability and growth.

Principle 6 **Consider Your Competition.**

Evaluating your competition is critical for strategic pricing in your architectural firm. It's not just about matching or undercutting prices, but understanding the full market landscape and where your services fit within that context. By analysing competitors, you can identify market gaps or areas where your firm excels, and leverage these strengths in your marketing and pricing strategy. For example, if your firm specialises in eco-friendly designs and your competitors are not emphasising sustainability, you could highlight this as a unique selling point, potentially justifying a premium price. Understanding competitive pricing also helps ensure you're not undervaluing your services, so safeguarding your margins while appealing to clients seeking your specialised expertise.

For example, ABC Architects Ltd., when researching competitor XYZ Design Studio, discovers it charges £50,000 for similar architectural services. ABC's total project cost is £30,000, aiming for a 20% profit margin, setting its price at £36,000. Based on these figures, ABC could justify increasing its price to £45,000 based on its unique sustainable design approach. This adjustment covers costs and improves profit margin, and positions ABC as a leader in eco-friendly architecture, differentiating it from XYZ Design Studio.

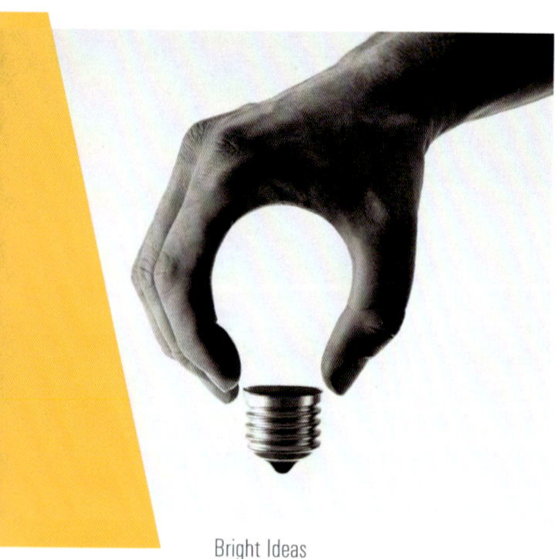

Bright Ideas

Principle 7 Identify Areas for Improvement.

Analysing your firm's operational and financial performance to identify areas for improvement can greatly enhance overall efficiency and profitability. This includes thoroughly examining fixed and variable costs, workflow efficiency, and the effectiveness of current technologies and methodologies. By leveraging detailed analytics and feedback, a firm can uncover hidden inefficiencies such as underutilised resources or processes that do not add value to the client experience. Implementing lean management, investing in employee training, and adopting cutting-edge design and project management technologies can yield substantial improvements. Periodic reviews of supplier contracts and service agreements can also uncover opportunities to negotiate better terms or find more cost-effective alternatives without compromising quality.

For example, ABC Architects Ltd. conducted a comprehensive audit of its project management cycle, revealing that the firm spent an average of 20% more time on design revisions than initially projected, impacting project timelines and profitability. By adopting a new collaborative software platform, the firm streamlined communication with clients, reducing the time spent on revisions by 15% and improving client satisfaction. This efficiency gain added £30,000 in profit per project due to reduced labour costs and shorter project durations, allowing for a higher project turnover rate. Furthermore, renegotiating supplier contracts led to a 5% reduction in material costs, saving £50,000 annually. These strategic optimisations significantly enhanced the firm's competitiveness and profitability.

Learning Points

- **Understand Direct and Indirect Costs:** Know the expenses directly and indirectly associated with projects for accurate pricing.
- **Track Time and Expenses:** Implement systems for detailed tracking to optimise billing and operational efficiency.
- **Determine Profit Margin:** Calculate the difference between service charges and total costs to guide pricing and investment decisions.
- **Consider Your Competition:** Analyze competitors' pricing and offerings to position your services competitively.
- **Identify Areas for Improvement:** Continuously evaluate and refine cost models and operational processes to enhance profitability and efficiency.

1.3 // Drive for Show, Putt for Dough

(Money / Turnover for Vanity / Profit for Sanity)

As an entrepreneur, it's tempting to focus on high turnover and rapid revenue growth as indicators of success. However, prioritising turnover alone can lead to financial strain and mental exhaustion. Instead, entrepreneurs should build a business model focused on profitability and gross margin, known as 'turnover for vanity, profit for sanity'. This philosophy emphasises sustainable growth and long-term success over short-term revenue gains.[1]

Putt for Dough

Why is this important?

High turnover can put a significant strain on a business, both financially and mentally. It can lead to a cash flow crunch and put pressure on suppliers, employees, and other stakeholders. Constantly chasing high turnover can also lead to exhaustion and burnout, negatively impacting an entrepreneur's mental health and well-being. By prioritising gross margin and profitability entrepreneurs can create a stable, profitable, more sustainable and successful business allowing for reinvestment and growth.[2] This approach also allows entrepreneurs to take a longer-term view of their business rather than chasing short-term gains.[3]

[1] Drucker, P.F., 2020. The essential Drucker. Routledge.

Economic Models for Profitability

- **The Profit Margin Model:** Profit margin measures a company's profitability by dividing net income by revenue. By focusing on building a business model with strong profit margins, entrepreneurs can ensure that they are generating sustainable profits. This, in turn, allows them to reinvest in their business and grow over time.

  Example: ABC Architects Ltd. calculates the profit margin by subtracting the total costs from the service charges. For Project Alpha, if the service charge is £40,000 and the total cost is £27,300, the profit is £12,700. The profit margin is calculated as (£12,700 / £40,000) * 100 = 31.75%. This robust profit margin indicates a healthy business capable of reinvesting in innovation and growth.

- **The Pareto Principle (80/20 Rule)**: The Pareto Principle states that 80% of effects come from 20% of causes. This often means that 80% of revenue comes from just 20% of customers or products. By identifying and focusing on the most profitable areas of their business, entrepreneurs can maximise their profits while minimising risk.[4]

  Example: ABC Architects Ltd. analyzes its client base and discovers that 80% of its revenue comes from 20% of its high-profile clients. They can maximise profitability and ensure steady revenue streams by focusing on maintaining and expanding services to these key clients.

- **The Cash Conversion Cycle Model:** The cash conversion cycle measures the time it takes for a business to convert its investments in inventory and other resources into cash. By optimising the cash conversion cycle, entrepreneurs can improve their cash flow and ensure they have the resources needed to reinvest in their business and pursue growth.[5]

  Example: ABC Architects Ltd. streamlines their project billing process to reduce the time between project completion and payment receipt. By shortening the cash conversion cycle, they improve cash flow, allowing for timely reinvestment in new projects and resources.

Practical Steps to Prioritize Profitability

- **Evaluate Financial Health Regularly:** Review financial statements regularly to assess your business's health. Focus on key metrics like profit margins, cash flow, and return on investment (ROI). Use these insights to make informed decisions about pricing, resource allocation, and cost management.[6]

  Example: Monthly financial reviews help ABC Architects Ltd. identify cost overruns in real-time and implement corrective measures, ensuring that profitability targets are met.

- **Focus on High-Margin Services:** Identify which services or products have the highest margins and focus on promoting and expanding those areas. This strategic focus ensures that your efforts are directed towards the most profitable aspects of your business.[7]

[2] Porter, M.E., 2008. Competitive advantage: Creating and sustaining superior performance. Simon and Schuster
[3] Collins, J., 2009. Good to Great: why some companies make the leap and others don't. HarperCollins

Example: ABC Architects Ltd. finds that their sustainable design services have higher profit margins compared to standard architectural services. By marketing these services more aggressively, they attract more clients interested in sustainability, increasing overall profitability.

- **Streamline Operations:** Look for ways to streamline operations and reduce waste. Implement efficient project management practices, invest in technology that automates routine tasks, and continuously seek ways to improve productivity [8]

  Example: By adopting a new project management software, ABC Architects Ltd. reduces project timelines and administrative overhead, leading to significant cost savings and improved profit margins.

- **Build Strong Client Relationships:** Strong client relationships can lead to repeat business and referrals, which are more cost-effective than acquiring new clients. To build lasting relationships, provide exceptional service, maintain open communication, and exceed client expectations.[9]

  Example: ABC Architects Ltd. implements a more effective client feedback system. Positive feedback leads to high client retention and increased referral-based projects, boosting profitability.

- **Regularly Review Pricing Strategies:** Ensure your pricing strategies reflect the true value of your services and cover all associated costs, including overheads and profit margins. Regularly adjust prices to keep up with market trends and cost increases.

  Example: ABC Architects Ltd. conducts an annual review of its pricing structure, adjusting rates to reflect increased material costs and market demand. This ensures that its pricing remains competitive while maintaining healthy profit margins.

Learning Points

- **Profitability Over Turnover:** Focus on building a business model that generates consistent profits.
- **Economic Models:** Apply the profit margin model, Pareto principle, and cash conversion cycle model to maximise profitability.
- **Sustainability:** Ensure long-term success by generating consistent profits and reinvesting in the business.

[4] Mornati, F., 2006. An Analytical-Epistemological Reconstruction of the Genesis of Pareto's Manuale di economia politica. International Review of Economics, 53(4), pp.579-591.
[5] Johnson, J., Whittington, R., Regnér, P., Angwin, D., Johnson, G. and Scholes, K., 2020. Exploring strategy. Pearson UK.
[6] Siemionek, M., 2010. Balanced scorecard as a possible key for business strategy. Baltic Management Review, p.51.
[7] Collins, J., 2009. Good to Great: Why some companies make the leap and others don't. HarperCollins

THE BUSINESS OF ARCHITECTURE

10 Common Areas of Failure //

- **Lack of Market Research:** Many new firms fail because they do not fully understand the needs of their target market. Comprehensive market research is crucial to identify your audience, understand their needs, and tailor your offerings accordingly.
- **Inadequate Financial Planning:** A common pitfall for new businesses is underestimating the capital required to sustain operations until becoming profitable. Detailed financial planning is essential, including cash flow management and securing adequate funding.
- **Poor Product-Market Fit:** Launching a product or service that doesn't adequately solve a problem or fulfill a need for your target market can lead to failure. Continuous feedback loops and willingness to pivot are necessary to ensure your offerings align with market demands.
- **Overlooking the Importance of a Strong Team:** The right team can make or break a new firm. A common area of failure is not investing in finding and retaining individuals who are both skilled and share the company's vision and culture.
- **Neglecting Customer Feedback:** Ignoring the feedback of your early customers is a significant oversight. Engaging with your customers and valuing their input is crucial for refining your product or service.
- **Underestimating the Competition:** Failure to accurately assess and strategise around the competitive landscape can leave a business vulnerable. Understanding your competition's strengths and weaknesses allows you to position your offerings effectively.
- **Scaling Too Quickly:** Expanding operations or scaling the business before establishing a solid foundation and understanding of the market can lead to resource drain and operational inefficiencies.
- **Ineffective Marketing:** Talent and creativity alone don't guarantee success. An inability to effectively communicate the value of your product or service to your target audience can fail to gain traction.
- **Lack of Adaptability:** The architectural and business landscape is ever-changing. A reluctance or inability to adapt to new trends, technologies, or market shifts can render a firm obsolete.
- **Ignoring Legal and Regulatory Requirements:** Overlooking the legal and regulatory aspects of running a business can lead to significant issues, including fines, penalties, and operational disruptions.

[8] Drucker, P.F., 2020. The essential Drucker. Routledge.
[9] Porter, M.E., 2008. Competitive advantage: Creating and sustaining superior performance. Simon and Schuster

NAVIGATING THE FINANCIAL LANDSCAPE

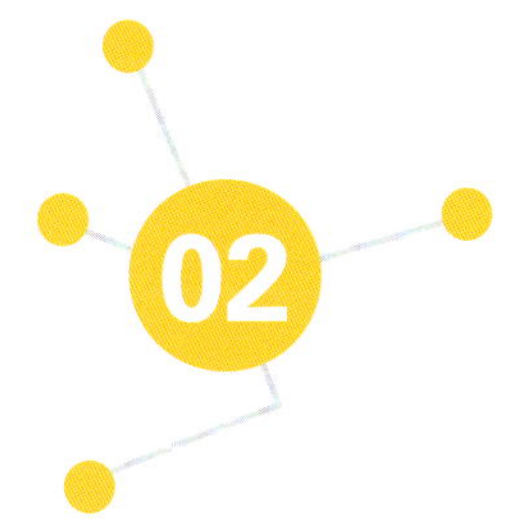

CHAPTER TWO

Navigating the Financial Landscape

Without solid financial backing and strategic partnerships, even the most innovative ideas may never come to fruition. This chapter explains various funding options available to architects and highlights the importance of choosing the right partners for your business. We examine various funding sources, from self-funding and bank loans to private equity, crowdfunding, and grants. Each offers unique advantages and challenges, and understanding these can help you make informed decisions about financing your projects. Real-life examples from renowned architects such as Renzo Piano and Jean Nouvel illustrate how such funding strategies have been effectively utilised to support their visionary work.

We then address the critical subject of business partnerships. Good partnerships can provide shared expertise, resources, and risk management, but they also require careful selection and management to avoid conflicts and legal disputes. We will explore the importance of corporate governance, record-keeping, and clear agreements through case studies of notable architects like Frank Lloyd Wright and Zaha Hadid. These examples offer valuable lessons on navigating the complexities of business partnerships.

2.1 // Go Fund Me

(Sources of Funding / Banks / Private Equity / DIY)

Transforming innovative ideas into tangible structures demands significant capital, which can be a daunting challenge for many entrepreneurs. However, just as an architect sees potential where others see space, the entrepreneurial architect can turn financial obstacles into opportunities by exploring various funding sources.

Option 1 Self-funding

Genoa Port: Renzo Piano

Self-funding, or bootstrapping, is financing a business using personal savings or assets. This funding method is popular among entrepreneurs who want to maintain complete control over their businesses without taking on external investors. The advantage of self-funding is that it allows the entrepreneur to retain full ownership of the company and avoid diluting equity. However, it can be challenging to fund a business entirely from personal savings, and the entrepreneur may eventually need to seek external funding.

Example: Renzo Piano, the founder of Renzo Piano Building Workshop, self-funded his business. Piano started his firm in 1981 after leaving his previous partnership and used his savings to finance the company. Today, the Renzo Piano Building Workshop is one of the world's leading architectural practices, known for its innovative and sustainable designs.

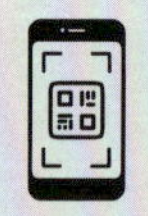

Useful Link: Guide to Bootstrapping Your Startup – A range of guides can be found here

Step-by-Step Guide:

1. Assess your savings and personal assets.
2. Create a detailed budget for your initial expenses.
3. Plan for future funding needs and consider contingency plans.

Genoa Port and Astrup Fearnley Museum in Tjuvholmen Quarter by Renzo Piano

Option 2 Bank Loans

Bank loans are a traditional source of funding for entrepreneurs. Banks offer various loan options, including term loans, lines of credit, and equipment financing. The advantage of bank loans is that they are often easier to obtain than other forms of funding, and the entrepreneur does not have to give up equity in the company. However, bank loans may require collateral, and the entrepreneur must have a good credit score and a solid business plan to be approved.

Example: Richard Rogers, the founder of Rogers Stirk Harbour + Partners, started his firm in 1977 with two partners, using bank loans to purchase their first office space. The loans enabled them to establish their practice and invest in the necessary resources to grow their business.

Step-by-Step Guide:

1. Prepare a comprehensive business plan.
2. Ensure your credit score is in good standing.
3. Identify potential collateral for the loan.
4. Research and compare loan options from different banks.
5. Apply for the loan with all required documentation.

Useful Link: **Guide to Applying for a Small Business Loan**

Option 3 Private Equity

Private equity funding is when an investor provides capital to a business in exchange for an ownership stake. Private equity investors are typically high-net-worth individuals or institutional investors looking for high investment returns. The advantage of private equity is that it provides access to significant amounts of capital, which can be used to fuel growth and expansion. However, the entrepreneur will need to give up a portion of the company's ownership, and the investor may require a say in the company's management.

Example: Renowned architect Jean Nouvel demonstrated the strategic use of private equity in his projects. In the early 2000s, Nouvel sought to bring his innovative designs to life, including the iconic Louvre Abu Dhabi. To overcome financial constraints, he turned to private equity investors who recognized the value of his architectural vision. With their investment, Nouvel's creative ideas took form, resulting in architectural marvels that reshaped skylines and enriched cultural landscapes.

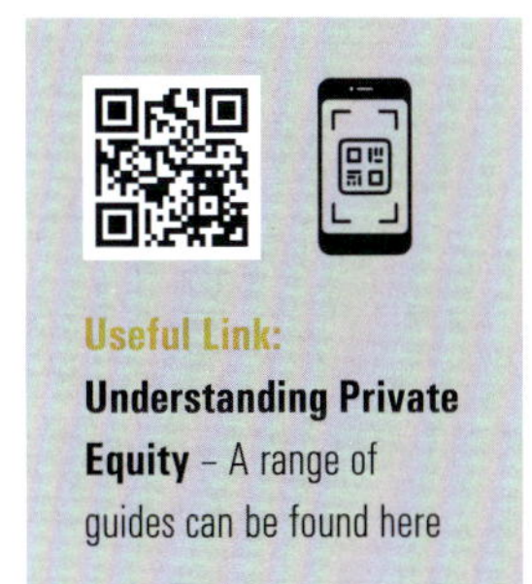

Useful Link: **Understanding Private Equity** – A range of guides can be found here

Step-by-Step Guide:

1. Prepare a compelling pitch and business plan.
2. Identify potential private equity firms or investors.

3. Network and build relationships with investors.
4. Negotiate terms and ownership stakes.
5. Finalize the investment agreement.

Option 4 Crowdfunding

Crowdfunding is a relatively new method of funding that involves raising capital from many people, typically through an online platform. Crowdfunding can take different forms, including rewards-based crowdfunding, equity crowdfunding, and debt crowdfunding. The advantage of crowdfunding is that it allows entrepreneurs to access capital without giving up equity or taking on debt. However, crowdfunding can be challenging to execute successfully, and the entrepreneur must have a compelling story and a solid marketing plan.

Example: In 2012, David Basulto launched a crowdfunding campaign to fund the development of an online platform to showcase architecture and design worldwide. The campaign was successful, and ArchDaily has since become one of the leading sources of architectural news and inspiration, with millions of monthly visitors.

Step-by-Step Guide:

1. Choose the right crowdfunding platform.
2. Create a compelling campaign with a clear goal and story.
3. Develop a marketing plan to promote the campaign.
4. Engage with your audience and provide updates.
5. Fulfill rewards and follow through on promises.

Useful Link: **Crowd Funding comparison platform**

Option 5 Grants and Subsidies

Grants and subsidies are a form of funding available to businesses in certain industries or regions. These funds are typically provided by governments or non-profit organizations and are designed to support innovation, research, and development. The advantage of grants and subsidies is that they do not need to be repaid and can provide significant financial support to the business. However, there is much competition for grants and subsidies, and the application process can be lengthy and complex.

Example: Alejandro Aravena, the founder of Elemental, received a grant to fund a project. In 2016, Aravena was awarded the Pritzker Architecture Prize, which includes a $100,000 grant to support a project of the laureate's choice. Aravena used the grant to fund a social housing project in his hometown of Santiago, Chile, providing affordable and sustainable housing to low-income families.

Step-by-Step Guide:

1. Research available grants and subsidies.
2. Prepare a detailed project proposal and budget.
3. Ensure compliance with eligibility criteria.
4. Submit the application with all required documentation.
5. Follow up and provide additional information if needed.

Useful Link:
Grant Opportunities for Architects –
See Funding Circle

Option 6 The Business Incubator

Business incubator buildings can be essential for start-ups and small businesses needing a dedicated space to work and grow their business. The Bower, where Allford Hall Monaghan Morris (AHMM), Hawkins\Brown, and ORMS shared a building, is an excellent example of a business incubator building that provided a collaborative environment and fostered a sense of community among different firms.

Such buildings can be especially valuable for architects who are starting their own firms. Business incubator buildings provide access to office space, shared resources, and professional networks that can be difficult to obtain independently. Architects can benefit from a collaborative environment that allows them to exchange ideas, share resources, and support one another as they grow their businesses. Business incubator buildings also often provide mentoring and coaching services to help entrepreneurs build their skills and develop their businesses. These resources can be invaluable for architects who may be skilled in design but need more business acumen to successfully launch and grow a practice.

Step-by-Step Guide:

1. Identify suitable business incubators in your area.
2. Apply to join the incubator with a detailed business plan.
3. Utilise shared resources and participate in networking events.
4. Seek mentoring and coaching from experienced professionals.
5. Collaborate with other start-ups and firms within the incubator.

Case Study Norma Merrick Sklarek & Patronage

Norma Merrick Sklarek's story is a powerful testament to what effort, talent, and the support of a patron can yield. Sklarek faced immense discrimination and challenges as a pioneering African American architect. Despite her impressive education and credentials, she struggled to secure architectural positions due to her gender and race. In the 1960s, Sklarek's fortunes began to change when she was introduced to the developer and real estate magnate William Pereira. Recognising her talent, Pereira hired Sklarek as the project director for the design of the Pacific Design Center in Los Angeles, California. This groundbreaking project made Sklarek the first African American woman to receive a license to practice architecture in the United States.

The Pacific Design Center project, completed in 1975, was a massive undertaking that consisted of multiple phases and buildings. Sklarek's leadership and design prowess were instrumental in its success. Her role in the project earned her recognition and respect within the architectural community, paving the way for more opportunities in the field. Sklarek went on to co-found one of the largest woman-owned architecture firms in the United States, leaving a legacy of resilience and achievement in the face of adversity. Pereira's belief in Sklarek's abilities not only propelled her career forward but also contributed to breaking down barriers for women and people of color in architecture.

2.2 // Choose Your Partners Carefully

(Tales from the Divorce Court)

Business partnerships can provide many benefits, including shared expertise, resources, and risk. However, they can lead to conflicts, financial losses, and legal disputes if not carefully chosen and managed. This section highlights the importance of good corporate governance and record-keeping in business partnerships and provides examples of architects whose business partnerships didn't work out.

The Importance of Good Corporate Governance and Record-Keeping

Good corporate governance and record-keeping are essential for any business partnership. Corporate governance refers to the rules, practices, and processes by which a company is directed and controlled. It ensures that a business is transparent, accountable, and responsible to all its stakeholders. It includes having a clear organisational structure, establishing roles and responsibilities, and maintaining accurate financial records. Record-keeping is also essential for business partnerships. Accurate record-keeping ensures that all transactions and decisions are properly documented, which can be critical in legal disputes, audits, or other investigations. It also helps partners track their financial performance, identify areas for improvement, and make informed decisions about the future of the business.

Essential Components of Good Corporate Governance:

- **Clear Organizational Structure:** Define roles and responsibilities to avoid confusion and overlap.
- **Regular Meetings:** Schedule regular meetings to discuss progress, resolve issues, and plan future actions.
- **Transparency:** Ensure that all partners have access to relevant information about the business.
- **Accountability:** Establish mechanisms to hold partners accountable for their actions and decisions.
- **Accurate Financial Records:** Maintain detailed and accurate financial records to track performance and facilitate audits.

// Examples of Architects Whose Business Partnerships Didn't Work Out

Case Study 1 Frank Lloyd Wright and William Masselink

Frank Lloyd Wright had a notoriously tumultuous relationship with his business partners, including William Masselink. Wright and Masselink formed a partnership in 1909 to develop and market Wright's designs, but the partnership quickly fell apart due to disagreements over finances, management, and design. Wright eventually bought out Masselink's share of the business and continued to work independently for the rest of his career.[1]

This case highlights the importance of aligning visions and expectations in a partnership and the potential consequences of failing to do so.

Lessons Learned:

- **Align Visions:** Ensure all partners share a common vision and goals.
- **Clear Agreements:** Have clear agreements regarding roles, responsibilities, and financial arrangements.
- **Regular Communication:** Maintain open and regular communication to address issues promptly.

[1] Gill, B., 1987. Many masks: a life of Frank Lloyd Wright. G P Putnam's Sons

The Gherkin London - Foster and partners

Case Study 2 Norman Foster and Ken Shuttleworth

In 2007, Norman Foster, the founder of Foster + Partners, faced legal action from his former business partner, Ken Shuttleworth. Shuttleworth had been a key figure at the firm for many years and played a vital role in its success. However, tensions arose, and Shuttleworth eventually left the firm to establish his own architectural practice, 'Make Architects'. Following his departure, Shuttleworth claimed that Foster had not upheld his side of an agreement regarding the ownership of certain projects and their associated profits. Shuttleworth filed a lawsuit against Foster, seeking financial compensation. The ensuing legal battle highlighted the importance of clear partnership agreements and communication within architectural firms. While the case was eventually settled out of court in 2009, it emphasised how disagreements among partners can escalate into legal proceedings if there are no formal agreements or clarity regarding ownership, responsibilities, and profit-sharing.[2]

Lessons Learned:

- **Formal Agreements:** Ensure that all agreements are documented and legally binding.
- **Clarity on Ownership:** Clearly define ownership and profit-sharing arrangements.
- **Conflict Resolution:** Establish mechanisms for resolving disputes amicably.

Case Study 3 Richard Rogers and Marco Goldschmied

Similarly, in 2019, the architect Richard Rogers was involved in a legal dispute with his business partner, Marco Goldschmied. Goldschmied had left the firm they co-founded, Rogers Stirk Harbour + Partners, and sought to sell his shares in the company. However, Rogers objected to the sale and took legal action to prevent it. The case was eventually settled, with Goldschmied selling his shares to Rogers.[3]

Lessons Learned:

- **Exit Strategy:** Have a clear exit strategy for partners leaving the firm.
- **Shareholder Agreements:** Ensure shareholder agreements cover all potential scenarios, including the sale of shares.
- **Dispute Prevention:** Proactively address potential disputes before they escalate.

Case Study 4 Daniel Libeskind and Bovis Lend Lease

In the early 2000s, renowned architect Daniel Libeskind faced significant challenges in his partnership with Bovis Lend Lease, the construction management firm selected to build the Freedom Tower at the World Trade Center site in New York City. Although Libeskind's groundbreaking design won the international competition, tensions quickly arose between him and the construction management firm regarding design changes, budget constraints, and project management.[4]

The conflict escalated to the point where Libeskind was effectively sidelined from the project, and significant modifications were made to his original design. This partnership breakdown underscored the importance of having clear agreements and understanding the roles and responsibilities of each party involved in a complex, high-profile project.[5]

Lessons Learned:

- **Clear Roles and Responsibilities:** Define and agree on the roles and responsibilities of each party from the outset.
- **Conflict Resolution Mechanisms:** Establish mechanisms for resolving conflicts before they escalate.
- **Respect for Vision:** Ensure all parties respect the original vision and design intent.

Case Study 5 Zaha Hadid and Patrik Schumacher

After the sudden death of Zaha Hadid in 2016, her firm Zaha Hadid Architects faced internal turmoil regarding the future direction of the company. Patrik Schumacher, Hadid's long-time partner and successor, sought to take the firm in a new direction, which caused significant friction with other senior members of the firm and Zaha Hadid's estate executors.[6]

[2] Moore, R. (2012). 'The Story of Ken Shuttleworth'. The Telegraph. Available at: https://www.telegraph.co.uk/culture/art/architecture/8998284/The-story-of-Ken-Shuttleworth.html

[3] Jenkins, S. (2019). 'Richard Rogers in Legal Battle Over Firm's Future'. The Guardian. Available at: https://www.theguardian.com/artanddesign/2019/nov/11/richard-rogers-in-legal-battle-over-firms-future

Heydar Aliyev Conference Centre, Baku, Azerbaijan Zaha Hadid Architects

The dispute revolved around differing visions for the firm's future, leading to public disagreements and legal challenges. This example highlights the critical importance of succession planning and having clear governance structures to manage transitions smoothly.[7]

Lessons Learned:

- **Succession Planning:** Develop a clear succession plan to ensure a smooth transition in leadership.
- **Governance Structures:** Establish governance structures that can manage internal disputes and differing visions.
- **Communication:** Maintain open and effective communication to align on the firm's future direction.

While partnerships can provide significant benefits, they also come with risks. By practicing good corporate governance, maintaining accurate records, and having clear agreements, architects can minimise risks and maximise their chances of success.

Heydar Aliyev Conference Centre, Baku, Azerbaijan

[4] Goldberger, P., 2005. Up from zero: politics, architecture, and the rebuilding of New York. Random House Trade Paperbacks.
[5] Ouroussoff, N. (2006). 'A Tower That Could Narrow the Gap Between Symbol and Substance'. The New York Times. Available at: https://www.nytimes.com/2006/04/27/arts/design/a-tower-that-could-narrow-the-gap-between-symbol-and-substance.html

Best Practices for Successful Business Partnerships

- **Due Diligence:** Conduct thorough due diligence before entering into a partnership. Understand the potential partner's strengths, weaknesses, and values.
- **Shareholder Agreement:** Have a detailed shareholder agreement outlining each partner's rights and responsibilities. Include provisions for decision-making, ownership, profit-sharing, and dispute resolution.
- **Communication:** Establish regular communication channels. Hold frequent meetings to discuss progress, resolve issues, and make decisions collaboratively.
- **Legal Advice:** Engage legal counsel to draft and review all partnership agreements and contracts.
- **Governance Framework:** Implement a strong corporate governance framework to ensure transparency, accountability, and effective decision-making.
- **Record-Keeping:** Maintain accurate and comprehensive records of all business transactions and decisions.
- **Exit Plan:** Develop an exit strategy for partners, detailing how departures will be handled to avoid conflicts and ensure a smooth transition.

2.3 // It's All in The Small Print

(Contracts / Copyright and Contentious Issues)

To succeed in the highly competitive and fast-paced architectural profession, architects must have strong design and technical skills and a good understanding of business contracts, copyright law, and how to deal with contentious issues that may arise in their practice.

Business Contracts

Business contracts define the terms and conditions of the business relationship between the architect and their clients, suppliers, contractors, and other parties involved in the project. Contracts also protect the interests of all parties involved and ensure that each party fulfils their obligations and responsibilities.

Architects need to understand the different types of business contracts and their contents, including terms and conditions, scope of work, payment terms, and dispute resolution mechanisms. They should also understand contract law and its practical application to ensure their contracts are enforceable and legally binding. It still amazes me how few professionals read their contracts and fully understand their scope of services before commencing work. In the same way that actors participate in table-reads before taking to the stage or film set, a Project Initiation Meeting (PIM) is an excellent way to get your team around the table to go through every part of a project scope and fully understand the responsibilities and services you are to provide.

[6] Barkham, P. (2016). 'The Cult of Zaha Hadid.' The Guardian. Available at: https://www.theguardian.com/artanddesign/2016/apr/05/cult-of-zaha-hadid

[7] Wainwright, O. (2016). 'Zaha Hadid Architects in Turmoil as Patrik Schumacher Angers Colleagues'. The Guardian. Available at: https://www.theguardian.com/artanddesign/2016/nov/25/zaha-hadid-architects-turmoil-patrik-schumacher-colleagues

A very common type of architecture contract is the owner-architect agreement. This outlines the architect's scope of work, payment terms, and project schedule. It also defines the architect's responsibilities, such as ensuring that the project complies with building codes and regulations, coordinating with contractors and other professionals, and delivering quality work. By having a well-drafted and comprehensive owner-architect agreement, architects can avoid misunderstandings, conflicts, and legal disputes.

Whilst the RIBA has published its own suite of documents for appointing architects on various project sizes, many clients prefer to have a bespoke set of professional appointment documents for their project teams. This is usually because it is easier to cross-reference scopes of services between consultants to ensure there are no gaps in service provision.

The common points of debate and discussion, however, remain:

- Limit of PI liability Required
- Net Contribution Clauses
- Number of Warranty assignments

Figure 6: Know your Copy-Rights!

Copyright Law

Copyright law protects creative works, including architectural designs, from unauthorised use, reproduction, or distribution. Architects need to understand copyright law and how it applies to their practice. They should also take steps to protect their intellectual property and avoid infringing on the rights of others.

One of the main challenges for architects is the thin line between inspiration and imitation. Architects often draw inspiration from existing designs, styles, and materials, which may lead to unintentional copyright infringement. To avoid this, architects should be careful when using existing works, ensure their designs are original, and seek legal advice when in doubt. Architects should also be aware of the different types of copyrightable works, such as drawings, plans, specifications, and models, and the duration of copyright protection. They should also consider registering their works with the relevant copyright office to strengthen their legal protection.

Copyright issues can arise in other areas as well:

[8] Barclays. (2015, July). Rise, created by Barclays. Retrieved from https://rise.barclays/

[9] EUR-Lex. (2015, January 28). Judgment of the Court (Fourth Chamber) of 28 January 2015, Harald Kolassa v Barclays Bank plc. Retrieved from https://eur-lex.europa.eu/

Case Study Rise vs Barclays Bank Plc

In April 2015, Barclays Bank Plc applied for a trademark of their new subsidiary Fintech company Rise.[8] The application was published in the Trademarks Journal in July 2015 for a specification of services in trademark class 35 (project and management consulting services). This was brought to my attention by our legal advisor, who monitors the protection of our trademark rights.

Our company objected to this application under the Trademarks Act 1994 based on an earlier trademark registration for the mark Rise under class 35 that we had made in September 2011. Our mark was disputed by Barclays, and the case went to the Technology Court. Extensive witness statements were made, and barristers were appointed. We were successful in our defense in this classification. Of note were the judges' comments that in assessing a mark, the 'visual, aural and conceptual similarities of the marks must be assessed by reference to the overall impressions created by them, bearing in mind their distinctive and dominant components' (Sabel BV v. Puma AG). Barclays was denied a mark under class 35 but was granted a trademark under class 43 for financial services (EUR-Lex, 2015).[9]

This was financially and emotionally costly, and very time-consuming, but ultimately a very educational experience.

Contentious Issues

Contentious issues are inevitable in any business, and architecture is no exception. Architects may face disputes with their clients, contractors, or other parties. These disputes may arise from delays, defects, cost overruns, or changes in project scope. Architects should understand dispute resolution mechanisms, such as mediation, arbitration, or litigation, to deal with contentious issues. They should also have a well-drafted dispute resolution clause in their contracts, which outlines the steps to be taken in case of disputes.

In addition to legal measures, architects should adopt a proactive approach to avoid contentious issues. This includes maintaining clear communication with all parties involved, documenting all decisions and changes, and managing expectations from the outset.

Case Study Frank Gehry and MIT

One notable illustrative example is the case of Frank Gehry and MIT.[10] In 2003, MIT commissioned Gehry to design a new building for the Stata Centre, completed in 2004. However, in 2007, MIT filed a lawsuit against Gehry's firm, alleging that the building was structurally unsound, had leaks and other defects, and that the firm had breached its contract by failing to deliver a quality building.

Ray and Maria Stata Center - Frank Gehry

Gehry's firm, in turn, countersued MIT, alleging that MIT had modified the building design without their consent and had infringed on their copyright by making unauthorised changes.[11] The legal dispute between Gehry and MIT lasted several years, resulting in millions of dollars in legal fees and damages. It highlights the importance of clear and comprehensive contracts, proper project management, and effective dispute resolution mechanisms in architecture.

The case also emphasised the need for architects to protect their intellectual property and be aware of copyright law. If Gehry's firm had registered its design with the relevant copyright office and had an explicit copyright clause in its contract with MIT, the copyright issue with MIT could have been avoided.

Architects need to understand business contracts, copyright law, and how to deal with contentious issues. Comprehensive and well-drafted contracts help architects avoid misunderstandings and conflicts with their clients, contractors, and other parties. Understanding copyright law and protecting intellectual property can help architects safeguard their designs and avoid infringement. Finally, by adopting a proactive approach to managing their projects and dealing with disputes, architects can ensure the success of their practice and maintain their reputation in the industry.

[10] Petrunia, P. (2010, April 14). Three years after suing Gehry, MIT settles with architect in Stata Center dispute. Archinect. Retrieved from https://archinect.com/news/article/98834/three-years-after-suing-gehry-mit-settles-with-architect-in-stata-center-dispute

[11] MIT News Office. (2010, March 30). Stata Center lawsuit amicably resolved. MIT News. Retrieved from https://news.mit.edu/2010/stata-lawsuit

NAVIGATING THE FINANCIAL LANDSCAPE

Key Learning Points //

- **Corporate Governance** is essential for transparency, accountability, and effective decision-making in business partnerships. It is important to have aligning visions and expectations to avoid conflict
- **Record-keeping:** Ensure all transactions and decisions are properly documented, which is critical in legal disputes and audits. This is crucial in maintaining transparency and accountability within partnerships.
- **Clear Agreements:** Detailed, legally binding partnership agreements help prevent conflicts and manage partnership expectations.
- **Choosing the Right Partners:** Conduct thorough due diligence, align visions, and establish clear roles and responsibilities to ensure successful collaborations.
- **Dispute Resolution:** Understand mediation, arbitration, and litigation mechanisms to address contentious issues.
- **Copyright Law:** Protecting intellectual property is essential. Knowing how to safeguard your designs and respect others' copyrights can prevent costly legal disputes.

FIRST DATE AND MAYBE EVEN A SECOND

De le Warr Pavillion by Mendelsohn & Chermayeff

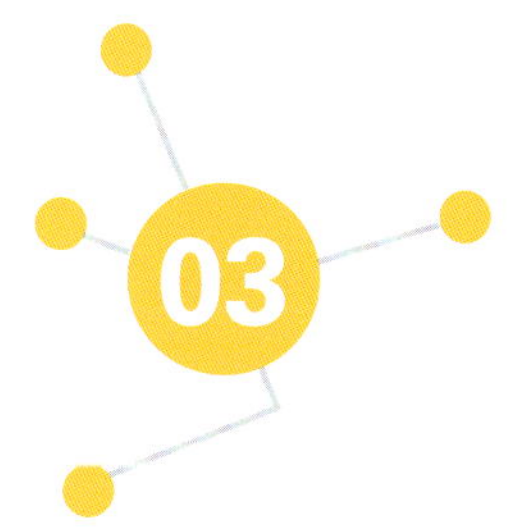

CHAPTER THREE

First Date and Maybe Even a Second

Architecture is a competitive profession, so securing new business and establishing strong client relationships is paramount. Chapter Three looks into the critical aspects of client engagement, starting with making a great first impression, conducting successful initial meetings, and maintaining momentum to secure follow-up interactions. The chapter emphasises the importance of thorough preparation, customised pitches, and strategic communication to ensure that architects capture the interest of potential clients and also lay the foundation for long-term, collaborative relationships.

Finally, the chapter discusses the importance of follow-up and continued engagement. It provides practical momentum-building strategies, such as prompt, personalised follow-ups, regular updates, and proactive problem-solving to strengthen client relationships and ensure project success.

3.1 // You never get a second chance to make a good first impression

(Conducting Successful First Meetings)

The first meeting with a potential client sets the stage for the project. Making a great first impression is crucial, as it establishes the foundation for trust, collaboration, and mutual understanding. Architects must employ effective strategies to ensure this initial interaction is positive, engaging, and leaves a lasting impression.

Preparation for First Meetings

Making a great first impression begins with professionalism and preparedness. Architects should arrive on time, dressed appropriately, and equipped with all necessary materials, such as portfolios, business cards, and presentation tools. According to Goman[1] non-verbal cues like punctuality, attire, and body language play a significant role in how others perceive us. By demonstrating professionalism through these cues, architects can establish credibility and earn the client's respect from the outset.

One effective technique for making a strong first impression is to start the meeting with a brief, well-prepared introduction. This introduction should succinctly cover the architect's background, experience, and the specific expertise they bring to the table. Highlighting past successes and relevant projects can help build the client's confidence in the architect's capabilities. As Bortz[2] suggests, a compelling introduction can capture the client's interest and set a positive tone for the rest of the meeting.

But remember you are there to talk about the client's project. Demonstrate a client-focused approach to help build rapport—the conversation should centre around the client's needs, goals, and vision for the project. Be measured in your presentation and avoid death by PowerPoint at all costs!

Understanding Client Needs and Market Trends

Thorough preparation is essential for making a strong first impression. By understanding the client's needs and the current market trends, architects can tailor their approach to address specific client concerns and demonstrate their knowledge and expertise.

- **Client Research:** Before the meeting, research the client's background, business, and past projects. Understand their values, goals, and the challenges they face. This will help you tailor your pitch and show that you are genuinely interested in their needs.
- **Market Trends:** Stay informed about the latest trends and developments in the architecture industry. Knowing market trends can provide valuable insights into what clients might be looking for and help you suggest innovative solutions that set you apart from competitors.
- **Competitor Analysis:** Understanding what your competitors are offering can help you identify gaps in the market and position your services more effectively. Highlighting your unique strengths can make a compelling case for why the client should choose your firm.

[1] Goman, C.K., 2011. The Silent Language of Leaders: How Body Language Can Help--or Hurt--How You Lead. John Wiley & Sons.
[2] Bowman, J.S., West, J.P., Berman, M. and Van Wart, M., 2016. The professional edge: Competencies in public service. Routledge.

3.2 // Hitting the Bullseye, Crafting Pitches that Resonate with Clients

(Customizing Pitches to Align with Client Goals)

During the initial meeting, actively listen to the client's goals and objectives. Ask questions that help you understand their vision and what they hope to achieve with the project. Based on the information gathered, tailor your proposal to align with their specific needs. Highlighting how your expertise and proposed solutions can directly benefit the client is more likely to resonate and be successful.

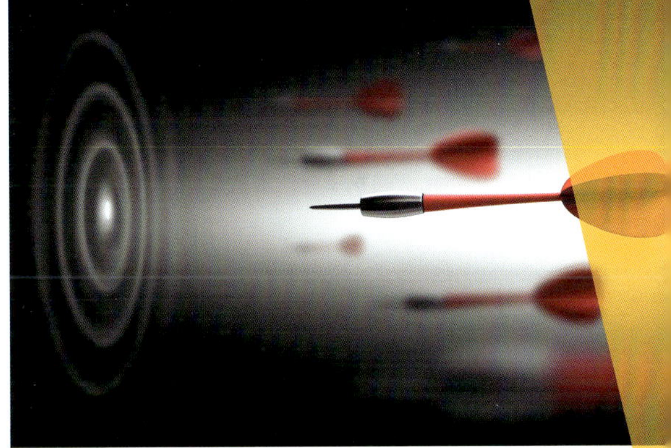

One effective strategy for customising pitches is aligning the proposal with the client's business goals. For instance, if the client is a retail company looking to redesign its flagship store, the architect should emphasise how the new design can enhance customer experience, increase foot traffic, and ultimately drive sales. By linking the architectural proposal to the client's business objectives, architects can demonstrate their understanding of the client's priorities and ability to deliver value beyond aesthetics.

According to Lewis and Bonollo,[3] visual representations, such as sketches, renderings, and 3D models can help clients visualise the proposed solutions and understand their potential impact. Architects should select project examples relevant to the client's industry and design preferences, showcasing their ability to handle similar projects successfully.

Clients may have specific budget limitations, regulatory requirements, or site constraints to consider. By proactively addressing these issues in the pitch, architects can demonstrate their problem-solving skills and commitment to finding practical solutions that meet the client's needs. This approach builds trust and shows that the architect is prepared to handle the project's challenges.[4]

Architects should articulate their ideas clearly and confidently, avoiding technical jargon that might confuse the client. Instead, they should focus on conveying the benefits of their proposals in straightforward terms that the client can easily understand. Clear and concise communication is key to ensuring that the client grasps the value of the proposed solutions and feels confident in the architect's ability to deliver.

[3] Lewis, W.P. and Bonollo, E., 2002. An analysis of professional skills in design: implications for education and research. Design studies, 23(4), pp.385-406.
[4] Guide, P.M.B.O.K., 2008. A guide to the project management body of knowledge. Project Management Inst.

Temporary Pavilion at the De La Warr Pavilion Bexhill - Niall McLaughlin Architects

Follow-Up Questions and Clarifications

Architects should encourage clients to ask questions and seek clarification throughout the meeting. This interactive dialogue ensures that clients fully understand the proposed designs and feel comfortable expressing their thoughts and concerns. By addressing these questions promptly and thoughtfully, architects can demonstrate their commitment to client satisfaction and their willingness to adapt and refine their proposals based on client input.[5]

Following Up

Maintaining momentum after the first meeting requires a strategic approach that combines effective communication, proactive follow-up, and continuous engagement. The following strategies can help architects secure follow-up meetings and ensure ongoing client involvement:

- **Prompt and Personalised Follow-Up:** According to Drucker,[6] timely and thoughtful follow-up can reinforce the positive impression made during the first meeting and set the stage for future interactions. Send a prompt and personalised follow-up email after the initial meeting. This email should thank the client for their time, summarise the key points discussed, and outline the next steps. Personalise the message by referencing specific details from the meeting to demonstrate your attentiveness and commitment.
- **Propose Specific Next Steps:** In the follow-up communication, propose specific next steps, such as scheduling a follow-up meeting to discuss detailed project requirements, presenting initial design concepts, or reviewing additional information provided by the client. By outlining clear and actionable next steps, you can create a sense of continuity and purpose, making it easier for the client to commit to further engagement.

5 Seitamaa-Hakkarainen, P., Viilo, M. and Hakkarainen, K., 2010. Learning by collaborative designing: Technology-enhanced knowledge practices. International Journal of Technology and Design Education, 20, pp.109-136.
6 Drucker, P.F., 2020. The essential Drucker. Routledge.

- **Regular Updates and Check-Ins:** Communicating regularly with the client between meetings keeps them engaged and informed. Provide regular updates on the progress of initial design concepts, industry trends, or relevant case studies to help sustain the client's interest and demonstrate the architect's proactive approach. According to Leonardi, et al.[7] consistent and transparent communication is key to building trust and fostering a collaborative relationship.
- **Utilise Collaborative Tools and Platforms:** Project management software, online collaboration platforms, and virtual design tools can facilitate ongoing engagement and make it easier for clients to provide feedback, review updates, and stay informed about project developments. These tools can enhance transparency and streamline communication, making coordinating follow-up meetings easier and ensuring the project remains on track.[8]
- **Addressing Client Concerns Proactively:** Architects can build trust and encourage the client to continue engaging with the project by demonstrating a proactive approach to addressing any concerns or questions the client raises after the initial meeting.[9] This might involve providing additional information, clarifying design concepts, or offering alternative solutions to address specific challenges.
- **Importance of a Follow-Up Meeting and Continued Engagement:** Securing a follow-up meeting after the initial client interaction is crucial for maintaining momentum and fostering a strong client-architect relationship. The follow-up meeting is an opportunity to build on the rapport established during the first interaction and delve deeper into the project's specifics. From experience, successful negotiations and collaborations often require multiple interactions, allowing both parties to understand each other's needs and expectations better.

During follow-up interactions, architects can motivate clients to remain actively engaged and committed to the project by showcasing the advantages of ongoing involvement.[10] This could involve highlighting the benefits of regular feedback, iterative design processes, and the opportunity for the client to shape the project's direction.

[7] Leonardi, P. M., Huysman, M., & Steinfield, C. (2013). Enterprise social media: Definition, history, and prospects for the study of social technologies in organizations. Journal of Computer-Mediated Communication, 19(1), 1-19.
[8] Majchrzak, A., Markus, M. L., & Wareham, J. (2016). Designing for digital transformation: Lessons for information systems research from the study of ICT and societal challenges. MIS Quarterly, 40(2), 267-278.
[9] Kelley, T. (2001). The Art of Innovation: Lessons in Creativity from IDEO, America's Leading Design Firm. Currency.
[10] Schön, D. A. (1983). The Reflective Practitioner: How Professionals Think in Action. Routledge

FIRST DATE AND MAYBE EVEN A SECOND
9 Key Learning Points //

1. **Thorough Preparation:** Research client backgrounds, understand their needs, and stay informed about market trends to tailor your approach effectively.
2. **Customised Pitches:** Align your proposals with client goals, demonstrating how your solutions can directly benefit them and address their specific needs.
3. **Active Listening:** Engage in active listening to show genuine interest in the client's objectives and concerns, fostering a sense of trust and collaboration.
4. **Professionalism:** Maintain a professional demeanour, including punctuality, appropriate attire, and preparedness with necessary materials.
5. **Clear Communication:** Use clear and concise language, avoiding technical jargon, to ensure the client easily understands your ideas and proposals.
6. **Visual Aids and Interactive Tools:** Utilise sketches, renderings, 3D models, and VR experiences to help clients visualise proposed solutions and engage more deeply with the project.
7. **Follow-Up Actions:** Send prompt, personalised follow-up communications summarising key discussion points and outlining the next steps to maintain momentum.
8. **Regular Updates:** Keep clients informed with regular updates on project progress, industry trends, or new ideas, reinforcing your commitment to their project.
9. **Securing a follow-up meeting:** After the initial client interaction, a follow-up meeting is crucial for maintaining momentum and fostering a strong client-architect relationship

Central St. Giles by Renzo Piano in London

ENCORE: KEEP THEM COMING BACK FOR MORE

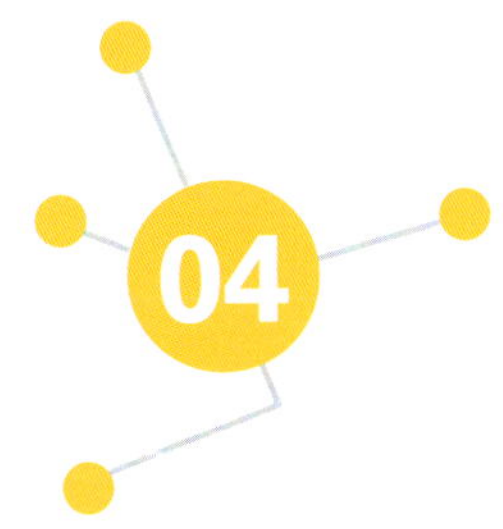

CHAPTER FOUR

Encore: Keep them Coming Back for More

In Chapter Four we delve into strategies and practices to help architects build lasting connections with their clients, ensuring not only repeat business but also a steady flow of referrals. This chapter underscores the importance of leveraging existing relationships to drive new business, presenting compelling evidence and practical examples.

We begin by exploring why it is generally easier and more cost-effective to generate new business from existing relationships rather than cultivating new ones. The chapter then transitions to practical strategies for architects, emphasising the importance of personalising interactions and maintaining constant engagement with clients. We then introduce the four pillars of a client-centric approach: Empathy, Active Listening, Client Education and Empowerment, and Proactive Problem-Solving. Each provides insights into how these principles can be applied to enhance client satisfaction and foster deeper connections.

4.1 // Hello Cold Caller

(It is easier to drive New Business from Existing Relationships)

Hello, Cold Caller

Building strong relationships is essential for success in architecture, as in most industries. Architects who already have robust connections with existing clients and partners hold a significant advantage, because generating business from existing relationships is generally more straightforward and cost-effective than cultivating new ones from scratch.

A primary reason it is easier to generate new business from existing relationships is the level of trust that has already been established. Trust is a critical component in any business relationship, and it is particularly important in architecture, where projects often involve significant financial investments and long-term commitments. According to

[1] Latham, S.M., 1994. Constructing the team. HMSO.

[2] Homburg, C., Wieseke, J. and Bornemann, T., 2009. Implementing the marketing concept at the employee-customer interface: the role of customer need knowledge. Journal of marketing, 73(4), pp.64-81.

Latham,[1] trust reduces perceived risk and uncertainty, facilitating smoother negotiations and project execution. Existing clients and partners are more likely to recommend an architect to their network if they have had a positive experience, creating a snowball effect that drives new business from a single relationship.

Architects who have worked with a particular client or partner already understand their needs, preferences, and working styles. This familiarity allows architects to tailor their approach to new projects or opportunities, making it more likely that they will win the business. Research by Homburg et al.[2] shows that familiarity enables more personalised service, which can significantly enhance client satisfaction and loyalty.

// Practical Tips for Leveraging Existing Relationships

Building and Maintaining Trust

- Deliver consistently high-quality work to reinforce your reliability.
- Be transparent and honest in all communications and dealings.
- Follow through on promises and commitments.

Staying Top-of-Mind

- Regularly update clients and partners on your latest projects and achievements through newsletters or social media.
- Host events or workshops to engage with clients and showcase your expertise.
- Send personalised messages or holiday greetings to maintain a personal connection.

Turning Successful Projects into New Opportunities

- Ask satisfied clients for testimonials or referrals.
- Conduct post-project reviews to gather feedback and identify areas for improvement.
- Offer to present completed projects to potential clients to demonstrate your capabilities.

How Can I Help you?

4.2 // How Can I Help You?

(The 4 Pillars of a Client-Centric Approach)

Understanding and addressing client needs is crucial in creating successful architectural projects. This means going beyond technical skills and design aesthetics to truly understand and respond to the client's unique architectural needs and aspirations.

[3] Goleman, D., 1998. Working with emotional intelligence. NY: Bantam Books.

[4] Celestin, M. and Vanitha, N., 2017. Breaking down silos: Collaborative strategies that actually work. International Journal of Applied and Advanced Scientific Research (IJAASR), 2(2), pp.391-397.

// The Four Pillars of a Client-Centric approach

Pillar 1 Empathy

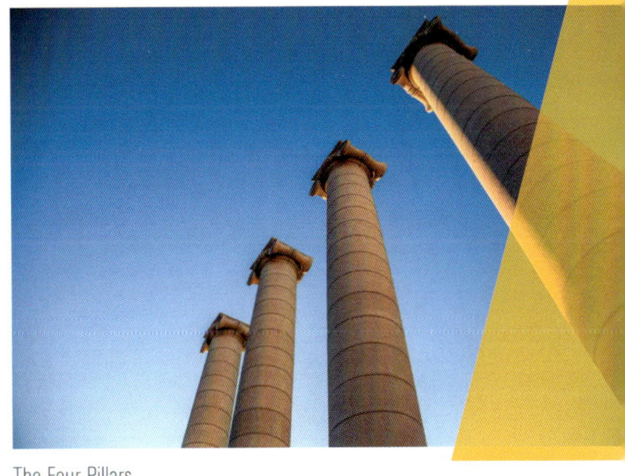
The Four Pillars

Empathy is an essential component of a client-centric approach in architecture. According to Goleman,[3] empathy is a key element of emotional intelligence, which involves being aware of, controlling, and expressing one's emotions and handling interpersonal relationships judiciously and empathetically. For architects, this means having an emotional and cognitive understanding of the client's experiences and feelings, and the personal significance of their projects. As Cooper and Evans[4] suggest, empathy bridges the gap between client expectations and the architect's vision. By understanding a client's emotional and psychological connection to their project, architects can create spaces that resonate more deeply with users.

Empathy

Empathy plays a vital role in building trust. Mayer[5] highlights that trust in professional relationships facilitates open communication and collaboration, which are crucial for the success of complex projects. Many architectural projects also carry emotional weight for clients. Understanding and acknowledging this can help architects deliver more satisfying results because clients who feel understood and valued are more likely to trust the architect's expertise and judgment.

Kosslyn et al.[6] suggest collaborative creativity thrives in environments where team members feel understood and supported. When architects demonstrate empathy, they encourage collaborative creativity with their clients, leading to a richer exchange of ideas and more personalised and innovative outcomes.

Moreover, empathy can significantly impact client satisfaction and loyalty. Empathetic interactions increase clients' satisfaction with the process and the final product. This often translates into client loyalty and advocacy. As Reichheld notes,[7] loyal clients are more likely to recommend a service they find deeply responsive to their needs, driving business growth through referrals.

[5] Mayer, R. C., Davis, J. H., & Schoorman, F. D. (1995). An integrative model of organizational trust. Academy of Management Review, 20(3), 709-734.
[6] Kosslyn, S.M. and Miller, G.W., 2015. Top brain, bottom brain: harnessing the power of the four cognitive modes. Simon and Schuster.
[7] Reichheld, F. F. (2003). The one number you need to grow. Harvard Business Review, 81(12), 46-55.

Architects can cultivate empathy by actively seeking to understand their clients' stories, backgrounds, and aspirations. This involves asking open-ended questions, listening without judgment, and showing genuine interest in the client's experiences and needs. Architects should also be aware of non-verbal cues, such as body language and tone of voice, which can provide additional insights into the client's emotional state.

Training in emotional intelligence can further enhance an architect's empathetic abilities. Programs that focus on developing skills like active listening, emotional regulation, and empathetic communication can be invaluable.

Pillar 2 **Active Listening**

Active Listening

Active listening begins with the listener's full presence in the conversation. Architects must set aside distractions and focus entirely on the client, ensuring that they capture not only the explicit content of the conversation but also the underlying emotions and concerns. According to Brownell[8] active listening is a dynamic and interactive process that involves paying attention, withholding judgment, reflecting, clarifying, summarising, and sharing. Each component plays a vital role in ensuring that the communication is effective, and that the client feels heard and understood.

Active listening significantly enhances the client-architect relationship. Clients who feel that their concerns and ideas are genuinely being listened to and considered, are more likely to engage openly and honestly. This can lead to a richer and more productive dialogue, enabling a deeper exploration of the client's needs and desires. One practical active listening technique is asking open-ended questions that encourage clients to share more about their vision and expectations. These often uncover detailed information that might not surface through simple yes-or-no inquiries. For instance, instead of asking, 'Do you like this design?' an architect might ask, 'How does this design align with your vision for the space?' to gather more comprehensive information.

Another active listening technique is reflecting and paraphrasing. By repeating back what the client has said in their own words, architects can ensure they have accurately understood the client's message. Active listeners might use phrases like, 'What I hear you saying is...' or 'It sounds like you're concerned about...' to demonstrate understanding and seek confirmation. This technique can also clarify any misunderstandings early in the conversation.

[8] Brownell, J. (2012). Listening: Attitudes, Principles, and Skills. Routledge

According to Mehrabian[9] non-verbal cues can convey more information than words alone. Architects must be attuned to their clients' body language, facial expressions, and tone of voice, to gather additional insights into their feelings. For instance, a client might verbally agree with a proposed design but show signs of hesitation through their body language. By noticing these cues, architects can address any underlying concerns before they become larger issues.

Active listening also involves providing constructive feedback. For example, if a client expresses concern about the environmental impact of a project, an architect might respond by discussing sustainable design options that address those concerns. This shows that the architect is listening and committed to finding solutions that meet the client's needs.[10] According to Carlson and Low,[11] clients who feel heard and understood are likelier to return for future projects and recommend the architect to others.

Pillar 3 Client Education and Empowerment

Educating clients about the architectural process demystifies the complexities of design and construction, making them feel more confident and involved in their projects. According to Mazur and Friar,[12] providing clients with a clear understanding of the architectural process, design principles, and sustainable practices can significantly enhance their trust and satisfaction. Empowering clients with knowledge equips them to participate more actively and make informed decisions, which fosters a sense of ownership and collaboration.

A key aspect of client education is explaining design principles in an accessible and engaging way. This involves breaking down complex architectural concepts into simple, understandable terms, such as explaining how natural light impacts a space's mood and energy efficiency. Schön[13] suggests that communicating design principles effectively can help clients appreciate the rationale behind design decisions and feel more connected to the project.

Client Education

With growing awareness of environmental issues, many clients are interested in incorporating sustainability into their projects but may not know where to begin. Educating clients about sustainable design practices, such as energy-efficient building systems, renewable materials, and green building certifications, empowers them to make more environmentally responsible choices and align their projects with greater sustainability goals.[14]

Empowering clients also means providing guidance on various design options and their implications, presenting various scenarios and explaining the benefits and trade-offs of each option, such as discussing the long-term cost savings of investing in high-quality insulation or the aesthetic and

[9] Mehrabian, A. (1971). Silent Messages. Wadsworth. [10] Dwyer, J., 2012. Communication for Business and the Professions: Strategies and Skills. Pearson Higher Education AU. [11] Mayer, J.D., Roberts, R.D. and Barsade, S.G., 2008. Human abilities: Emotional intelligence. Annu. Rev. Psychol., 59(1), pp.507-536. [12] Agarwal, N. and Rathod, U., 2006. Defining 'success' for software projects: An exploratory revelation. International journal of project management, 24(4), pp.358-370.
[13] Schön, D.A., 2017. The reflective practitioner: How professionals think in action. Routledge.

functional benefits of open-plan living spaces to help clients make decisions that best meet their needs and preferences.[15]

Client education and empowerment are vital in managing expectations and reducing potential conflicts. When clients are well-informed about what to expect at each project stage, they are less likely to encounter surprises that could lead to dissatisfaction or disputes. Clear, consistent communication about timelines, budgets, and potential challenges ensures clients have a realistic understanding of the project's scope and limitations.

In practice, holding a workshop at the beginning of the project to explain the design process and discuss initial ideas can set a positive tone for collaboration. Providing clients with detailed drawings and 3D models can help them visualize the final outcome and feel more engaged in the design process.[16] Interactive design software, online resources, and virtual reality (VR) technologies can provide clients with immersive experiences that deepen their understanding of architectural concepts and their specific projects, making the design process more transparent and interactive and fostering a stronger partnership between the architect and the client.[17]

Pillar 4 **Proactive Problem-Solving**

Problem Solving

Proactive problem-solving emphasises anticipating and addressing potential issues before they arise. It involves risk assessment, contingency planning, and transparent communication about potential challenges. Proactive problem-solving shows clients that their architect is vigilant, prepared, and dedicated to ensuring the project's success despite unforeseen obstacles.

Anticipating potential issues begins with a thorough understanding of the project's scope and the environment in which it will be executed. Architects must engage in comprehensive risk assessments that identify potential challenges early in the project lifecycle. According to Ward & Chapman,[18] risk assessments in project management involve identifying risks, analysing their potential impact, and developing mitigation strategies. In architecture, this could mean assessing environmental conditions, regulatory requirements, and stakeholder expectations to foresee any complications that might arise during the project.

Contingency planning involves developing alternative plans and strategies to address potential risks. Kerzner emphasises that contingency planning is about preparing for unexpected events and having predefined responses ready to implement.[19] For architects, this could include preparing for delays due to weather conditions, unforeseen site issues, or changes in client requirements. With contingency

[14] Guy, S. and Farmer, G., 2001. Reinterpreting sustainable architecture: the place of technology. Journal of Architectural Education, 54(3), pp.140-148. [15] Spector, T., 2012. The ethical architect: the dilemma of contemporary practice. Chronicle Books. [16] Whitney, D.E., 1990. Designing the design process. Research in engineering design, 2(1), pp.3-13. [17] Al-Qawasmi, J., 2005. Digital media in architectural design education: Reflections on the e-studio pedagogy. Art, Design & Communication in Higher Education, 4(3), pp.205-222.

plans, architects can quickly adapt to changing circumstances without significant disruptions to the project timeline or budget.

Architects should regularly review and update their risk assessments and contingency plans throughout the project based on new information and developments. This ongoing vigilance ensures that potential issues are identified and addressed promptly, minimizing their impact on the project.

Proactive problem-solving includes transparent communication about potential challenges. According to Olander,[20] this can significantly improve stakeholder satisfaction and project outcomes. For architects, this means being upfront about foreseeable issues and regularly updating clients on progress and changes in the risk landscape, and measures being taken to mitigate them.

As Turner[21] notes, proactive risk management is critical for delivering projects on time, within budget, and to the required quality standards. In practice, regular team meetings and project reviews can help identify potential issues early. Engaging with all stakeholders, including clients, contractors, and regulatory bodies, can provide valuable insights into potential risks and effective mitigation strategies. Project management software enhances proactive problem-solving by providing tools for risk assessment, contingency planning, and communication.

[18] Ward, S. and Chapman, C., 2003. Transforming project risk management into project uncertainty management. International journal of project management, 21(2), pp.97-105.

[19] Kerzner, H., 1989. A systems approach to planning, scheduling, and controlling. Project management, pp.759-764.

[20] Olander, S. and Landin, A., 2005. Evaluation of stakeholder influence in the implementation of construction projects. International journal of project management, 23(4), pp.321-328.

[21] Turner, J.R., 2009. The handbook of project-based management. The McGraw-Hill Companies, Inc.

ENCORE: KEEP THEM COMING BACK FOR MORE

Key Learning Points //

Techniques for Active Listening and Empathy

- Maintain eye contact and nod to show you are engaged.
- Repeat back what the client has said to confirm understanding.
- Avoid interrupting while the client is speaking.

Empathy

- Put yourself in the client's shoes and consider their perspective.
- Acknowledge their emotions and validate their feelings.
- Show genuine concern for their needs and aspirations.

Questions to Ask to Better Understand Client Needs

- What are your primary goals for this project?
- Can you describe any specific preferences or requirements you have in mind?
- What challenges have you faced in previous projects?
- How do you envision the final outcome of this project?
- Are there any particular styles or elements that you are drawn to?

Personalisation Techniques: Personalising your interactions shows clients that you value them as individuals and are committed to addressing their unique needs. This approach can significantly enhance trust and satisfaction.

- Address clients by their names and remember details about their lives and preferences.
- Tailor your communication style to match theirs, whether formal or casual.
- Offer personalised solutions that align with their specific needs and goals.

Building Trust and Understanding

- Be transparent about your process and timelines.
- Keep clients informed about project progress and any potential issues.
- Follow up after project completion to ensure satisfaction and gather feedback.

Educating and Empowering Clients

- Conduct workshops to explain the architectural process, design principles, and sustainable practices.
- Use visual aids, such as drawings, 3D models, and virtual tours, to help clients understand complex concepts.
- Share informative articles, videos, and guides about architecture and design.
- Create a client-friendly handbook that outlines key aspects of the project process.
- Invite clients to site visits and design review meetings.
- Encourage clients to ask questions and provide feedback at every stage.

Proactive Problem-Solving

Risk Assessment

- Conduct comprehensive risk assessments at the start of the project to identify potential challenges.
- Regularly update risk assessments based on new information and developments.
- Contingency Planning
- Develop contingency plans for identified risks, outlining alternative strategies and solutions.
- Ensure that contingency plans are communicated clearly to the client and all project stakeholders.

Transparent Communication

- Keep clients informed about potential risks and the measures to mitigate them.
- Provide regular updates on project progress and any changes in the risk landscape.

Effective, long term client relationships are about building trust, demonstrating value, and fostering collaboration throughout each project lifecycle. By following the strategies outlined in this chapter, architects can ensure they meet and exceed client expectations, paving the way for repeat business and positive referrals.

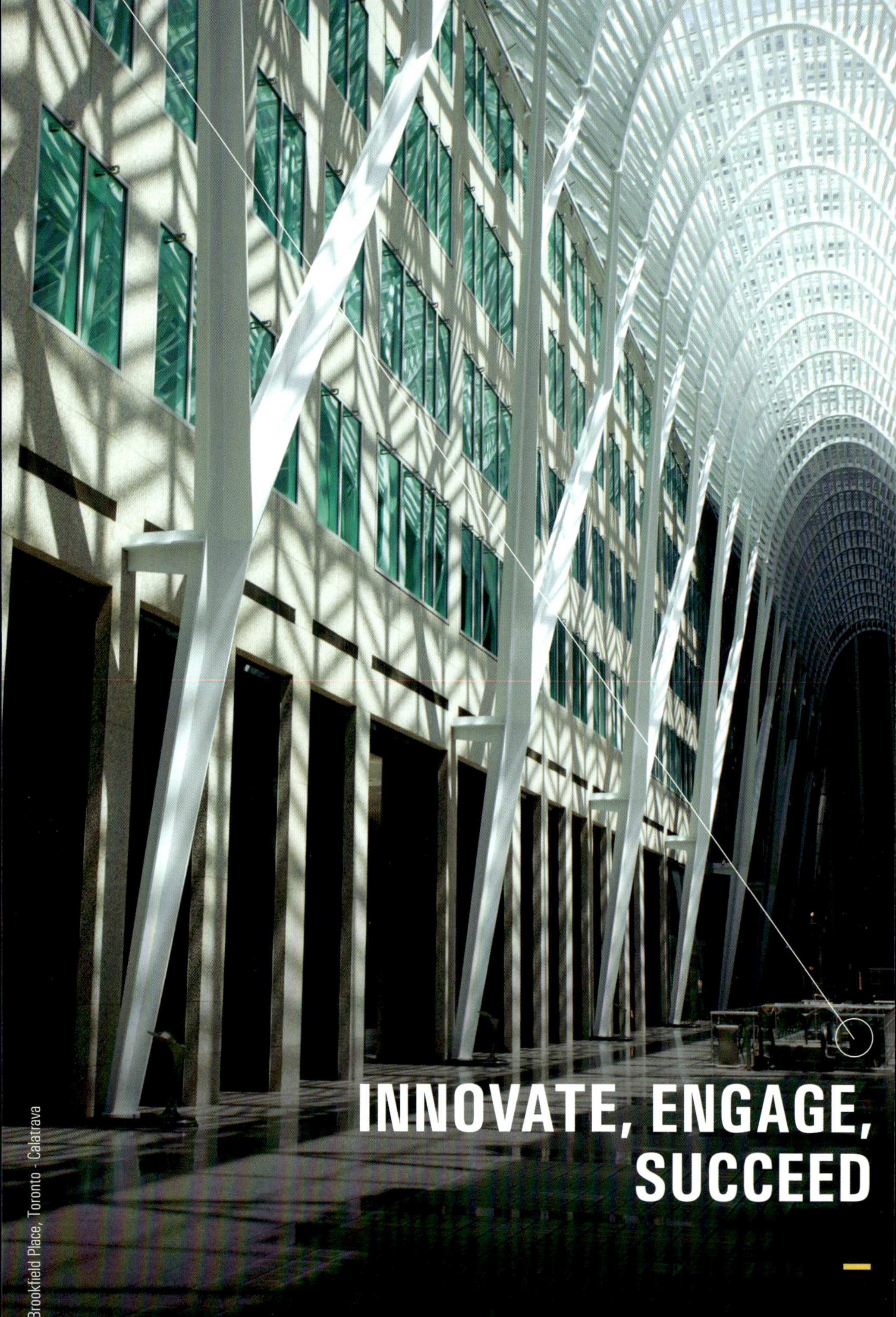

INNOVATE, ENGAGE, SUCCEED

Brookfield Place, Toronto - Calatrava

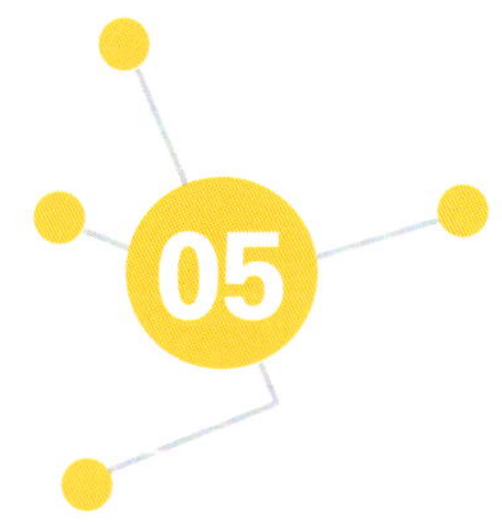

CHAPTER FIVE

Innovate, Engage, Succeed: Avoiding Pitfalls and Fostering Loyalty

Chapter Three discussed client engagement and Chapter Four offered strategies to help architects build long-lasting connections with clients. Chapter Five addresses strategic client relationship management, emphasising the importance of vigilance against complacency, avoiding common mistakes, integrating effective business management practices and the strategic use of technology. Architects can enhance client satisfaction, foster loyalty, and drive business growth by focusing on these key areas.

5.1 // The Complacency Trap:

(Don't Take Your Eye Off the Ball)

When architects become complacent, they risk taking their clients for granted; over time, this erodes trust and satisfaction, driving clients to seek more attentive competitors. Complacency can thus create a dangerous feedback loop where reduced client engagement leads to declining service quality and even less client engagement.

Complacency can arise from the assumption that existing clients will remain loyal without continuous effort. Reichheld[1] states client loyalty is built on consistent, high-quality interactions. He emphasises that retaining clients requires as much effort as acquiring new ones, highlighting that complacency can be just as detrimental as losing a new client lead. Additionally, complacency can lead to missed opportunities for upselling or cross-selling services, further limiting business growth.[2] Word-of-mouth referrals are crucial in architecture, where personal recommendations often influence client decisions. Studies show dissatisfied clients are more likely to share their negative experiences. Negative reviews and diminished referrals can spread rapidly in professional networks, significantly harming a firm's reputation[3] and ultimately affecting the firm's ability to attract new clients.

Complacency can result in failure to innovate. When architects become too comfortable, they might cease staying abreast of the latest knowledge and trends, and their designs may become

[1] Reichheld, F.F., 2003. The one number you need to grow. Harvard business review, 81(12), pp.46-55..
[2] Gronroos, C., 1994. From marketing mix to relationship marketing: Towards a paradigm shift in marketing. Asia-Australia Marketing Journal, 2(1), pp.9-29.
[3] Anderson, E.W., 1998. Customer satisfaction and word of mouth. Journal of service research, 1(1), pp.5-17.
[4] Drucker, P.F., 1986. Innovation and entrepreneurship: practice and principles. Harper & Row.

old-fashioned. Drucker[4] notes that continuous innovation is essential for staying relevant in any industry where more dynamic competitors are constantly evolving and improving their offerings.

Complacency

When leadership displays a complacent attitude, it can undermine internal team dynamics, leading to a general decline in motivation and productivity. Mediocrity becomes acceptable, further eroding the quality of work delivered to clients. Complacency can also hinder the ability to respond when the market or a client's needs change. According to Kotter,[5] the ability to change and adapt is critical to long-term success in any industry. Maintaining a proactive stance towards client engagement and market trends is essential for sustained growth and competitiveness.

// Practical Tips for Avoiding Complacency

Continuous Engagement Strategies

- **Regular Check-Ins:** Schedule periodic meetings with clients to discuss project progress and address concerns. This demonstrates commitment and provides opportunities to identify and resolve issues early.
- **Personalised Communications:** Tailor communications to individual clients, addressing their needs and preferences.
- **Client Feedback Loops:** Implement mechanisms for regularly gathering client feedback. Use this feedback to keep improving service delivery.

Keeping Up with Industry Trends and Innovations

- **Professional Development:** Encourage team members to keep skills and knowledge up-to-date by attending industry conferences, workshops, and training sessions.
- **Research and Development:** Invest in R&D to explore new materials, technologies, and design approaches. Sharing these innovations with clients can enhance their trust and confidence in the firm's capabilities.
- **Networking:** Engage with industry peers through professional organisations and social media to provide insights into emerging trends and best practices that can be shared with clients.

By implementing these strategies, architects can avoid the complacency trap and ensure that their client relationships remain strong and productive.

5.2 // Common Mistakes

(........and How to Avoid Them)

Relationship management is critical in architecture, but common mistakes can undermine your efforts. One pitfall is failing to set clear expectations with clients. Misunderstandings can arise without well-defined project scopes, timelines, and deliverables, leading to dissatisfaction and conflicts. Clients may assume certain aspects are included in the project when they are not or misunderstand the time and resources required for specific phases. Such lack of clarity can lead to scope creep, where clients continuously request additional work not originally planned, straining resources and extending timelines.

Another mistake is neglecting regular communication. Clients expect timely updates on project progress, and not getting them can cause anxiety and frustration. Transparent and consistent communication is vital for maintaining client trust and satisfaction. Regular updates, even to inform clients the project is on track, are reassuring and help prevent doubts about its status. Without updates, clients might assume the worst, leading to unnecessary stress.

Overpromising and underdelivering is a significant mistake. While it might be tempting to make ambitious promises to win a project, failing to meet them can severely damage a firm's reputation. Setting realistic expectations and delivering on them is crucial for long-term client relationships,[5] and clients are more likely to appreciate honest assessments and realistic timelines over promises that lead to disappointments. This approach builds a foundation of trust, where clients feel confident in the firm's ability to deliver what has been agreed upon. A lack of follow-up after project completion is also a mistake. Post-project follow-ups can provide valuable feedback and reinforce client relationships, showing that the firm cares about the client's satisfaction even after the project is finished. According to Kotler,[6] this can lead to repeat business and referrals. By neglecting follow-ups, firms miss out on opportunities to learn from their experiences and to demonstrate their commitment to long-term client care.

Client feedback is essential for continuous improvement and a better understanding of client needs. When firms disregard client feedback out of complacency they miss the chance to improve, and also signal to clients that their opinions are not valued. Implementing a structured feedback process helps gather insights that can be used to refine services and processes, ultimately leading to higher client satisfaction.[7]

[5] Kotler, P., Keller, K.L., Brady, M., Goodman, M. and Hansen, T., 2016. Marketing Management 3rd edn PDF eBook. Pearson Higher Ed..
[6] Aaker, D.A. and Moorman, C., 2023. Strategic market management. John Wiley & Sons.
[7] Reichheld, F.F., 2003. The one number you need to grow. Harvard business review, 81(12), pp.46-55.

Case Study The Leadenhall Building by Rogers Stirk Harbour + Partners

The Leadenhall Building, also known as the 'Cheesegrater', is a prominent skyscraper in London designed by Rogers Stirk Harbour + Partners (RSHP). This case study examines the challenges faced during its construction, highlighting issues related to communication, project delays, and scope management, and the subsequent strategies employed by RSHP to overcome them.

The 'Cheesegrater' on Leadenhall St - Rogers Harbour Stirk

Background and Challenges

British Land commissioned the building, at 122 Leadenhall Street in the City of London. The project was much anticipated due to its unique design and significant impact on the London skyline. However, several challenges tested the firm's project management and client relationship capabilities.[8]

Initially, RSHP set ambitious timelines to meet the client's expectations and secure the project, but the site's complexity and unforeseen regulatory requirements caused significant delays. The project's unique slanted design, intended to preserve the sightlines of St. Paul's Cathedral, introduced additional engineering challenges that were not fully anticipated during the planning phase.[9]

Furthermore, the project scope was not clearly defined at the outset. British Land frequently requested additional features and modifications as construction progressed, leading to scope creep. This strained the project's budget and timeline, frustrating both the client and the firm. A lack of regular and transparent communication exacerbated these issues, leading to a strained relationship between RSHP and British Land.[10]

[8] 'The Leadenhall Building' Rogers Stirk Harbour + Partners, www.rsh-p.com/projects/the-leadenhall-building.
[9] Eastman, C.M., 2011. BIM handbook: A guide to building information modeling for owners, managers, designers, engineers and contractors. John Wiley & Sons.

Recovery and Lessons Learned

To address these issues, RSHP implemented several strategies to improve communication and project management:

- **Comprehensive Review and Realignment:** RSHP held a comprehensive review meeting with British Land to openly discuss the challenges and develop a realistic revised timeline and budget. This helped realign the project goals with the client's expectations and set a new path forward. The firm's transparency in acknowledging the issues and willingness to collaborate on solutions helped rebuild trust.
- **Enhanced Communication Plan:** RSHP introduced a robust communication plan that included weekly updates on the project's progress to provide detailed information about the work completed, upcoming tasks, and any potential issues. Visual aids such as 3D models and site photographs were used to help the client visualize progress and understand the project's status. Regular status meetings were also scheduled to address any new concerns promptly.[11]
- **Stringent Project Scoping Procedures:** RSHP implemented detailed project scoping procedures to manage scope creep. They developed comprehensive project charters outlining the scope, budget, and timeline. Any changes to the project were documented and required client approval through a formal change management process. This ensured that all parties were aware of the implications of changes and agreed on the necessary adjustments before proceeding.
- **Investment in Training:** RSHP invested in training for their project managers and design team on effective project management and communication skills. This emphasised setting realistic expectations, maintaining transparency, and managing client relationships throughout the project lifecycle.
- **Leveraging Technology:** The firm also leveraged Building Information Modeling (BIM) to enhance project planning and coordination. BIM allowed detailed visualization and integration of various project aspects, improving stakeholder communication and reducing errors. Client portals and collaboration platforms were used to facilitate real-time communication and document sharing, ensuring that British Land was always informed and involved in the project process.

Reflection

The Leadenhall Building experience underscores the critical importance of clear communication, realistic timelines, and effective scope management in maintaining strong client relationships. By acknowledging and addressing communication and project management issues proactively, firms can rebuild trust and ensure successful project outcomes. Integrating advanced technologies such as BIM and maintaining transparency with clients are essential strategies for managing complex projects and fostering long-term client relationships.

[10] Azhar, S., 2011. Building information modeling (BIM): Trends, benefits, risks, and challenges for the AEC industry. Leadership and management in engineering, 11(3), pp.241-252. [11] Whyte, J., 2007. Virtual reality and the built environment. Routledge.

// Practical Tips for Avoiding Mistakes

Strategies for Proactive Management

- **Set Clear Expectations:** Develop detailed project charters that outline scope, deliverables, timelines, and budgets. Ensure that the client reviews and agrees to these documents before the project commences.
- **Regular Communication:** Establish a communication plan with regular updates and client check-ins. Use project management software to track progress and share updates transparently.
- **Manage Scope Creep:** Implement a formal change management process to handle any modifications to the project scope. Ensure all changes are documented, approved by the client, and reflected in the project timeline and budget.

Best Practices for Maintaining Strong Relationships

- **Build Trust Through Consistency:** Consistently deliver on promises and maintain high quality standards. This builds client trust and reinforces the firm's reputation for reliability.
- **Foster Transparency:** Be open and honest about potential challenges and how they will be addressed. This transparency helps manage client expectations and builds credibility.
- **Seek Continuous Improvement:** Regularly evaluate client feedback and use it to improve processes and services. Show clients that their input is valued and acted upon, which strengthens the relationship.

Conclusion

Chapter Five underscores the importance of avoiding complacency, learning from common mistakes, and integrating effective business management practices and technology to maintain strong client relationships. By maintaining vigilance against complacency, architects can prevent the erosion of trust and satisfaction that often drives clients to competitors. Clear expectations, regular communication, and a proactive approach to client feedback are essential strategies to avoid common pitfalls in relationship management.

AVOIDING PITFALLS AND FOSTERING LOYALTY

9 Key Learning Points //

- **Avoid Complacency:** Continuous engagement and proactive relationship management are essential to prevent complacency and ensure client satisfaction.
- **Set Clear Expectations:** Develop detailed project charters outlining scope, deliverables, timelines, and budgets to avoid misunderstandings and scope creep.
- **Regular Communication:** Establish a communication plan with regular updates and client check-ins to maintain transparency and trust.
- **Manage Scope Creep:** Implement a formal change management process to handle modifications to the project scope effectively.
- **Professional Development:** Encourage team members to attend industry conferences and training sessions to stay updated with the latest trends and technologies.
- **Client Feedback Loops:** Implement mechanisms for regularly gathering and acting on client feedback to continuously improve service delivery.
- **Financial Transparency:** Maintain detailed budget reports and cost forecasts to build client trust and ensure effective project management.
- **Personalised Client Interactions:** Use CRM systems to track client interactions and preferences, enabling personalised and tailored service.
- **Continuous Improvement:** Regularly evaluate and refine business practices based on client feedback and performance data to enhance client satisfaction and project outcomes.

KEEPING IT ALL IN CHECK

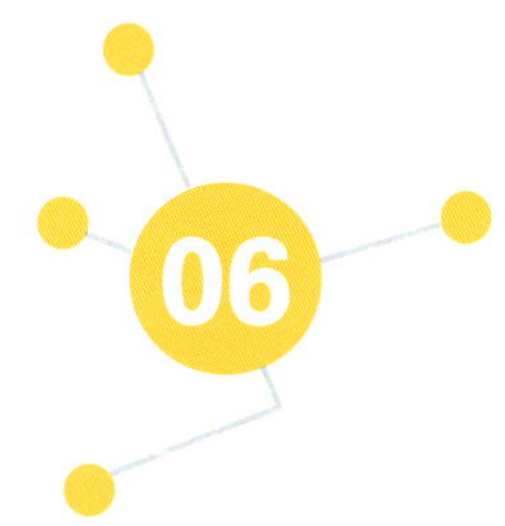

CHAPTER SIX

Keeping It All In Check

Chapter Six explores the essential practices that underpin a thriving architecture firm, providing a comprehensive guide to creating a culture of balanced and sustainable growth. It highlights how effective business strategies and the strategic integration of cutting-edge technology can strengthen client relationships, improve operational efficiency, and drive long-term success. The chapter also emphasises the role of key performance indicators (KPIs) in measuring and optimising performance. By focusing on key metrics and tracking progress, architects can identify how well the business is doing and make data-driven decisions to improve their business performance.

6.1 // Balancing Acts

(Mastering Business Management)

Effective business management is integral to maintaining strong client relationships. Well-managed operations provide a stable foundation, allowing architects to focus on creative and client-facing work while ensuring professional, organised, and efficient client interactions to create an environment where clients feel valued and confident in the firm's ability to deliver on its promises. Key practices—such as clear organisational structures, robust financial management, and efficient operational processes—ensure projects are completed on time, within budget, and to the client's satisfaction.

Clear organisational structures define roles and responsibilities within a firm. When team members know their duties and how they contribute to the project, communication and decision-making processes are streamlined. Robust financial management ensures projects stay within budget, further building client trust and satisfaction. Integrating relationship management into business practices via regular client surveys, feedback loops, and dedicated client relationship management (CRM) systems enables firms to tailor their services to meet specific client needs and expectations. By formalising feedback processes, architects can monitor client satisfaction and improve outcomes, demonstrating a commitment to client satisfaction and continuous improvement.

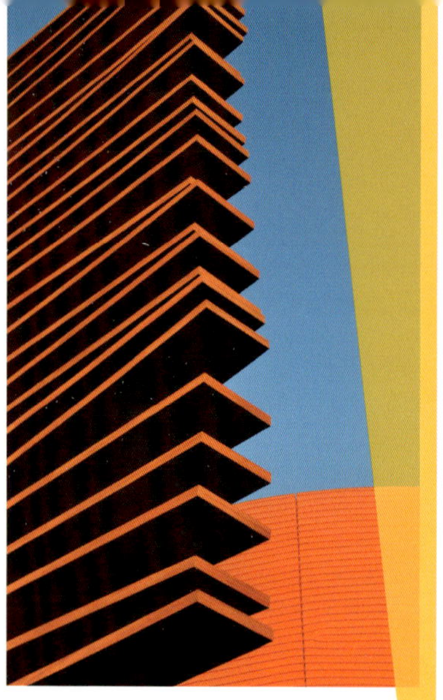

The Balancing Act

Efficient operational processes, including streamlined workflows, effective use of technology, and regular performance evaluations are essential for architecture firms. Streamlined workflows ensure every project phase is meticulously planned and executed to minimise delays and errors. Technology, like project management software and collaborative platforms, can facilitate real-time communication and document sharing among team members and clients.[1] Regular performance evaluations help maintain high standards of service delivery. This ensures that projects stay on track and reinforces a culture of accountability and excellence. Sound financial management, including careful budgeting and regular financial reviews, supports the firm's financial health. This allows firms to reinvest in their operations by upgrading technology, training staff, or expanding services, which can enhance client satisfaction and loyalty.

// Practical Tips for Effective Business Management

Techniques for Improving Business Management

- **Implement CRM Systems:** Use CRM software to track client interactions, manage contact information, and monitor feedback to maintain organised and efficient communication with clients.
- **Utilise Project Management Tools:** Invest in project management software tools like Trello, Asana, and Microsoft Project to track project progress, allocate resources, and provide real-time updates.
- **Adopt Financial Management Practices:** Use accounting software to track expenses, ensure accurate budgeting, forecasting, and financial reporting.

Tools and Technologies for Better Management Practices

- **Collaborative Platforms:** Use Slack or Microsoft Teams for internal communication and collaboration to facilitate quick information sharing and decision-making.
- **Client Portals:** Develop portals that provide secure access to project documents, progress reports, and communication logs. This transparency enhances client trust and satisfaction.
- **Data Analytics:** Leverage data analytics tools to gain insights into project performance, client satisfaction, and operational efficiency in order to make informed business decisions.

[1] Kerzner, H., 2009. Project Management: A systems approach to planning, scheduling, and controlling. Wiley.

6.2 // Tech Toys and Real Joys

(Strategic Technology Investment)

Technology is pivotal to supporting relationship management in architecture. Technological tools can streamline communication, enhance collaboration, and improve client satisfaction. By leveraging technology, architects can offer more accurate project updates, faster response times, greater efficiency, and a more transparent and engaging client experience, crucial for building and maintaining strong client relationships.

Tools like Building Information Modeling (BIM) enable detailed and accurate project planning and visualisation, and improve communication and coordination among project stakeholders, so reducing errors and improving project outcomes. BIM software provides a comprehensive platform where architects can integrate various aspects of the design and construction process while offering clients a transparent view of the project, which helps manage expectations and build trust. Additionally, client portals and collaboration platforms facilitate real-time communication and document sharing, allowing clients to access project updates, review documents, and provide feedback at their convenience, which enhances their sense of involvement and control over the project.

Clean Modern Tech

Virtual Reality (VR) and Augmented Reality (AR) are transformative for client engagement. VR and AR offer immersive virtual walk-throughs that help clients visualise the outcome of proposed designs more accurately and provide more informed feedback. Realistic design representation also enables adjustments before construction begins, enhancing client satisfaction. Additionally, project management software like Asana, Trello, and Microsoft Project can streamline task allocation, deadline tracking, and team collaboration, ensuring efficient project management and maintaining transparency and trust throughout the project lifecycle.

Customer Relationship Management (CRM) systems enable architects to tailor their services to meet specific client needs and expectations. CRM systems support personalised service by maintaining detailed client histories and preferences, significantly enhancing client satisfaction and loyalty. Digital technology improves operational efficiency through automated workflows and digital documentation, reducing the time spent on administrative tasks. Data analytics tools further boost productivity by providing insights into project performance, client satisfaction, and market trends. By analysing data from past projects, firms can identify patterns and areas for improvement, enabling them to make data-driven decisions that enhance project outcomes and client satisfaction.[2]

[2] Davenport, T.H. and Harris, J.G., 2007. Competing on analytics: the new science of winning. Harvard Business Review press, Language, 15(217), p.24.

Bobby Moore Academy School, Stratford - Perkins and Will

Case Study Leveraging Technology to Enhance Client Relationship Management in Architecture

This case study examines how Perkins and Will, a global architecture firm, successfully leveraged technology to improve client engagement, communication, and satisfaction, ultimately leading to better project outcomes and a stronger competitive position in the market.

Background: Established in 1935, Perkins and Will is renowned for its innovative designs and commitment to sustainability. With a diverse portfolio that spans healthcare, education, commercial, and residential projects, the firm has always prioritised client satisfaction and project excellence. However, as the firm expanded globally, maintaining consistent and effective client communication became increasingly challenging. Perkins and Will embarked on a strategic initiative to integrate advanced technology into their client relationship management processes.

// Implementation of Building Information Modeling (BIM):

Perkins and Will adopted BIM.

Benefits Realised

- **Enhanced Visualisation:** BIM enabled Perkins and Will to create highly detailed and accurate visualisations of their designs. Clients could virtually explore these models, and the immersive experience helped bridge the gap between client expectations and the actual design, significantly improving client satisfaction.

- **Improved Coordination:** BIM facilitated better coordination among architects, engineers, and contractors by integrating various facets of the project into a single model. This reduced the likelihood of errors and conflicts, ensuring smoother project execution. Clients appreciated the seamless process, which enhanced their trust in the firm's capabilities.
- **Real-Time Updates:** BIM permits real-time updates to the design model. Any changes made were instantly reflected across the project, ensuring that all stakeholders always worked with the most current information. This transparency and accuracy were critical in maintaining client confidence and satisfaction.

// Adoption of Client Portals and Collaboration Platforms

Perkins and Will implemented client portals and collaboration platforms to further enhance client engagement.

Benefits Realised

- **Centralised Communication:** Client portals served as a centralised, single point of access for all project-related information, streamlining communication and reducing the risk of information silos. Clients could log in at their convenience to review progress reports, access design documents, and communicate with the project team.
- **Enhanced Collaboration:** Features like instant messaging, video conferencing, and collaborative document editing enabled more interactive and efficient discussions among project stakeholders. Clients could actively participate in design reviews and provide immediate feedback, fostering a more collaborative relationship.
- **Increased Transparency:** Perkins and Will ensured high transparency by providing clients with real-time access to project updates and documents. Clients could track the project's progress, understand the rationale behind design decisions, and see how their feedback was being incorporated. This transparency was crucial in building trust and confidence in the firm's processes.

// Integration of Virtual Reality (VR) Technology

Perkins and Will also explored using VR technology to create immersive design experiences for their clients.

Benefits Realized

- **Immersive Visualisation:** VR technology allows clients to experience the design in a way that 2D drawings or even 3D models could not. Clients could better understand the design's spatial relationships, lighting, and material choices by virtually walking through the space. This helped clients make more informed decisions and provided valuable feedback early in the design process.

- **Enhanced Client Engagement:** VR's interactive qualities made design presentations more engaging and enjoyable for clients. This heightened level of engagement encouraged clients to spend more time reviewing and discussing the design, leading to a deeper understanding and stronger buy-in.
- **Early Issue Identification:** By allowing clients to explore the design, potential issues or concerns could be identified and addressed early in the process, reducing the risk of costly changes or delays later in the project and ensuring that the final design met the client's expectations and needs.

// Utilisation of Customer Relationship Management (CRM) Systems

Perkins and Will implemented a robust CRM system to manage client interactions effectively.

Benefits Realized

- **Personalised Client Interactions:** The CRM system allowed Perkins and Will to maintain detailed records of each client's history, preferences, and feedback. This enabled the firm to address each client's unique needs and expectations. Clients welcomed the tailored approach, reinforcing their trust and loyalty to the firm.
- **Proactive Feedback Management:** By systematically collecting and analysing client feedback, Perkins and Will could identify trends and areas for improvement, ensuring client needs and concerns were addressed promptly and effectively, helping the firm build stronger, more resilient relationships.
- **Improved Client Retention:** The CRM system facilitated better client retention by enabling Perkins and Will to stay engaged with clients after project completion. Regular follow-ups, personalised communications, and continuous engagement helped maintain strong client relationships, leading to repeat business and referrals.

The strategic integration of technology has significantly enhanced Perkins and Will's client relationship management practices. As a result, Perkins and Will has strengthened its competitive position in the market, demonstrating the critical role of technology in modern architectural practice.

Practical Tips for Strategic Technology Investment

- **Assess Needs and Goals:** Conduct a thorough needs assessment to identify areas where technology can improve your firm's operations and client management.
- **Research Solutions:** Investigate various technology solutions and evaluate their features, benefits, and costs. Consider factors like ease of use, scalability, and integration with existing systems.

- **Pilot Testing:** Implement a test of the chosen technology to evaluate its effectiveness and gather user feedback. Based on the results, make necessary adjustments.
- **Training and Support:** Provide comprehensive training for all team members on the new technology. Ensure that ongoing support is available to address any issues or questions.
- **Integration with Existing Systems:** Ensure the new technology seamlessly integrates with your firm's existing systems and processes. This will minimise disruption and enhance efficiency.
- **Continuous Evaluation:** Regularly evaluate the technology's performance and its impact on your operations and client relationships. Make adjustments as needed to maximise benefits.

6.3 // Track It

(KPIs and Performance Results)

KPIs are powerful tools for measuring and optimising architectural practice performance. By tracking progress against key metrics such as client satisfaction, project profitability, employee productivity, revenue growth, and project delivery time, architects can make data-driven decisions to optimise their business performance and overall contribution to society and the built environment.

Client Satisfaction

Client satisfaction is a critical KPI for architectural practice, measurable through feedback surveys, customer reviews, and repeat business. High client satisfaction drives positive word-of-mouth advertising, essential in this industry due to the personalised nature of services, while low satisfaction risks negative reviews and impacts the firm's reputation, so reducing future business prospects. Hence, monitoring and improving client satisfaction is crucial for sustainable growth.

Track it

Project Profitability

Project profitability is measured by comparing actual project costs to the estimated costs, and tracking billable hours and expenses. High project profitability indicates effective cost management and efficient use of resources, while consistent overruns and unprofitable projects can strain the firm's resources and threaten its viability. Analysing profitability helps architects identify cost-saving opportunities and areas to generate additional revenue, ensuring long-term business sustainability.

Employee Productivity

Employee productivity is measured by tracking billable hours, project completion rates, and employee utilisation rates. High productivity indicates that employees manage their time and resources effectively, leading to timely project completion and increased profitability. Low productivity suggests inefficiencies and a need for better management practices or additional training. Monitoring productivity allows firms to implement targeted improvements to enhance efficiency and performance.

Revenue Growth

Revenue growth is tracked through sales and new client acquisitions. Sustained revenue growth demonstrates the ability to attract and retain clients, indicating market competitiveness and effective business strategies. A decline in revenue growth can signal issues in marketing or client retention. Focusing on revenue growth enables firms to make strategic decisions to attract new clients and increase their revenue.

Project Delivery Time

Measured by tracking project completion time, timely project delivery enhances client satisfaction and maximises profitability by allowing the firm to take on more projects. Delays lead to dissatisfaction and resource strain. Monitoring delivery times helps identify bottlenecks and improve delivery.

Sustainability Metrics

Tracking sustainable practices, such as the use of environmentally friendly materials, energy efficiency improvements, and water conservation efforts, can attract environmentally conscious clients and help meet regulatory requirements. Failing to meet these standards risks reputational damage and loss of potential clients. Sustainability metrics can demonstrate a firm's commitment to responsible design and improve their marketability.

Design Awards and Recognition

Winning or being shortlisted for prestigious design awards can be a valuable KPI. It reflects the quality and innovation of the architect's work, enhancing their reputation within the industry. This can lead to increased client interest and opportunities for high-profile projects. A lack of awards and recognition might suggest a need for creative improvements or improved marketing.

Project Diversity

A diverse portfolio demonstrates a firm's versatility, adaptability and expertise across various sectors—from residential to commercial, cultural, and educational. This diversity can mitigate business risks by enabling access to different market segments and attracting a broader client base.

Client Referrals

Tracking the number of new clients acquired through referrals from existing clients is a powerful indicator of client satisfaction. High referral rates demonstrate high client trust and satisfaction, which can significantly reduce marketing costs and ensure a steady stream of new business.

BIM Utilisation

Tracking BIM usage measures how effectively a firm integrates this technology. High BIM utilisation improves project outcomes, while low usage may indicate a need for better technology integration.

Community Engagement

Active community engagement, such as outreach programs or collaboration with non-profits, can be tracked as a KPI. Participation reflects a firm's commitment to social responsibility and can enhance its reputation, while limited engagement suggests a need for stronger community ties and corporate social responsibility initiatives.

Technology Integration

Integrating and utilising new technologies, such as VR, AR, and advanced visualisation tools, indicates a firm's commitment to innovation. Effective integration enhances design and client communication. Failure to keep up with technological advancements risks competitive disadvantage.

Employee Retention and Satisfaction

Low turnover rates and high employee satisfaction point to a positive work environment, which boosts productivity and lowers recruitment costs. High turnover suggests underlying issues that need attention to maintain team stability.

Social and Ethical Responsibility

Measuring involvement in pro bono projects, community improvement initiatives, or projects focused on social justice can serve as KPIs that reflect a firm's commitment to making a positive social impact, strengthening their reputation. A lack of such activities might indicate a need for stronger ethical commitments.

Conclusion

Integrating effective business management and technology streamlines operations and facilitates personalised interactions and immersive experiences, crucial for building lasting client relationships. As the industry evolves, firms that leverage these practices will remain competitive, innovative, and client-focused, ensuring long-term success and growth.

KEEPING IT ALL IN CHECK

7 Key Learning Points //

- **Regular Communication:** Establish a communication plan with regular updates and client check-ins to maintain transparency and trust.
- **Professional Development:** Encourage team members to attend industry conferences and training sessions to stay updated with the latest trends and technologies.
- **Leverage Technology:** Utilise BIM, VR, AR, and CRM systems to enhance project planning, client engagement, and operational efficiency.
- **Client Feedback Loops:** Implement mechanisms for regularly gathering and acting on client feedback to continuously improve service delivery.
- **Financial Transparency:** Maintain detailed budget reports and cost forecasts to build client trust and ensure effective project management.
- **Personalised Client Interactions:** Use CRM systems to track client interactions and preferences, enabling personalised and tailored service.
- **Continuous Improvement:** Regularly evaluate and refine business practices based on client feedback and performance data to enhance client satisfaction and project outcomes.

Use those KPIs…..

Bullring, Birmingham - Future Systems

ROYAL OPERA HOUSE

SAIL
INNOVATION

THE CLOCKS TICKING

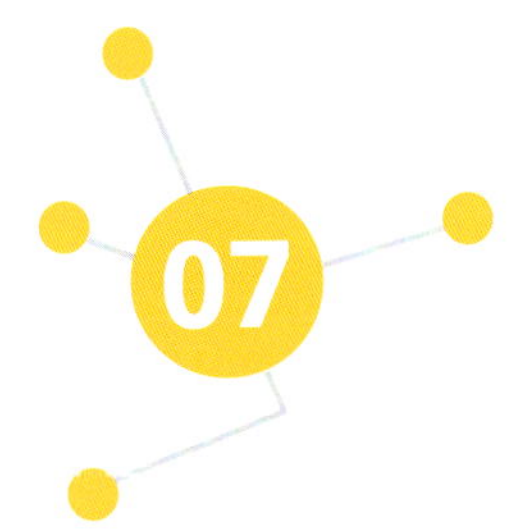

CHAPTER SEVEN

The Clock's Ticking: The Time Trap

Chapter Seven explores time management and productivity for architects, balancing the demands of creativity and professional practice. It covers balancing project deadlines and client expectations while maintaining a fertile ground for innovation. It highlights transformative strategies for effective time management, advocating for a holistic approach that integrates goal setting, prioritisation, and embracing technology to enhance efficiency. Here, we offer practical insights and illuminating case studies for architects striving to harmonise their creative aspirations with professional commitments and personal well-being.

7.1 // Time Management

(It's Not All About Timesheets)

Effective time management plays a critical role in the success of architects at all stages of their careers. While the goal remains constant, there are notable similarities and differences in how undergraduates and early career professionals approach this skill. Nevertheless, despite the differences, the underlying principle of effective time management remains consistent. All groups must cultivate organisational skills, set realistic goals, and harness tools and techniques that enhance productivity, and all must recognise the value of periodic breaks and self-care to prevent burnout and maintain sustained performance.

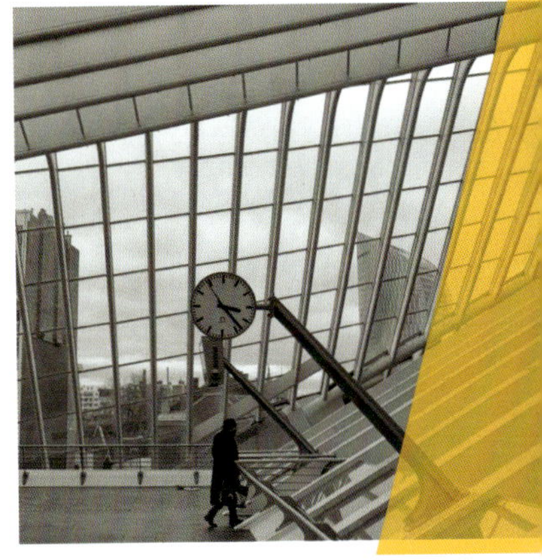

Time ticks away

For undergraduates, time management involves balancing coursework, studio projects, exams and personal commitments, and requires careful planning and prioritisation. Undergraduates must learn to allocate sufficient time for research, conceptualisation, drafting, and revisions, so developing effective study habits and strategies becomes paramount. While the stakes may feel high within the academic setting, the consequences of poor time management are primarily centred around individual academic performance and personal growth.

Early career professionals face a shift in the complexity of responsibilities. Time management extends beyond academic assignments to encompass multifaceted project schedules, client interactions, team coordination, and business development efforts. Architects in this phase of their careers must seamlessly integrate design tasks with administrative duties, such as meetings, documentation, and budget management. Now, balancing creativity with project management requires a refined sense of prioritisation. The consequences of inadequate time management at this stage are broader, affecting project timelines, client relationships, team dynamics, and even the reputation of the architectural firm.

For established architects, a comprehensive approach to time management, particularly when billing clients and monitoring project performance and key performance indicators (KPIs) is necessary to optimise their productivity, meet client expectations, and achieve project goals.

Budget Adherence

A study by Ashworth and Perera[1] highlights the importance of early cost planning and control in maintaining budget adherence. Budget overruns can occur from inaccurate cost estimations and time tracking, unanticipated changes in material costs, design modifications, or project delays. Therefore, it is crucial to include contingency plans during the budgeting process.

Tools: Use time-tracking software linked to billing systems and cost estimation software early in the design phase. Software like TSheets, Toggl, or Harvest can help track time accurately. Tools like CostX or PlanSwift assist in precise cost estimation, enhance transparency and accountability, and ensure that hours worked and expenses incurred are documented. Adopting a phased budgeting approach—reviewing and adjusting costs at the end of each project phase—can help identify and address potential overruns early. Regular financial reporting and variance analysis also ensures projects remain on track financially.

Unrealistic Expectations

According to Winch,[2] clear communication and realistic goal-setting are critical to managing client expectations effectively. Unrealistic expectations can lead to project delays and client dissatisfaction, and may arise from ambitious timelines, insufficient understanding of project complexities, or the desire for quick project delivery.

Tools: Ensure that project goals are specific, measurable, achievable, relevant, and time-bound (SMART). Use tools like Slack or Microsoft Teams for real-time communication and collaboration. Tools like Gantt charts and project management software like Trello or Asana can help clients understand the project's scope and duration. They also allow architects to break down the project into manageable tasks, assign deadlines, and track progress aiding time management.

[1] Ashworth A, Perera S., 2015. Cost studies of buildings. Routledge.
[2] Winch, G.M., 2012. Managing construction projects. John Wiley & Sons.

Practical Elements and Tips

- **Utilise Project Management Software:** Streamline workflow and communication with architecture-specific project management tools, ensuring projects stay on schedule and within budget. Software like ArchiCAD, Revit, and BIM 360 can enhance project management efficiency.
- **Implement Agile Methodologies:** Break projects into manageable sprints for flexibility and continuous improvement. According to Rigby et al.[3], agile methodologies can significantly improve project outcomes.

Enhancing productivity in architectural practice involves a multifaceted approach. By integrating the following frameworks into daily practice, architects can optimise their workflows, improve project outcomes, and foster an environment that values efficiency and creativity.

Frameworks for Enhancing Productivity

- **Prioritise High-Value Tasks:** The Pareto principle, also known as the 80/20 rule, posits that 20% of tasks contribute 80% of outcomes.[4] Identifying and focusing on high-value tasks ensures the most critical aspects of a project are addressed first, leading to better overall results. This might include prioritising design phases, client interactions, or critical project milestones that have the most substantial impact on the project's success.
- **Eliminating Non-Essential Tasks:** Minimise distractions and unnecessary meetings. Organise tasks into actionable steps, ensuring time is spent on meaningful work rather than administrative overhead. For example, implement no-meeting days or schedule brief, focused meetings with clear agendas to waste less time and enhance productivity.
- **Automating Routine Processes:** Use tools like Zapier to automate routine tasks such as scheduling meetings, sending follow-up emails, or updating project statuses to save time and allow architects to focus on complex, value-adding activities. Automation tools can also reduce the risk of human error, ensuring that routine processes are handled consistently and efficiently.
- **Outsourcing Delegable Tasks:** According to Dainty et al.[5], effective delegation can enhance productivity and team efficiency. Tasks such as social media management, basic administrative duties, or even aspects of project documentation can be outsourced to external services or in-house roles supporting the core team, allowing architects to focus on design and client interaction. Delegation also allows team members to focus on their strengths, contributing to overall project efficiency.
- **Adopting an Experimental Mindset:** An experimental approach promotes continuous improvement and innovation.[6] Encourage testing and iteration using new tools, techniques, and workflows to discover more efficient ways to manage projects and teams.

[3] Breakspear, S., 2017. Embracing agile leadership for learning-how leaders can create impact despite growing complexity. Australian Educational Leader, 39(3), pp.68-71. [4] Koch, R., 2011. The 80/20 Principle: The Secret of Achieving More with Less: Updated 20th anniversary edition of the productivity and business classic. Hachette UK. [5] Dainty, A., Moore, D. and Murray, M., 2007. Communication in construction: Theory and practice. Routledge. [6] Thomke, S., 2003. Experimentation Matters: Unlocking the Potential of New Technologies for Innovation. Harvard Business School Press.

- **Leveraging Collaborative Technologies:** Collaborative technologies can bridge the gap between remote and on-site team members. Use collaborative software like Basecamp, Slack, and Miro for real-time collaboration, information sharing, and tracking project progress efficiently.

Strategies for Implementing Frameworks

Effective implementation of the above frameworks for enhancing productivity requires a structured approach to ensure that they are not only adopted but also become integral parts of an architect's workflow. The following practical strategies offer actionable steps to enhance productivity:

- **Setting Daily Top Three Priorities:** Identify three critical tasks at the beginning of each day that will significantly impact projects. This approach helps maintain focus and ensures that the most important tasks are completed first. This way, architects can align their efforts with their most pressing goals, leading to more effective time management and higher productivity.
- **Practicing Mindfulness and Stress Management:** Incorporate mindfulness practices such as meditation and deep breathing exercises to improve concentration and well-being. Kabat-Zinn's mindfulness-based stress reduction techniques can be beneficial. These can help architects manage stress, enhance focus, and maintain a calm, clear mind even in high-pressure situations.
- **Mastering the Art of Rejection:** Saying 'No' to less critical tasks allows architects to protect their time and focus on tasks that deliver the most value. This skill is crucial for avoiding overcommitment and ensuring that energy is directed towards high-priority activities that advance project and career objectives.
- **Single-Tasking:** Research by Ophir et al. , shows that multitasking reduces efficiency and performance. Dedicating full attention to one task until completion before moving on to the next minimises errors, enhances creativity, and increases productivity by reducing the cognitive load of switching between tasks.
- **Prioritising Breaks:** Regular breaks, especially lunch breaks, help maintain productivity. The Pomodoro Technique suggests taking short breaks to improve focus and productivity. Structured breaks throughout the day permit mental rest and rejuvenation, permitting high levels of productivity over extended periods without burnout. Scheduled breaks also provide opportunities for physical activity and social interaction, which can boost overall well-being.
- **Leveraging Small Windows of Time:** Utilise brief periods of downtime for minor tasks. This approach maintains a steady workflow and prevents small tasks from accumulating. For instance, use short breaks between meetings or design sessions to reply to emails or organise files.

- **Implementing the Two-Minute Rule:** Address minor tasks immediately to prevent them from building up. Allen popularised the principle that if a task takes less than two minutes, it should be done immediately rather than deferred. This approach keeps the to-do list manageable and ensures time is used efficiently.

// Optimising Meetings in Architectural Practice

Meeting Types

- **Information Sharing:** These meetings distribute knowledge or updates. They are typically straightforward and can often be replaced with written reports or digital updates.
- **Discussion and Feedback:** These meetings are designed to gather input, decide directions, or foster connections. They are essential for collaborative decision-making and brainstorming.
- **Decision and Permission Seeking:** Focused on obtaining approval or consensus, these meetings are critical for moving projects forward but should be well-structured to avoid unnecessary delays.

Optimising Meetings

- **Clarify the Purpose:** Before scheduling a meeting, clearly define its purpose and desired outcomes. This ensures only relevant participants are involved, and the discussion remains focused.
- **Leverage Digital Platforms:** Tools like Slack, Basecamp, or Notion can be used to share information and gather feedback asynchronously. This minimises the need for frequent meetings and allows team members to contribute at their convenience.
- **Establish Clear Agendas:** Setting a clear agenda with specific topics and time allocations ensures meetings are concise and productive. Adhering to the agenda prevents discussions from veering off-track and helps keep the meeting within the allotted time.

By implementing these strategies, architects can ensure that meetings serve their intended purpose without draining time and resources. This enhances efficiency and fosters a more productive and focused work environment.

Effective Planning Strategies in Architectural Practice

In architectural practice, effective planning is a cornerstone of productivity. Prioritising tasks and focusing on the most critical ones ensures significant projects receive the attention they deserve.

Planning Strategies

- **Prioritise Critical Tasks:** Distinguish between essential tasks and those that only appear urgent. Schedule necessary tasks during peak productivity hours to ensure they receive the required focus and energy.
- **Guard Your Productive Time:** Identify and safeguard your most productive hours for uninterrupted deep work. Inform your team and clients about these time blocks to minimise disturbances and protect these periods for high-value tasks.
- **Utilise the Eisenhower Matrix:** Use this matrix to differentiate between urgent and important tasks. This helps you structure your workday, ensuring that crucial tasks are prioritised and less critical activities are scheduled for later.
- **Commit to Time Tracking:** Thoroughly track your time for a few weeks to gain insight into how you spend your day. This can reveal where you waste time and facilitates optimisation.
- **Embrace Elimination:** As Clear suggests, focusing on what truly matters can dramatically improve productivity. Recognise that not all tasks contribute equally to your goals, and eliminate those that are not essential.
- **Tackle Challenging Tasks Early:** Address the most daunting tasks first to prevent procrastination. Completing these tasks early in the day can boost morale and free up time for other activities.
- **Establish Accountability:** Set realistic deadlines, even artificial ones, and hold yourself accountable, preferably to another person. This external accountability can motivate timely task completion.
- **Leverage Project Management Tools:** Digital tools like Basecamp, Streamtime, Monday, and Notion are invaluable to assign tasks, set deadlines, and track progress. Breaking down projects into smaller milestones with clear checklists encourages steady progress without constant supervision.
- **Manage Expectations:** Be realistic about the time required for tasks to avoid the planning fallacy. Accurate time estimation prevents undue pressure and ensures quality work.
- **Organise Your Workspace:** Whether digital or physical, a well-organized workspace streamlines your workflow. Having all necessary tools within reach minimises distractions and keeps you focused on the task.

In the digital age, architects are inundated with distractions ranging from email alerts and social media notifications to the constant buzz of their workplace. Adopting proactive strategies to minimise interruptions facilitates personal time management and overall productivity. This involves creating a physical and digital workspace that fosters concentration and focused work.

Practical Strategies for Minimising Distractions

- **Designate 'Focus Hours':** Block out specific times in your schedule as 'Focus Hours' to enable the uninterrupted work needed for the creativity and problem-solving architecture demands. During these periods, ensure that all notifications are silenced and that colleagues are aware you are unreachable for non-urgent matters.
- **Leverage Technology Wisely:** Use technology to your advantage; turn off non-essential notifications and schedule specific times to check emails and messages. Tools and apps designed to enhance focus, such as Freedom, Focus@Will, or StayFocusd, can be invaluable in structuring your day for maximum productivity. Utilising project management software can streamline communication and reduce the need to constantly check emails.
- **Physical Workspace Management:** A tidy, organised workspace can significantly reduce mental clutter and distractions. Organising your physical environment by decluttering your desk, ensuring that necessary tools and resources are easily accessible, and creating a visually calm environment can pay dividends in heightened focus and efficiency.
- **Avoid the Perfectionism Trap:** Striving for perfection can lead to procrastination and unnecessary delays. Embrace the principle of 'Done is better than perfect' to maintain momentum in your projects and avoid getting stuck in the details.
- **Cultivate a Mindset of Continuous Improvement:** Instead of aiming for perfection, focus on continuous improvement and learning. This mindset allows you to adapt and evolve your strategies for productivity and creativity over time. Methodologies such as Kaizen, which emphasises small, incremental changes, can significantly improve efficiency and output.

7.2 // Don't Forget to Be Creative

(Our Lifeblood)

Creativity is the essence of architecture, propelling innovation and shaping spaces. It differentiates exceptional designs from merely functional ones, giving life to the structures surrounding us. However, creativity does not occur in a vacuum; it requires an environment that enables deep thinking and experimentation. This section sets out the principles necessary for unleashing creativity and provides a framework for integrating them into everyday practice.

// Principles for Unleashing Creativity

Nurturing Experimentation

Encourage risk-taking and curiosity. According to Amabile, creativity flourishes in environments that support freedom, autonomy, and encourage experimentation. Architectural firms can create an environment where creativity is allowed to run wild, enabling architects to explore uncharted territories, by promoting a culture that views failures not as setbacks but as stepping stones toward innovative solutions. For instance, incorporating design charrettes or brainstorming sessions can provide a safe space for experimenting with new ideas without fearing immediate criticism or failure.

The playground of creativity

Striking the Balance

Architects must balance creativity with practical considerations to achieve design excellence. The concept of 'design thinking', as popularised by Tim Brown, emphasises empathy, ideation, and experimentation within the constraints of real-world challenges. By embracing these constraints, architects can find innovative solutions that are not only creative but also practical and feasible.

Significance of Deep Thinking

Architects must carve out time for introspection, research, and analytical thinking. According to Csikszentmihalyi's concept of 'flow', deep thinking is facilitated by uninterrupted periods of focus where individuals can immerse themselves fully in their creative tasks. Scheduling regular 'think tank' sessions or retreats for architects to step away from routine tasks and engage in deep, reflective thinking can significantly enhance creativity.

Application of Principles in Architectural Practice

Implementing these principles requires a structured approach that integrates creativity into the core of architectural practice. Here are some practical applications:

- **Design Studios and Innovation Labs:** Establish dedicated spaces within architectural firms as design studios or innovation labs. These spaces should be equipped with the latest technology and materials, allowing architects to experiment freely with new designs and concepts. Regularly scheduled innovation sessions can provide opportunities for architects to collaborate on experimental projects outside of client constraints.

- **Cross-Disciplinary Collaboration:** Foster collaboration with professionals from other disciplines such as engineering, art, and environmental science. This interdisciplinary approach can bring fresh perspectives and inspire innovative solutions.
- **Incorporating Feedback and Reflection:** Create a feedback-rich environment where ideas are continuously evaluated and refined. Constructive feedback sessions and peer reviews can help architects refine their ideas and overcome creative blocks. Self-reflection through journaling or portfolio reviews can help architects track their creative progress and identify areas for improvement.
- **Flexible Work Schedules:** Allow architects flexible work schedules to accommodate their creative processes. Some individuals may find their creativity peaks at certain times of the day or in specific environments. Enabling them to work during these optimal times can enhance creative output.
- **Professional Development and Continuous Learning:** Encourage continuous learning through workshops, seminars, and courses focused on creative skills and methodologies.

7.3 // No Time to Be a Perfectionist

(Whilst Protecting Your Values)

Striking a Balance

For undergraduates, managing perfectionism involves balancing project quality with academic commitments. They must learn to manage their time to allow for exploration, experimentation, and iteration while ensuring they meet assignment deadlines.

Early career professionals might find themselves grappling with the pressure to deliver flawless designs within tight timelines. Here, the lesson lies in leveraging experience and sound judgment to identify the pivotal points where perfection is necessary and where it might be counterproductive. Striving for perfection in foundational design concepts and key project aspects while allowing flexibility in less critical elements enables professionals to achieve high-quality outcomes without sacrificing efficiency.

Everyone should recognise that pursuing perfection is admirable but must be tempered by a pragmatic approach. It's a matter of cultivating the ability to discern when perfection adds value and when it hinders progress, and adapting this wisdom to the context of each project and phase of their career.

Figure X: Caption

Case Study Sydney Opera House / Architect Jørn Utzon: The Integration of Time Management, Productivity, and Creativity

Background: The Sydney Opera House, designed by Danish architect Jørn Utzon, stands as an iconic example of 20th-century architecture. The project faced numerous challenges, including time management issues, productivity hurdles, and the need for creative solutions within practical constraints. Despite these obstacles, the final product is a testament to innovative design and engineering. This case study explores how these elements were managed and integrated throughout the project.

Time Management: The Sydney Opera House project was initially scheduled for completion in four years, but ultimately took 14 years (1957-1973). The extended timeline highlights the challenges of managing such a complex project. Factors contributing to the delay included changes in design, construction difficulties, and political issues. Originally estimated to cost AU$7 million, the project ended up costing AU$102 million.

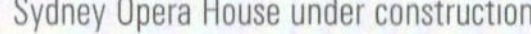

Sydney Opera House under construction

Tools and Techniques

- **Phased Construction Approach:** The project was divided into three phases—podium, roof shells, and interiors—each requiring different time management strategies. This phased approach allowed for better allocation of resources and adjustments based on the project's evolving needs.
- **Regular Milestones and Adjustments:** It was necessary to monitor and adjust schedules to address unforeseen challenges and delays. Using milestones helped track progress and make necessary adjustments to keep the project on track.

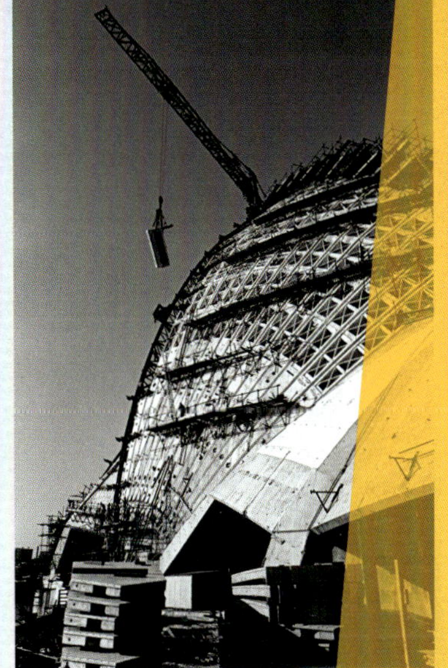

Shell under construction

- **Collaborative Planning:** Frequent consultations and planning sessions between the design and construction teams helped realign project goals and timelines. This collaborative effort ensured that all stakeholders were on the same page, reducing miscommunication and delays.

Productivity: Productivity was a significant challenge due to the innovative design and construction methods required for the Opera House's unique shell structures, and required continuous improvements in productivity techniques.

Frameworks and Strategies:

- **Innovative Construction Techniques:** The introduction of pre-cast rib segments and the use of computer-aided design (CAD) were groundbreaking at the time and significantly enhanced productivity.
- **Team Collaboration:** The collaborative efforts between Utzon's team and engineers like Ove Arup played a critical role in overcoming technical challenges. The synergy between architectural creativity and engineering precision was crucial in solving complex problems.
- **Task Prioritization:** Critical tasks, such as the design and construction of the roof shells, were prioritised to maintain momentum and focus on key project components. Prioritising these elements ensured that the most challenging aspects were addressed first, paving the way for smoother progress in later stages.
- **Creativity:** Creativity was at the core of the Sydney Opera House project. Utzon's vision for the building's unique design required innovative problem-solving and bold architectural decisions.

Sail Detail

Principles Applied:

- **Nurturing Experimentation:** Utzon's design process involved extensive experimentation with forms and materials. Using scale models and full-scale mock-ups allowed for creative exploration and refinement. For example, the spherical geometry solution for the roof shells emerged from such experimental processes.
- **Balancing Creativity with Practicality:** While Utzon's initial designs were ambitious, practical considerations such as material limitations and construction techniques guided the final execution. This balance was essential to achieving the project's aesthetic and functional goals. The final design used pre-cast concrete segments to form the shells, a practical solution that maintained the artistic integrity of Utzon's vision.
- **Deep Thinking and Reflection:** Utzon spent considerable time in deep thought and reflection, often drawing inspiration from natural forms and ancient architecture. His ability to think deeply about the project's design ensured that the final product was innovative and timeless. This reflective approach was crucial in navigating the project's numerous challenges and finding creative solutions.

Entrance steps to the Opera House

Conclusion: The Sydney Opera House case study demonstrates the intricate interplay between time management, productivity, and creativity in architectural projects. Despite significant challenges, the project's success was rooted in its ability to effectively adapt and integrate these elements. Utzon's innovative approach, combined with collaborative efforts and continuous improvement, ultimately resulted in one of the world's most iconic buildings.

SYDNEY OPERA HOUSE CASE STUDY
Key Learning Points //

- **Adaptability:** Flexible time management and the ability to adapt to changing circumstances are crucial for successfully completing complex projects. The phased construction approach and regular adjustments were key in managing the project's timeline.
- **Collaboration:** Collaboration between architects, engineers, and other stakeholders can significantly enhance productivity and innovation. The synergy between Utzon and Arup exemplifies the power of collaborative problem-solving
- **Balance:** Balancing creative vision with practical constraints ensures that architectural projects are aesthetically pleasing but also functional and feasible. The practical solutions for the roof shells illustrate how creativity and practicality can synergise.

By studying the Sydney Opera House project, architects can gain valuable insights into managing time, enhancing productivity, and fostering creativity in their practices. This case study underscores how integrating these elements can achieve architectural excellence.

DYELINES TO BYTES

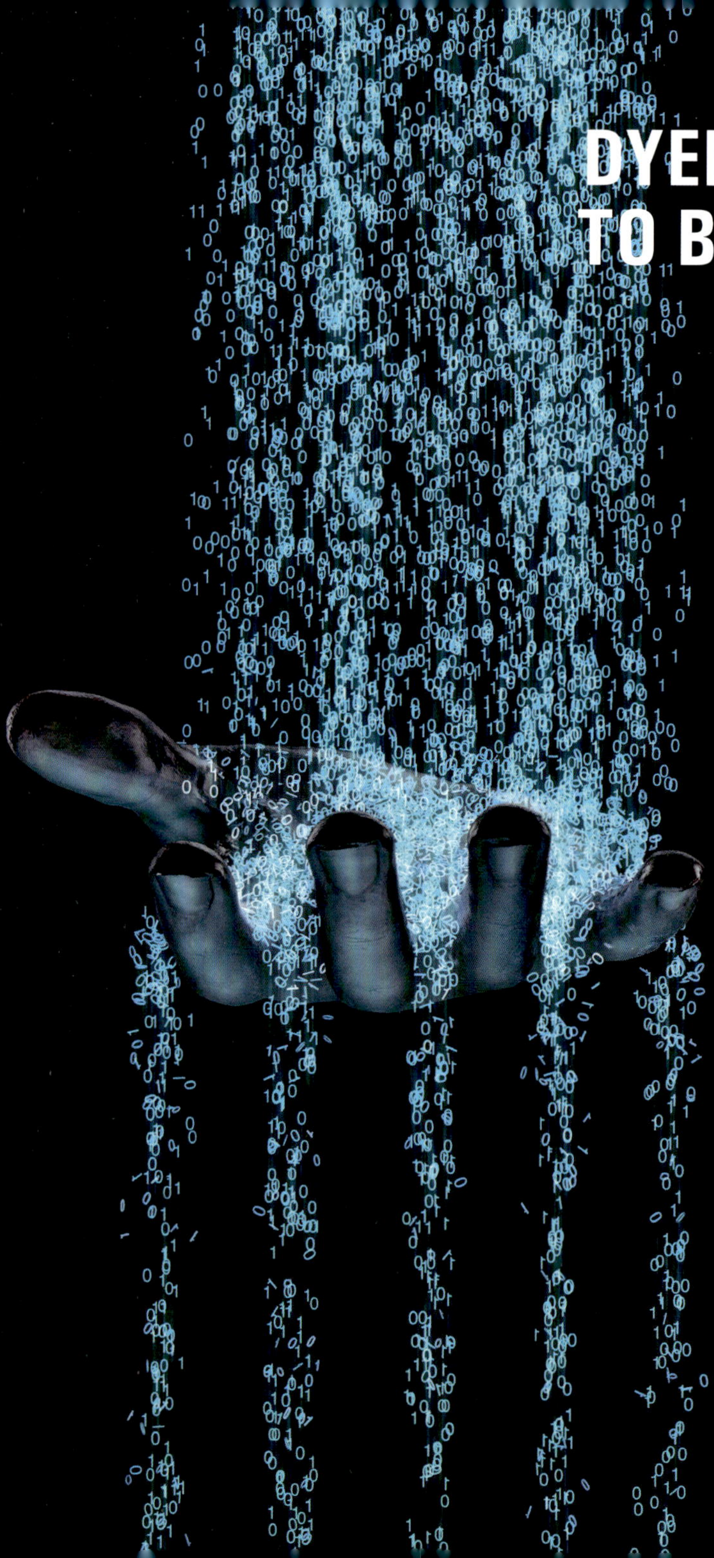

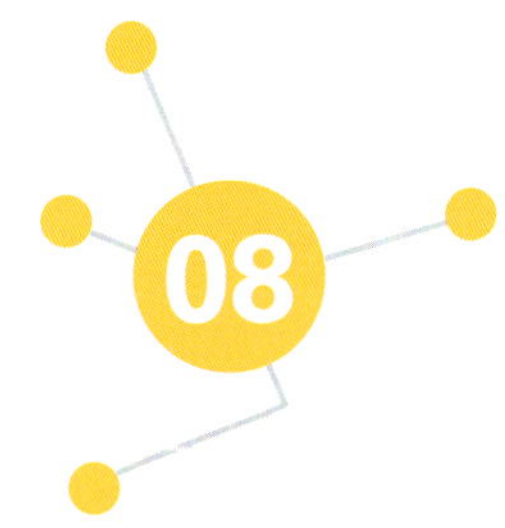

CHAPTER EIGHT

Dyelines to Bytes

In this chapter, we explore architecture and artificial intelligence, where the boundaries of creativity and technology blur. We see how AI—particularly Generative Adversarial Networks (GANs)—revolutionises architectural practice by redefining the architect's toolkit, offering new avenues for innovation, efficiency, and sustainability. Here, we equip practitioners with actionable insights and strategies to harness AI's transformative potential.

8.1 // 3-Dimensional Chess

(Architecture Is a Way of Thinking and Solving Problems)

Complexity theory highlights the non-linear and dynamic essence of systems, where minor alterations can lead to significant, unforeseen outcomes.[1] In this light, architecture is understood as a complex system, an intricate tapestry of interdependent components interacting with each other and their environment in elaborate ways, within which architects emerge as system designers tasked with crafting structures that both fulfil the functional needs of their occupants and adapt to their surroundings' dynamic and evolving nature.

The advent of artificial intelligence, primarily advanced algorithms and machine learning, heralds a pivotal transformation in the methodologies available to navigate and exploit architectural complexity.[2] By weaving AI into the core of architectural thinking and problem-solving, architects amplify their ability to analyse, forecast, and innovate, facilitating the design of adaptive, resilient, and sustainable ecosystems.

3-D Chess and Problem Solving

[1] Mitchell, M., 2009. Complexity: A guided tour. Oxford University Press

[2] Gero, J.S., 1994. Computational models of creative design processes. In Artificial intelligence and creativity: An interdisciplinary approach (pp. 269-281). Dordrecht: Springer Netherlands.

8.2 // GANs

(More than Just Pretty Pictures)

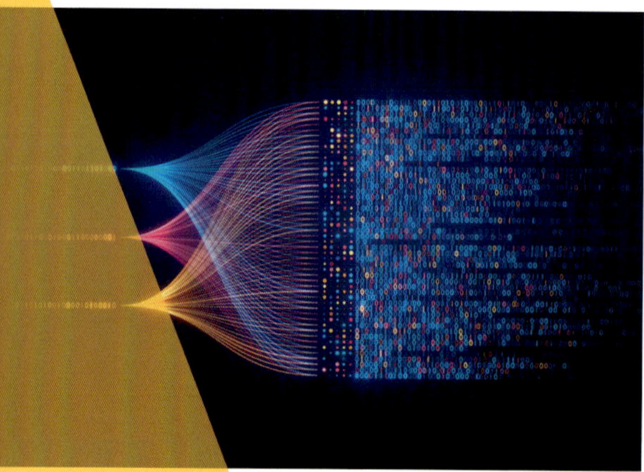

Zeros and Ones

Generative Adversarial Networks (GANs) are a class of artificial intelligence algorithms used in unsupervised machine learning, implemented by two neural networks contesting each other in a zero-sum game framework.[3] Essentially, GANs consist of a generator and a discriminator working in tandem. The generator's role is to create data that mimic a given distribution while the discriminator evaluates the authenticity of the generated data against a real dataset. The process is iterative and adversarial: the generator attempts to produce increasingly convincing data, and the discriminator becomes better at distinguishing between genuine and generated samples. Over time, the generator's output quality improves, enabling the creation of highly realistic synthetic data. GANs represent a groundbreaking approach in artificial intelligence, particularly in generative models.[4]

GANs have profound implications in architecture, offering a novel methodology for generating diverse and innovative architectural forms, layouts, and textures.[5] By training on architectural datasets, GANs learn stylistic nuances and spatial arrangements from various architectural movements or contexts, allowing architects and designers to explore many design possibilities beyond traditional constraints.

The advent of GANs in architectural design not only revolutionises the way designs are conceived and developed but heralds a new era of profoundly innovative, sustainable yet deeply human-centric design.

Entrepreneurs can capitalise on this by developing GAN-based tools and services that offer faster, more efficient, and creatively unrestricted design solutions. Start-ups can develop software solutions that harness GANs for automated design generation, enabling rapid prototyping and iteration of design concepts. Platforms leveraging GAN technology could customise designs to fit specific client needs or environmental contexts, reducing time and cost associated with the design phase.

[3] Goodfellow, I., Pouget-Abadie, J., Mirza, M., Xu, B., Warde-Farley, D., Ozair, S., Courville, A. and Bengio, Y., 2014. Generative adversarial nets. Advances in neural information processing systems, 27.

[4] Radford, A., 2015. Unsupervised representation learning with deep convolutional generative adversarial networks. arXiv preprint arXiv:1511.06434.

[5] Zhu, J.Y., Park, T., Isola, P. and Efros, A.A., 2017. Unpaired image-to-image translation using cycle-consistent adversarial networks. In Proceedings of the IEEE international conference on computer vision (pp. 2223-2232).

8.3 // Beyond Blueprints

(The Comprehensive Impact of AI)

Ten Steps to Effectively Integrate GANs in Architectural Design:

1. **Educate and Train:** Learn the fundamentals of GANs and their application in generative design through workshops, courses, and seminars focused on AI in architecture to build a solid foundation in this emerging field.
2. **Collaborate with AI Experts:** Partner with data scientists and AI experts to integrate GAN technology into your design processes. Their expertise can help tailor GAN models for specific architectural needs and projects.
3. **Curate Diverse Data Sets:** Collect and curate diverse architectural data sets to train GAN models, ensuring they include a wide range of styles, periods, and contexts to ensure varied design solutions.
4. **Experiment with Design Generation:** Use GANs to generate design proposals and explore new architectural forms, especially in early design stages where multiple options must be considered quickly.
5. **Implement Iterative Design Processes:** Blend AI-generated innovation with human creativity and expertise by refining and developing GAN-generated designs using traditional design methods.
6. **Focus on Customisation and Personalisation:** Train GAN models based on specific client preferences or site-specific conditions to offer highly customised and personalized design solutions for unique project requirements.
7. **Explore Sustainable Design Solutions:** Use GANs to generate designs optimising for sustainability, including energy efficiency, material use, and reduced environmental impact.
8. **Develop New Business Models:** Entrepreneurs and architectural firms can create new business models based on GANs' capabilities, offering AI-driven design consultancy services, design platforms, or software tools that integrate GANs into existing architectural software ecosystems.
9. **Engage in Continuous Learning:** AI and generative design are rapidly evolving. Stay updated on GAN technology and its evolving applications in architecture to refine and enhance your practice.
10. **Share Knowledge and Insights:** Participate in professional networks and forums to share experiences and insights, helping to advance the field and uncover new opportunities for innovation.

But What of the Design Process?

GANs revolutionise how architects can generate and analyse 2D and 3D designs from specific styles. By curating training datasets tailored to particular styles or themes, architects can control the fidelity and diversity of generated designs, enabling precise customisation and innovation. Techniques for improving the visual quality of generated designs with small datasets demonstrate GANs' versatility even with limited data.

GANs also allow architects to quickly explore many design options, making concept exploration more dynamic. Their analytical capabilities can help uncover novel design patterns or styles, fostering innovation and enhancing the creative process. At a tactical level, architects can integrate GANs into various design stages to enhance efficiency and creativity.

Actionable steps for leveraging GANs in architectural design:

1. **Curate and Customise Training Sets:** Architects can curate datasets tailored to specific styles or themes they wish to explore, using these to train GANs to generate unique designs that reflect the desired architectural characteristics.
2. **Utilise GANs for Concept Exploration:** GANs can rapidly generate a wide range of design options in the initial project stages, accelerating ideation and allowing multiple design directions to be considered.
3. **Enhance Design with Analytical Insights:** GANs' analytical capabilities help architects explore novel design patterns or styles, fostering innovation through new perspectives and ideas that might not emerge through traditional design methods.
4. **Apply GANs Across Design Phases:** From conceptualisation to detailed development, GANs can be integrated at various stages of the design process to enhance both efficiency and design quality.
5. **Bridge Traditional and Computational Design:** A hybrid approach blending GAN-generated proposals with traditional design methods leverages the strengths of both methodologies.
6. **Foster Collaborative Design Processes:** GANs encourage collaboration between architects and AI specialists. Merging architectural knowledge with advanced computational techniques leads to more innovative and technically sophisticated projects by pushing the boundaries of design.
7. **Advance Sustainable and Contextual Design:** Training GANs on datasets of sustainable or contextually significant architectures helps architects generate innovative designs responsive to environmental and cultural contexts, promoting sustainable and relevant architectural design.

This approach opens new avenues for architectural creativity and efficiency, challenging architects to rethink their roles in the design process. By blending their expertise with the capabilities of generative deep learning, architects can make the future of architectural design more innovative, responsive, and sustainable.

// The Comprehensive Impact of AI Beyond GANs

Building upon GAN's transformative potential in architectural design, Artificial Intelligence (AI) opens even more expansive horizons. Beyond generating novel design forms, AI's role extends into automated design assistance, sophisticated simulation and analysis, and the management of vast datasets, enhancing architects' ability to innovate and tackle complex challenges, redefining what's possible in architectural practice.

1. Automated Design Assistance

AI driven design assistance can significantly streamline the architectural design process by automating tedious tasks such as drafting, zoning analysis, and code compliance checks using machine learning algorithms. This allows architects to focus more on creative design exploration. AI tools like Autodesk's Revit for automated drafting and Rhino's Grasshopper for parametric design scripting have become essential in modern architectural practices. AI can also suggest design modifications to enhance functionality, aesthetics, or sustainability, offering a powerful tool for rapid prototyping and iteration. As AI systems learn from vast design datasets, they become increasingly adept at offering innovative and contextually appropriate solutions.

Action Points:

- **Learn and Apply:** Familiarize yourself with AI tools like Autodesk's Revit for automated drafting and Rhino's Grasshopper for parametric design scripting. Engage in online tutorials to understand their application in automating design tasks.
- **Incorporate AI Tools:** Integrate AI-driven design assistants like TestFit or Spacemaker into the planning phase to optimise site layout and building configurations, enhancing efficiency and innovation in the early design stages.
- **Iterate Creatively:** Use AI to automate routine tasks, freeing time for creative exploration. Regularly update your toolkit with the latest AI software to stay at the forefront of design technology.

2. AI-Driven Simulation and Analysis

AI-driven simulation and analysis tools enable architects to evaluate design performance in virtual environments before construction begins. These tools can simulate factors like structural stress, energy efficiency, and environmental impact, providing valuable insights into a design's viability and sustainability. By using AI for predictive analysis, architects can anticipate potential issues and make informed decisions early in the design process, optimising performance and ensuring compliance with environmental standards.

Action Points:

- **Embrace Simulation Tools:** Use simulation software such as Autodesk's Insight for environmental and energy analysis to ensure sustainable and efficient designs.
- **Predictive Analysis:** Apply predictive models using tools like Ladybug + Honeybee in Grasshopper to analyse climate data and environmental conditions, influencing design decisions for better performance.

3. Data Analysis and Management

AI's ability to analyse and manage large datasets is invaluable. AI can uncover insights that inform more nuanced and responsive design solutions, from processing complex urban planning data to analysing historical architectural data to identify trends, or it can sift through environmental data to guide the design of buildings that better adapt to their surroundings. This data-driven decision-making enhances the architect's ability to create innovative designs deeply rooted in context.

Action Points:

- **Leverage Big Data:** Employ AI platforms like CityCAD that can process vast datasets to inform smarter, more contextually integrated urban planning and design..
- **Innovate with AI Insights:** Use AI to analyse trends in architectural design or client preferences, utilising tools like IBM Watson for advanced data analysis to guide innovation and ensure designs meet evolving needs.
- **Data-Driven Design:** Encourage a culture of data-driven decision-making within your practice. Invest in training for your team to effectively utilise AI in data analysis and management to enhance the architectural design process.

4. Client Interaction and Customisation

AI enhances meaningful client interaction and customisation in architectural design. By harnessing data analytics and machine learning, architects can gain insights into client preferences and behaviours and create tailored design solutions that resonate personally with clients, offering them a previously unattainable sense of involvement and satisfaction. AI tools can analyse feedback, past projects, and even social media to build detailed client profiles, ensuring designs are aligned with the client visions and lifestyles.

Action Points:

- **Deep Learning for Client Insights:** Engage with platforms like Spacemaker AI or Morpholio Trace, which utilise deep learning to analyse client data and generate design options that align with their preferences.
- **Client Feedback Analysis:** Incorporate NLP technologies to parse and understand client feedback, enabling a dynamic response to their needs. Tools such as IBM Watson can be instrumental in this area.
- **Customised Experience with VR:** Use Virtual Reality (VR) platforms, like IrisVR, to immerse clients in customisable design environments where they can interact with and modify their future spaces in real-time.

5. Construction and Fabrication

Integrating AI into construction and fabrication boosts efficiency, precision, and sustainability. Predictive analytics help project managers foresee potential issues, manage resources and adjust timelines, reducing the risk of delays and cost overruns. AI-driven automation in fabrication processes speeds up construction and ensures a level of precision that minimises waste and maximises material efficiency. Robots, powered by AI, are deployed on-site for tasks ranging from bricklaying to component assembly, demonstrating a shift towards a more innovative, controlled, and safe construction environment.

Action Points:

- **Leverage Predictive Analytics:** Tools like PlanGrid and Procore offer AI-driven project management capabilities that predict project flow and resource needs.
- **AI in Robotic Fabrication:** Be aware of and explore the use of robotics for automated construction tasks. Systems like those developed by Boston Dynamics provide AI-powered robots capable of performing various construction tasks efficiently and precisely
- **Sustainability through AI Optimization:** Adopt AI tools such as algorithms for cutting patterns that maximise material efficiency to optimise material usage and reduce waste.

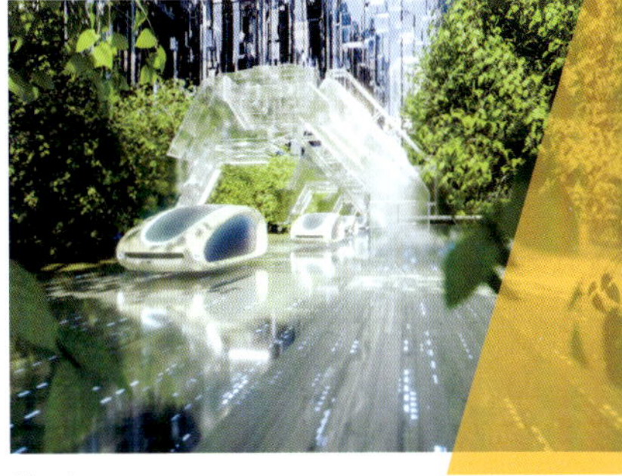

AI and you

These AI applications not only augment the architect's toolkit but also open new avenues for innovation and efficiency. Embracing AI enables architects to tackle modern design challenges with precision and creativity, leading to sustainable and responsive outcomes that meet society's evolving needs.

8.4 // Building the Future

(The Marriage of AI and Human Ingenuity)

Neri Oxman

Case Study Neri Oxman

Neri Oxman is an architect, designer, and professor at the Massachusetts Institute of Technology (MIT), working at the intersection of architecture, biology, and computer science. Her pioneering work introduces us to the groundbreaking concept of 'material ecology', exemplified by her compelling project 'Aguahoja'. This endeavour harnesses the power of machine learning algorithms to refine and optimise the architecture of 3-D-printed structures, inviting us to witness the remarkable synergy between human creativity and technological sophistication.

Material Ecology and Digital Fabrication

Oxman's concept of material ecology integrates computational design, additive manufacturing, and synthetic biology to create forms and structures inspired by nature. This approach challenges traditional architectural practices by promoting a seamless integration of design and fabrication, where materials and structures are conceived as interdependent components of a unified system. Through this lens, Oxman's work exemplifies a shift towards a more holistic and sustainable design philosophy that respects and mimics the inherent efficiencies of natural processes.

Example The Aguahoja Project

Utilising a blend of natural materials such as chitosan (a biopolymer derived from the shells of crustaceans) and pectin (found in plant cell walls), Aguahoja explores the potential of biodegradable structures that can be digitally fabricated. Machine learning algorithms play a crucial role in optimising these structures, enabling the creation of functionally effective and environmentally benign forms.

Perspective view showing the distribution of chemic interactions between five pectin skin composites anc two chitosan/cellulose shell composites

Implications of Oxman's Work

Oxman's creative exploration has sparked transformative ripples, leaving a trail of potential implications that stretch across various domains. However, there are potential criticisms and challenges associated with her work:

Rigid cellulose-based elements printed onto a flexible skin

Close view of a backlit section of the Aguahoja Pavilion and a Close-up shot of the Aguahoja Pavilion displaying its surface pattern

- **Disruption of Natural Ecosystems:**
  One potential criticism is that Oxman's 'material ecology' approach might inadvertently disrupt the balance of natural ecosystems. By introducing synthetic materials and digitally fabricated structures into natural environments, there is a risk of unforeseen ecological impacts. This criticism underscores the importance of rigorous environmental assessments and the development of sustainable practices in applying material ecology.
- **Loss of Human Touch:** Another critique is that AI-infused designs might remove the human touch from architectural creation, diluting the emotional resonance embedded in traditional craftsmanship. While AI and machine learning offer unprecedented precision and efficiency, there is a concern that they might lead to the loss of unique, hand-crafted elements.
- **Homogenised Aesthetic:** Lastly, a speculative concern might hint that Oxman's work could lead to a homogenised aesthetic, where all structures and objects produced through digital fabrication begin to resemble one another. This risk of aesthetic convergence emphasises the need for continuous innovation and the integration of diverse cultural and contextual influences in digital fabrication.

Neri Oxman's work at the intersection of architecture, biology, and computer science represents a significant leap forward in architectural design. Her approach to material ecology and the integration of AI in design challenges conventional practices and opens new pathways for sustainable and innovative architectural solutions. While potential criticisms and risks are associated with her methods, the benefits of her pioneering work far outweigh the challenges. Oxman's legacy will likely inspire future architects to embrace interdisciplinary approaches and harness the power of technology in their creative endeavours.

THE ETHICAL ARCHITECT

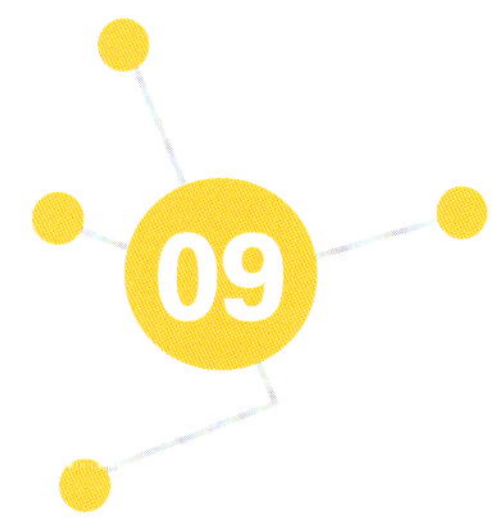

CHAPTER NINE

The Ethical Architect

Integrity is the moral compass that steers entrepreneurs to make principled decisions and act fairly and truthfully. In the architectural profession, integrity encompasses multiple dimensions that contribute to a firm's success and sustainability. Upholding integrity ensures long-term success by cultivating reliability and dependability among clients, customers, and stakeholders. Ethical decision-making, a key aspect of integrity, helps architects earn the respect and loyalty of their clients, laying a strong foundation for sustainable growth. This chapter addresses the importance of ethics in architectural practice, the challenges of maintaining professional integrity, and strategies for navigating ethical dilemmas and promoting ethical standards within the industry.

9.1 // The Ethical Blueprint

(Foundations of Integrity)

According to the Royal Institute of British Architects (RIBA), ethical practice in architecture involves honesty, fairness, and respect for others.[1] This extends beyond adherence to laws and regulations; it includes continuous professional development, staying updated with the latest industry trends and technologies, and maintaining a commitment to ethical practices in all aspects of an architect's work. Adhering to these standards not only enhances the credibility of individual architects but also elevates the overall standards of the profession.

Key Ethical Principles in Architecture:

- **Integrity and Honesty:** Integrity involves being truthful and transparent in all professional activities. This includes providing accurate information to clients, avoiding conflicts of interest, and maintaining transparency in financial matters.
- **Societal Well-being:** Architects are often entrusted with designing spaces intended to enhance the quality of life for individuals and communities. Architects should ensure accessibility, inclusivity, and community benefit by actively engaging with the communities

they serve, involving them in the design process to ensure that their needs and values are reflected in the outcome.[2]

- **Environmental Stewardship:** The American Institute of Architects (AIA) emphasises that architects should work towards creating resilient and sustainable built environments that positively impact future generations.[3] Ethical and sustainable design and construction practices include choosing eco-friendly materials, minimizing waste, designing energy-efficient buildings, incorporating energy-efficient systems and minimising waste. By prioritising sustainable practices architects help promote the planet's long-term health.[4]
- **Respect for Clients and Stakeholders:** Architects must ensure transparent and honest communication with clients about project details, potential challenges, and realistic outcomes. Treating employees fairly includes ensuring safe working conditions, providing fair wages, and fostering an inclusive workplace culture. Ethical dealings with contractors and suppliers include fairness in negotiations, timely payments, and respect for contractual agreements.[5] It also includes respecting the rights and interests of all the other stakeholders, including the public, who may be affected by architectural projects.
- **Project Execution:** Architects should implement rigorous quality control measures to ensure that all projects are functional, safe, and sustainable. This involves selecting materials responsibly, ensuring sustainable construction practices, and complying with all relevant regulations and codes. Regular site inspections and thorough documentation are key practices.
- **Professional Competence:** Maintaining professional competence involves continuous learning and staying updated with the latest developments in the field. Architects must possess the necessary skills and knowledge to deliver high-quality work and uphold professional standards.
- **Fairness and Justice:** Fairness requires architects to treat all parties equitably, without discrimination or bias. This principle applies to hiring practices, client interactions, and contractors' negotiations. It also involves advocating for the fair distribution of resources and opportunities within the community.
- **Enhancing Public Trust:** Architects prioritising integrity influence the norms within their firms and the broader industry, promoting a culture of ethical behaviour that enhances overall performance and reputation with the public. Architects who consistently demonstrate ethical behaviour are also more likely to be seen as leaders and innovators within the industry.[6]

[1] RIBA (2020). Code of Professional Conduct. London: Royal Institute of British Architects, p. 12.
[2] Brown, J. (2006). Ethical Leadership: Creating and Sustaining an Ethical Business Culture. Oxford: Oxford University Press, p. 50.
[3] AIA (2017). Code of Ethics and Professional Conduct. Washington, DC: American Institute of Architects, p. 30.
[4] Hopkins, R. (2018). Sustainable Architecture: Design for an Energy-Conscious Future. London: Wiley-Blackwell, p. 45.

9.2 // The Architect's Dilemma

(Navigating Ethical Quandaries)

Ethical dilemmas are situations where conflicting values or principles make determining the right course of action challenging. Architects must navigate these challenges by adhering to ethical principles and seeking solutions that align with professional standards, personal values, and contribute to the greater good of society and the environment.[7]

Understanding Ethical Dilemmas in Architecture

Ethical dilemmas in architecture can arise from various scenarios, such as:

- **Client Demands vs. Public Good**

  Scenario: A client requests a design that maximises their private benefit but compromises public safety or environmental sustainability.

  Challenge: Balancing the client's desires with broader social responsibilities.

  Resolution: Architects must engage in open dialogue with clients, educating them about the broader implications of their requests and advocating for designs that serve the public good. This approach is rooted in the ethical principle of beneficence, which emphasises actions that promote the well-being of others.[8]

- **Financial Pressures**

  Scenario: Financial constraints may tempt architects to cut corners, compromising the quality and safety of a project.

  Challenge: Maintaining professional integrity while managing budget limitations.

  Resolution: Architects should uphold the principles of honesty and transparency, ensuring that all stakeholders understand the financial constraints and the potential impact on the project. Adopting a transparent approach helps in maintaining trust and mitigating risks associated with financial pressures.[9]

- **Conflicting Stakeholder Interests**

  Scenario: Different stakeholders, such as clients, contractors, and the community, have conflicting interests and expectations from a project.

  Challenge: Balancing these interests without compromising ethical standards.

  Resolution: Architects must practice fairness and justice by giving all stakeholders a voice in the decision-making process. This can be achieved through inclusive design practices and participatory planning methods that consider diverse perspectives and needs.[10]

[5] Dutton, T. A. (2009). Architects and Cultural History: Ethics and Identity in the 21st Century. Minneapolis: University of Minnesota Press, p. 112.
[6] Feldman, R. (2000). Ethics in Urban Planning: Principles and Practice. New York: McGraw-Hill, p. 89.
[7] Fisher, T. (2013). Ethics for Architects: 50 Dilemmas of Professional Practice. New York: Princeton Architectural Press, p. 78.

Ethical Frameworks for Decision-Making

Navigating ethical dilemmas effectively requires a structured approach to decision-making. Several ethical frameworks can guide you as an architect:

- **Deontological Ethics (Duty-Based)**

  Principle: Actions are judged based on adherence to rules and duties, regardless of the consequences.

  Application: Architects should follow professional codes of conduct and legal requirements, ensuring their actions are morally right even if they face adverse outcomes. For instance, despite client pressure to reduce costs, refusing to use substandard materials aligns with deontological ethics.

- **Utilitarian Ethics (Consequentialism)**

  Principle: Actions are judged based on their outcomes, with the best action maximising overall happiness or well-being.

  Application: When faced with design choices, architects can evaluate the potential outcomes of each option, choosing the one that provides the greatest benefit to the most people. For example, opting for a sustainable design that benefits the environment and the community, even with higher initial costs, reflects utilitarian principles.[11]

- **Virtue Ethics**

  Principle: Focuses on the moral character of the individual making the decision rather than the action itself.

  Application: Architects should cultivate virtues such as honesty, courage, and empathy to guide their professional behaviour. By embodying these virtues, architects can navigate ethical dilemmas with integrity and moral clarity.[12]

- **Rights-Based Ethics**

  Principle: Emphasises the importance of respecting and protecting individual rights.

  Application: Architects must ensure that their actions do not infringe on the rights of others. This includes respecting workers' rights to fair wages and safe working conditions and the rights of the public to a safe and healthy environment.[13]

Practical Strategies for Navigating Ethical Dilemmas

- **Developing a Personal Ethical Code:** Architects should establish ethical guidelines that align with professional standards and personal values. This personal code can be a reference point when faced with difficult decisions.
- **Ethical Decision-Making Models:** Structured models like the 'Four-Component

[8] Dhirani, L. L., Mukhtiar, N., & Chowdhry, B. S. (2023). Ethical Dilemmas and Privacy Issues in Emerging Technologies: A Review. Sensors, 23(3), 1151, p. 24.
[9] Luxmi, D., Mukhtiar, N., & Chowdhry, B. S. (2023). Ethical Dilemmas and Privacy Issues in Emerging Technologies: A Review. Sensors, 23(3), 1151, p. 31.
[10] Emerald Insight. (2023). Ethical consideration dilemma: Systematic review of ethics in qualitative data collection through interviews. Emerald Insight, p. 18.

Model of Morality' described by James Rest can help architects systematically analyse and resolve ethical dilemmas. This model involves four psychological processes which describe the sequence of thoughts and actions that result in ethical behaviour:

Moral Sensitivity: Recognizing the presence of an ethical issue.

Moral Judgment: Determining the right course of action.

Moral Motivation: Prioritizing ethical values over other considerations.

Moral Character: Implementing the ethical decision despite potential obstacles.

- **Seeking Diverse Perspectives:** Engaging with colleagues, clients, and other stakeholders to gather diverse viewpoints can provide valuable insights and help identify the best ethical course of action. This collaborative approach ensures that decisions are well-grounded and factor in all impacts.
- **Continuous Education:** Staying informed about the latest ethical and industry standards. Regularly attending ethics training and workshops can enhance architects' ability to navigate complex ethical situations.
- **Reflective Practice:** Regular reflection on past decisions and their outcomes can help architects learn from experience and improve their ethical decision-making skills. This involves critically analysing what went well, what could have been improved, and how similar situations might be handled in the future.

9.3 // Virtues and Vices

(Real-World Ethical Case Studies)

- **Ethical Dilemma in Sustainable Design**

  Scenario: An architect is hired to design a luxury resort in a sensitive ecological area. The client demands a design that maximises commercial potential, while the local community and environmentalists advocate for minimal environmental impact.

  Resolution: The architect adopts a participatory design process, engaging with the client, community, and environmental experts to develop a sustainable design that balances all interests. This approach demonstrates the application of utilitarian ethics, aiming for the greatest good for the most stakeholders.[14]

- **Financial Pressure and Quality Compromise**

  Scenario: A client pressures an architect to use cheaper, lower-quality materials to reduce costs. The architect knows that this compromise could lead to safety issues.

  Resolution: The architect refuses to compromise on quality, explaining the long-term

[11] Shaw, W. H. (1998). Contemporary Ethics: Taking Account of Utilitarianism. Oxford: Blackwell, p. 62.
[12] Annas, J. (1993). The Morality of Happiness. Oxford: Oxford University Press, p. 27.
[13] Traer, R. (2009). Doing Environmental Ethics. Boulder: Westview Press, p. 103.
[14] Rosen, M. (2013). The Bullitt Center: A Model for Sustainable Design. Seattle: University of Washington Press, p. 56.

risks and potential legal implications to the client. By adhering to deontological ethics, the architect upholds professional integrity and prioritizes safety.[15]

- **Conflicting Stakeholder Interests**

  Scenario: During the redevelopment of a historical site, the interests of developers, preservationists, and the local community conflict. The developers prioritize profit, preservationists focus on maintaining historical integrity, and the community desires accessible public spaces.

  Resolution: The architect facilitates a series of workshops to mediate between stakeholders, leading to a design that incorporates commercial, historical, and community elements. This inclusive approach aligns with rights-based ethics, ensuring that the rights and interests of all parties are considered.[16]

9.4 // Promoting Ethical Standards

(Sub-Heading?)

Professional organisations, educational institutions, and individual firms all play a role in upholding and advancing ethical standards, benefiting the profession and society as a whole.

Establishing Clear Guidelines

- **Professional Codes of Conduct:** Professional organisations such as the American Institute of Architects (AIA) and the Royal Institute of British Architects (RIBA) provide comprehensive codes of conduct that serve as benchmarks for professional behaviour and offer guidance on addressing ethical issues. For example, the AIA's Code of Ethics and Professional Conduct includes provisions for environmental responsibility, equity, and justice. Similarly, the RIBA's Code of Professional Conduct emphasises honesty, integrity and competence, as well as concern for others and the environment, as a foundation for ethical practice.
- **Regulatory Frameworks:** Architects must adhere to various regulatory frameworks that govern ethical practice, such as the UK's Building Regulations. These usually include guidelines on health and safety, environmental sustainability, fair labour practices, and standards for the design and construction of buildings to ensure safety and accessibility.
- **Ethics Policies in Firms:** To guide decision-making and behaviour, individual architectural firms should develop and implement a consistent ethical framework that also aligns with broader professional standards.

15 Feldman, R. (2000). Ethics in Urban Planning: Principles and Practice. New York: McGraw-Hill, p. 78.
16 Yoder, R. (2016). Architectural Ethics: Theory and Practice. New York: Routledge, p. 138.
17 Cuff, D. (1991). Architecture: The Story of Practice. Cambridge, MA: MIT Press, p. 123.
18 Borden, I. (2001). The Ethical Architect: The Dilemma of Contemporary Practice. London: Routledge, p. 134.
19 Feldman, R. (2000). Ethics in Urban Planning: Principles and Practice. New York: McGraw-Hill, p. 89.
20 Dutton, T. A. (2009). Architects and Cultural History: Ethics and Identity in the 21st Century. Minneapolis: University of Minnesota Press, p. 112.

Fostering a Culture of Integrity

- **Leadership and Role Modeling:**Ethical leadership is crucial to foster integrity within architectural firms. Leaders must demonstrate honesty, transparency, and accountability in all professional activities to inspire their teams to uphold ethical standards and create a positive organisational culture.[17]
- **Ethics Training and Education:**Professional organisations and firms should offer regular training programs such as ethics workshops and seminars that cover ethical theories, decision-making models, and case studies to enhance architects' understanding of ethical principles and improve their ability to navigate complex ethical dilemmas.
- **Encouraging Open Dialogue:**Open dialogue fosters a culture of transparency and trust, enabling firms to identify and resolve ethical issues effectively.[18] Firms should encourage employees to voice their ethical concerns and provide platforms for discussing ethical dilemmas. This can include regular ethics meetings, confidential reporting channels, and mentorship programs.

Ensuring Accountability

- **Monitoring and Reporting Mechanisms:** Firms should establish effective procedures for monitoring compliance with ethical standards and addressing violations to help maintain ethical standards and hold individuals accountable for their actions.[19] These can include regular audits, ethics committees, and whistleblower protections.
- **Performance Appraisals:** Recognising and rewarding ethical behaviour in addition to technical skills and project outcomes in performance appraisals can motivate employees to prioritise ethics in their work.[20]
- **Consequences for Unethical Behavior:** Firms must outline the repercussions for violating ethical policies, ranging from warnings and retraining to termination of employment. Enforcing these consequences consistently ensures that ethical standards are upheld and deters unethical behaviour.[21]

Role of Professional Organizations and Educational Institutions

- **Professional Organizations:** Organisations like the AIA and RIBA promote ethical standards by providing resources, training, and support to their members. Additionally, these organisations advocate for ethical practices within the industry and contribute to developing regulatory standards.[22 23]
- **Educational Institutions:**By integrating ethics education into their curricula to foster a strong ethical foundation, educational institutions contribute to developing ethically responsible professionals.[24] Courses on professional ethics, case studies, and practical applications can prepare students to face ethical dilemmas in their careers.

- **Collaboration Between Institutions:** Collaboration between professional organisations, educational institutions, and architectural firms to advance the understanding and application of ethical principles in architecture can take the form of ethics conferences, publications, and research projects. Such collaborations can also provide platforms for sharing knowledge and best practices across the industry.[25]

Case Studies and Real-World Examples

- **The Ethics of Sustainable Design:** The Bullitt Center in Seattle is a prime example of ethical and sustainable design. Designed by the Miller Hull Partnership, it incorporates cutting-edge sustainable technologies and materials, making it one of the greenest commercial buildings in the world. The project demonstrates a commitment to environmental responsibility and the ethical imperative to design for sustainability.[26]
- **Navigating Client Relationships:** The architectural firm Mecanoo's renovation of the New York Public Library highlights the ethical challenges of balancing client desires with public interest. The project required careful negotiation to preserve the library's historical integrity while meeting modern needs. The architects' transparent communication and commitment to public welfare exemplify ethical practice in managing client relationships.[27]
- **Promoting Diversity and Inclusion:** The architectural firm MASS Design Group is renowned for its commitment to social justice and inclusive design. Their work in underserved communities, such as the Butaro District Hospital in Rwanda, shows how architecture can promote social equity and improve public health. MASS Design Group's approach underscores the ethical responsibility to serve diverse populations and address social inequalities.[28]

Visit the **IBE website** to access their comprehensive resources and support your commitment to ethical excellence in architectural practice. ibe.org.uk

For architects seeking to deepen their understanding of ethical practices and enhance their professional integrity, the Institute of Business Ethics (IBE) is an invaluable resource. The IBE offers a wealth of materials, including case studies, guidelines, and training programs tailored to foster ethical behaviour in business. These help professionals navigate complex ethical dilemmas, promote a culture of integrity, and implement robust accountability mechanisms. By engaging with the IBE's offerings, architects can stay informed about the latest ethical standards and best practices, ensuring that their work meets regulatory requirements and contributes positively to society and the environment.

[21] Fisher, T. (2013). Ethics for Architects: 50 Dilemmas of Professional Practice. New York: Princeton Architectural Press, p. 78.
[22] RIBA (2020). Code of Professional Conduct. London: Royal Institute of British Architects, p. 12.
[23] AIA (2017). Code of Ethics and Professional Conduct. Washington, DC: American Institute of Architects, p. 22.
[24] Schön, D. A. (1983). The Reflective Practitioner: How Professionals Think in Action. New York: Basic Books, p. 56.

THE ETHICAL ARCHITECT
10 Key Learning Points //

1. **Understanding the Scope of Ethics in Architecture:** Ethics in architecture extends beyond legal compliance to include societal well-being, environmental stewardship, and stakeholder respect.
2. **The Role of Professional Organizations:** Organisations such as the American Institute of Architects (AIA) and the Royal Institute of British Architects (RIBA) provide comprehensive codes of conduct that guide ethical behaviour in the profession.
3. **Developing Firm-Specific Ethics Policies:** Establish ethics policies that also align with broader professional standards. These should address issues like conflict of interest, confidentiality, and fair treatment of employees.
4. **Fostering a Culture of Integrity:** Create an environment where ethical behavior is valued and rewarded is essential.
5. **Importance of Ethics Training and Education:** Continuous ethics education through training programs, workshops, and seminars is crucial for maintaining high ethical standards and navigating complex ethical dilemmas.
6. **Encouraging Open Dialogue about Ethics:** Promote open dialogue about ethical issues, encouraging employees to voice concerns and discuss dilemmas to foster a culture of transparency and trust.
7. **Implementing Accountability Mechanisms:** Establish robust monitoring and reporting mechanisms to ensure compliance with ethical standards and address violations
8. **Ethical Leadership and Role Modeling:** Leaders are critical in promoting ethics by demonstrating honesty, transparency, and accountability in all professional activities, setting the tone for the organisation.
9. **Enhancing Public Trust through Ethical Practice:** High ethical standards build public trust and credibility, which is crucial for the success and reputation of architectural projects and the profession.
10. **Collaboration Between Professional Entities:** Joint efforts between professional organizations, educational institutions, and firms are necessary to advance and maintain ethical standards, which will benefit the entire architectural community and society.

[25] Brown, J. (2006). Ethical Leadership: Creating and Sustaining an Ethical Business Culture. Oxford: Oxford University Press, p. 74.
[26] Rosen, M. (2013) The Bullitt Center: A Model for Sustainable Design. Seattle: University of Washington Press. P102
[27] Yoder, R. (2016) Architectural Ethics: Theory and Practice. New York: Routledge. P138
[28] Kries, M. (2017) For the Common Good: Prefabrication and Sustainable Architecture. Basel: Birkhäuser. P 88

SECTION 3

AFTERWORD

Embracing the Future of Architectural Practice

Beware the quiet man in a t-shirt in a meeting room full of suits - he's earned the right to wear it.

Architects are more than just building designers; they are visionaries, problem solvers, and innovators who shape the way we live and interact with our surroundings. In an ever-evolving world, architects' roles extend far beyond architecture's traditional boundaries. They are at the forefront of addressing some of the most pressing global challenges, from climate change to social inequality. By integrating ethical principles and sustainable practices into their work, architects can create solutions that meet today's needs and ensure a better future for future generations.

Architects have a unique ability to transform visionary ideas into tangible realities. Their capacity for innovative thinking, combined with their technical expertise, positions them to drive significant change across various domains. Whether it's designing energy-efficient buildings, planning resilient urban spaces, or developing cutting-edge technology solutions, architects continuously demonstrate their potential to make a profound impact.

Throughout this book, we've explored the critical aspects of client engagement, business management, ethics, and sustainability, providing you with the tools and insights needed to navigate the complexities of modern architectural practice.

Successful client engagement is about meeting project requirements and understanding and exceeding client expectations. By fostering trust and collaboration, architects can create lasting partnerships that lead to repeat business and referrals, which are essential for sustaining and growing a practice.

Effective business management is another cornerstone of a thriving architectural practice. From managing finances and operations to leveraging technology and strategic planning, architects must be adept at navigating the business side of their work. The strategies and tools discussed in this section will help you streamline your operations, enhance productivity, and ensure the long-term success of your practice.

Ethics and professionalism are integral to the credibility and reputation of the architectural profession. Adhering to high ethical standards can build trust with clients, colleagues, and the broader community. This commitment to integrity and accountability is essential for maintaining the public's confidence in the profession and for driving positive social change.

Sustainability is no longer a choice but a necessity. As stewards of the built environment, architects are responsible for promoting sustainable design and construction practices. This involves reducing the environmental impact of their projects and creating spaces that enhance the well-being of their occupants and the community. Architects can contribute to a healthier, more resilient world by embracing sustainable practices.

As you move forward in your architectural career, remember that the potential for innovation and impact is limitless. The knowledge and strategies outlined in this book are just the beginning. Continue to seek out new opportunities, challenge conventional thinking, and push the boundaries of what is possible. Embrace your role as a leader, not only within your practice but also within your community and the broader architectural profession. The future of architecture is bright, and you are well-equipped to shape it. So, the next time you have an idea, know you have the skills, knowledge, and passion to bring it to life. The journey ahead is filled with possibilities, and your contributions have the power to create lasting change.

Thank you for embarking on this journey with us. We look forward to seeing the incredible innovations and solutions you will create. Keep pushing the envelope, stay committed to your values, and continue positively impacting the world.

The architectural profession holds a unique and vital place in shaping the future, and with your expertise and dedication, the possibilities are endless. Embrace the future of architectural practice with confidence and inspiration. The world is waiting for your ideas.

ACKNOWLEDGEMENTS

For Sarah, Ben, Isobel, Charis and Charlie.

Thanks to Stew & Sarah Smith for helping bring this book to life.

And

Unicorn

Lucy Duckworth, Eva Menhuin and the late David Breuer,

Henley Business School

Prof Bernd Vogel and Dr Fabio Oliveira

Prof Anastasiya Saraeva, Prof Jane McKenzie, Prof Chris Dalton, Dr Liza Castro Christiansen, Prof Ben Laker, Louise Hillier, Becky Kite. Ayo Ajanaku, Muzi Dladla, Darren Franklin and Booshan Parikh.

Oxford University

Prof Ngaire Woods, Mike Wigg and Sir John Hood

Cardiff University

Prof Wayne Forster and Prof Sarah Lupton,

In Practice

Prof Ian Ritchie CBE

Russell Brown & Morag Morrison, Roger Hawkins.

Patrick Walsh and Nigel Follows. Brad Fauteux, Jim Eyre, Stafford Critchlow, Keith Brownlee, Simon Alford, Jack Pringle, Ben Cousins, Nick Ling and the late Dennis Sharp and Chris Wilkinson.

Clients and Collaborators

Michael Freeman.

Claire Kramer

Joel Cadbury, Dame Susie Sainsbury, Dame Julia Peyton-Jones, Julie Burnell, Michael Bloomberg and the Bloomberg Foundation, Sir Nicholas Bacon, Col Dan Rex, Ruth Evans, Col Gary Sullivan, Lady Sarah Younger, Simon Ruck, Baroness Caroline Cox Emma Kennedy, Philip Sharman, Peter Rogers, Troy Hinson, Peter Carroll, and Catherine Vasseur. Rebecca Craddock, Victoria Firth, Annalie Howling, Abigail Ings, Lana Parise and Anna Prior. Kevin Lenane, Brendan Morrisey, Lee Mears, and Charlie Hodgson.

and

Nigel & Rowena Stapleton, Andrew & Sarah Rogers, Malcolm & Jo Bonner, Casey & Amanda Stine, Guvna B, Paul Woodward, Ric Child, and Loz Moon, David & Sue Llewelyn, Steve Anderson, Steve Charlton, and Chris & Kate Finch.

Without the kind support of all these people, my career and this book would not have been possible.

IMAGE CREDITS

Chapter	Title	Credits
Cover (Front Back)	The Architects Edge	Stewart Smith / Gareth Stapleton
About The Author	Gareth Stapleton	Claire Kramer
Introduction		Stewert Smith
Section One	Pexels	Alexadebache
Chapter 1	Warwick Hall	Clews Architects
	David	Gareth Stapleton / Stewart Smith
	Reggio Emilia, Italy, Railway Station	Massimo1y
Chapter 2	The End	Gareth Stapleton / Stewart Smith
	Start	Alex Si
Chapter 3	Make an Impact	Nikada
	Who are you ?	Isobel Stapleton
	Dior Omotesando, Tokyo by SANAA	Roysei Watanabe
	Dior Omotesando, Tokyo by SANAA	Roysei Watanabe
	Apartments - Copenhagen, Hovedstaden, Denmark	Paolo Graziosi
	Worcester Cathedral Visitor Centre	Clews Architects
	Worcester Cathedral Visitor Centre	Clews Architects
	Worcester Cathedral Crypt Refurbishment	Clews Architects
	Worcester Cathedral	Clews Architects
	Arab Institute Paris	Ulysse Pixel
Chapter 4	Wooden ceiling at the Art Gallery in Auckland, New Zealand - FJMT	Imago Dens
	Snohetta, Oslo Opera House	Mike UK
	Drone Photogrammetry Scan - Tomas Millar,	Millar Howard
	The Dursley Tree House	Grand Designs
	Millar Howard Offices	Issac orr
	Livid in Custom Build	Livedin in Custom Build
	The Yarrows Deck	Tomas Millar
Chapter 5	Linbury Theatre Royal Opera House	Luke Hayes
	Apple HQ	Barabara AAA
	Apple HQ	Barabara AAA
	Aqua Tower Chicago - Studio Gang	Christophe Merceron
	V&A Dundee	mcKensa
	V&A Dundee - Detail	Jim McDowall
	The Bosco Verticale skyscrapers in Milan	Silva Cozzi
	Smart Cities	Jarmo Piironen
Chapter 6	Snohetta, Oslo Opera House	Mike UK
	Host Logo	Stewart Smith / Gareth Stapleton
	Arkan Theatre Cairo	Braker / ritchie*studio.
	Arkan Theatre Cairo	Braker / ritchie*studio.
	Arkan Theatre Cairo	ritchie*studio.
	Arkan Theatre Cairo	Braker / ritchie*studio.
	Arkan Theatre Cairo	Braker / ritchie*studio.
	Arkan Theatre Cairo	Braker / ritchie*studio.
	Mirror - Architectural Detail	Erc Falco
Chapter 7	Newcastle Millennium bridge at sunset with the Tyne Bridge	Sol Stock
	Belfast Stones	Laura McClorey
	External View of Archive Square	Laura McClorey
	External View of Archive Square	Laura McClorey
	City View	Laura McClorey
	Belfast Stones - Perspective Section	Laura McClorey
	Technical Model	Laura McClorey
	The Voyage of Ituna	Rolex
	Itunas arrival in New York	Prof Chris Dalton
	Telegram from Frank Lloyd Wright to Desmond Dalton	Prof Chris Dalton
	Telegram from Frank Lloyd Wright to Desmond Dalton	Prof Chris Dalton
Chapter 8	Biome at Eden Project Botanic Gardens in Cornwall	Paul Mcguire
	Serpentine Summer Pavilion	Iwan Baan
	Sou Fujimoto Serpentine Pavilion	Iwan Baan
	Sou Fujimoto Serpentine Pavilion	Iwan Baan
	Sou Fujimoto Serpentine Pavilion	Iwan Baan
	Space frame detail	Iwan Baan
	Eden Project	Brian Scantlebury
Chapter 9	Penny for your thoughts	Simon Kr
Afterward	Pexels	Alinerliraa

Section Two	Concept	Ralwel
Chapter 1	Penny for your thoughts - Title needs to be changed	Stewart Smith
	Neural Network	Gareth Stapleton
	Wear out your Shoe Leather	Ozgurcankaya
	Help others up the ladder of success	Gareth Stapleton
Chapter 2	Stand up Speak Up	Photoman
	Brene Brown	University of Texas at Austin
	High Line New York	Ferrantraite
	High Line New York	Ferrantraite
	Stavros Niarchos Foundation Cultural Centre	Alexandros Michalidis
	Stavros Niarchos Foundation Cultural Centre (small image)	Photoman
	The Table Cloth	Stewart Smith
	Serpentine Summer Pavilion - Sketch	Gareth Stapleton
Chapter 3	Office Image	Ariel Perspective Works
	Boats	Ilker Celik
	Atrium Biochemistry - Oxford University	Hawkins Brown Architects
	Matrix Management	MF3d
	Team Based Structure	Tadamichi
	Market Sector	Torston Asmus
	Apple Market	Chris Dalton
Chapter 4		
	Lifting the Bonnet	Stewert Smith
	Gender Pay gap	Gareth Stapleton
	Chiswick Bridge	Stocklapse
	Clove Office Fit-out	Useful Studio
	Foundry Office Fit Out	Useful Studio
	University Reception	Useful Studio
	St Mary's University Master Plan	Useful Studio
Chapter 5	Antwerp Port	Andreja Potocnik
	Wellness	Thitareesarmkasat
	Salk Institute	HaoboHu
	Salk Institute - Exterior Office Building	softservegirl
	National Assembly Building, Sher-e-Bangla	Pixhound
	Ergonomics	Warchi
	Peter Zumthor Thermal Baths	Wirestock
	Galaxy Soho by ZHA	ispyfriend
	Hudsons Yards New York by ZHA	AI Photographic
Chapter 6	The power of No	Stewart Smith
Chapter 7	Royal Ontario Museum , Toronto	Gareth Stapleton
	Playbarn Buildings - Hawkins Brown Architects	Gareth Stapleton
	Playbarn Buildings - Hawkins Brown Architects	Hawkins Brown Architects
	Playbarn Buildings - Hawkins Brown Architects	Hawkins Brown Architects
	Playbarn Buildings - Hawkins Brown Architects	Hawkins Brown Architects
	Royal Opera House	Hawkins Brown Architects
	Royal Opera House	Luke Hayes
	New Linbury Theatre Foyer	Luke Hayes
	New Linbury Studio Theatre	Luke Hayes
	New Linbury Theatre	Luke Hayes
	Royal Ballet Bridge - Wilkinson Eyre	Luke Hayes
Chapter 8	RenewalMatyas	Margaret Sha
	Stepping Stones	Levente Sipos
	Bouncing Back	Leighcol.
	Design Museum Concept Sketch	Afzalkhan M
	Design Museum Front elevation	Andy Groarke
	Design Museum Front Model	Carmody Groarke Architects
	Brick Making Process	Carmody Groarke Architects
	Brick Making Process	RomaninNoceto.
	Brick Making Process	RomaninNoceto.
	Brick Making Process	RomaninNoceto.
	Brick Making Process	RomaninNoceto.
	Brick Making Process	RomaninNoceto.
	The finished Ghent Brick	RomaninNoceto.
Afterward	Unsplash	Bart-van-Leuven
		Pang-Yuhao

Section Three	Railroad station at dusk, Liege, Guillemins, Belgium	BIM
Chapter 1	The Business of Architecture	Gareth Stapleton
	Business Planning	Gareth Stapleton
	Bright Ideas	Anilakkus
	Putt for Dough	JJ Neff
	Vancouver Chandelier	Gareth Stapleton
Chapter 2	Navigating the Financial Landscape	Pete Sherrard
	Genoa Port: Renzo Piano	Claudio Arnese
	Genoa Port: Renzo Piano	Massimo 1G
	Astrup Fearnley Museum in Tjuvholmen Quarter by Renzo Piano	JJ Farquitectos
	The Gherkin London - Foster and partners	
	The Gherkin London - Foster and partners	
	Heydar Aliyev Conference Centre, Baku, Azerbaijan Zaha Hadid Architects	Sharrocks
	Heydar Aliyev Conference Centre, Baku, Azerbaijan Zaha Hadid Architects	Rusian Kaln
	Heydar Aliyev Conference Centre, Baku, Azerbaijan Zaha Hadid Architects	Orkhan Mammadov
	Know your Copy-Rights!	JL Gutierrez
	Ray and Maria Stata Center - Frank Gehry	AP Corrtizas Jr
Chapter 3	The De La Warr Pavilion and Milky Way	Wirestock
	First Date and Maybe Even a Second	Serpbelu
	Hitting the Bullseye	Cosmin 4000
	The De La Warr Pavilion Temporary Structure - Niall McLaughlin	Dave Collins
	The De La Warr Pavilion Temporary Structure - Niall McLaughlin	Victor Liew
	Renzo piano - Façade Details	Cold Snow Storm
Chapter 4	Encore	Team Jackson
	Hello Cold Caller	Ordasi Tatyjana
	How can I help you	Marcus Lindstom
	Empathy	Shivendu Jauhari
	Four Pillars	Leo Patrizi
	Active Listening	Oleksandr Shchus
	Client Education	Neu Stock Images
	Problem Solving	Mario31
Chapter 5	181 Bay Street Toronto - S. Calatrava	P Giam
	Complacency	Nuthawut Somsuk
	The 'Cheesegrater' on Leadenhall St - Rogers Harbour Stirk	Lance B
Chapter 6	Keeping it all in Check	M Bolina
	The Balancing Act	NadimIK
	Clean Modern Tech - The Sumida Hokusai Museum	Ben Bryant
	Bobby Moore Academy School, Stratford - Perkins and Will	Esther Barry
	Track It	BIM
	Bull Ring Birmingham - Future Systems	Chris Hepburn
Chapter 7	Sail Innovation	Simon Bradfield
	The Clocks Ticking	VTT Studio
	Time Ticks Away	WireStock
	The playground of creativity	HalfPoint
	SYDNEY OPERA HOUSE - VIEW ACROSS THE BAY	SIMON BRADFIELD
	SYDNEY OPERA HOUSE - CONSTRUCTION PHOTOS	JOHN CARNEMOLIA
	SYDNEY OPERA HOUSE - CONSTRUCTION PHOTOS	JOHN CARNEMOLIA
	SYDNEY OPERA HOUSE - CONSTRUCTION PHOTOS	JOHN CARNEMOLIA
	SYDNEY OPERA HOUSE - SHELL UNDER CONSTRUCTION	JOHN CARNEMOLIA
	SYDNEY OPERA HOUSE - SAIL DETAIL	SCM JEANS
	SYDNEY OPERA HOUSE - SAILS IN PROFILE	RUGLI G
	Entrance steps to the Opera House	Sergio Capuzzimati
Chapter 8	Dyelines to Bytes	Grand Educ
	3-D Chess and Problem Solving	Seruvenci
	Zeros and Ones	Nico Einino
	AI and You	Gremlin
	Neri Oxman	Noah Kalina
	Perspective view showing the distribution of chemical interactions between five pectin skin composites and two chitosan/cellulose shell composites	The Mediated Matter Group. Courtesy of The Mediated Matter Group.
	Close view of a backlit section of the Aguahoja Pavilion	The Mediated Matter Group. Courtesy of The Mediated Matter Group.
	Close-up shot of the Aguahoja Pavilion displaying its surface pattern	The Mediated Matter Group. Courtesy of The Mediated Matter Group.
	Rigid cellulose-based elements printed onto a flexible skin	The Mediated Matter Group. Courtesy of The Mediated Matter Group.
Chapter 9	The Ethical Architect	Claudio Devizia
Afterward	Pexels	Tracehudson

INDEX